KEITH CARTER'S interest in the great outdoors was kindled on a school trip to Snowdonia which hooked him for life. Work became what he did between walks and he has since explored almost every corner of the British Isles with occasional forays into France, Austria and the USA.

Writing articles for magazines led him into guidebook writing and he now spends most of his time re-discovering Scotland, cultivating organic vegetables and growing willow. He is co-author of *The Pennine Way*, also from Trailblazer.

Offa's Dyke Path
First edition: 2004

Publisher
Trailblazer Publications
The Old Manse, Tower Rd, Hindhead, Surrey, GU26 6SU, UK
Fax (+44) 01428-607571, info@trailblazer-guides.com
www.trailblazer-guides.com

British Library Cataloguing in Publication Data
A catalogue record for this book is available from the British Library

ISBN 1-873756-59-3

© Trailblazer 2004
Text and maps

Editor: Henry Stedman
Series editor: Charlie Loram
Typesetting: Henry Stedman
Layout: Henry Stedman and Bryn Thomas
Proof-reading: Anna Jacomb-Hood
Illustrations: © Nick Hill (pp58-61; C4: HG Adams and W Egmont Kirby
Photographs (flora): C1: middle left © Charlie Loram; bottom © Keith Carter
C2: top right © Charlie Loram
C3: top left © Keith Carter
C3: top right, middle left, bottom left and centre © Charlie Loram
C3: bottom right © Edith Schofield
C1-3 all others © Bryn Thomas
Cover photograph: ©John Cleare/Mountain Camera 2004
All other photographs: © Keith Carter 2004
Cartography: Nick Hill
Index: Jane Thomas

The maps in this guide were prepared from out-of-Crown-
copyright Ordnance Survey maps amended and updated by Trailblazer.

Warning: mountain walking can be dangerous
Please read the notes on when to go (p19) and health and outdoor safety (p198).
Every effort has been made by the author and publisher to ensure that the information
contained herein is as accurate and up to date as possible. However, they are unable
to accept responsibility for any inconvenience, loss or injury sustained by anyone
as a result of the advice and information given in this guide.

Printed on chlorine-free paper by
D²Print, Singapore

OFFA'S DYKE PATH

PRESTATYN TO CHEPSTOW
planning, places to stay, places to eat,
includes 88 large-scale walking maps

KEITH CARTER

TRAILBLAZER PUBLICATIONS

Dedication

I should like to dedicate this book to the farmers through whose fields much of the trail wends, for their patience and fortitude in difficult times. Good luck to them.

Acknowledgements

Thanks to those who helped me do this book particularly the series editor, Charlie Loram, for his insistence on attention to detail. Also at Trailblazer, thanks to Henry Stedman for editing and laying down the text, Nick Hill for all his work on the maps, Anna Jacomb-Hood for proof-reading and Jane Thomas for the index.

Thanks also to my companions on the trail, Annie my wife, and family and friends.

A request

The author and publisher have tried to ensure that this guide is as accurate and up to date as possible. However, things change even on these well-worn routes. If you notice any changes or omissions that should be included in the next edition of this guide, please email or write to us at Trailblazer (address on p2). You can also contact us via the Trailblazer website at 🖥 www.trailblazer-guides.com). Those persons making a significant contribution will be rewarded with a free copy of the next edition and an acknowledgement in the front of that edition.

Updated information will shortly be available on:
🖥 **www.trailblazer-guides.com**

Front cover: On the Offa's Dyke Path above Llangollen
© John Cleare/Mountain Camera 2004

CONTENTS

INTRODUCTION

Wherever I have been in Wales, I have experienced nothing but kindness and hospitality, and when I return to my own country, I will say so. **George Borrow *Wild Wales* 1862**

For 177 miles (285km), from Prestatyn in the north of Wales to Chepstow in the south, the Offa's Dyke Path winds along the English-Welsh border, roughly following the line of the 1200-year-old frontier earthwork which gives it its name. This magnificent long-distance footpath ranges over terrain diverse as any you will find in Britain; it traverses the whaleback ridges of the Clwydian Hills, along canal towpaths and old drovers' roads, beside the banks of the meandering Severn and Wye rivers, through the Shropshire hills and over the Black Mountains. The Border Country is the land of Merlin and Arthur, a land of history and legend, from which sprang Owain Glyndwr and the Lord of the Rings. To journey through it on foot is the finest way to discover one of Britain's best-kept secrets.

You leave the North Wales coastline for a bracing walk over the Prestatyn hillside with its awesome views of the mountains of Snowdonia before you take to the small lanes and hedgerows of the Vale of Clwyd. This farmland introduction gives way to the splendid ridges of the Clwydian Range and fine walking. Beyond Llandegla you enter a region that might be part of Tolkien's Middle Earth, the limestone cliffs and screes of the Eglwyseg Crags above the festival town of Llangollen. Then you follow the canals, crossing the magnificent Pontcysyllte Aqueduct; the inspiring views of the Marcher castle of Chirk herald your first glimpse of the Dyke itself.

You continue across the Severn Plain on a more modern man-made embankment with panoramic views of the Breidden Hills and then up to the Iron Age hill-fort of Beacon Ring with its crown of trees. As you approach the halfway mark at Knighton, 'the town on the dyke', you come to a part of the route aptly named the Switchbacks. Then it's on to Kington and the Hergest Ridge, a place of heather, gorse and wild ponies, with extensive views of the 'blue-remembered' hills of Shropshire and the Black Mountains of the Brecon Beacons National Park. Hay-on-Wye with its thirty or so second-hand book shops is a welcome stop for a night. From here the trail climbs over Hay Bluff to the Hatterrall Ridge following the spine of this fine massif.

From Pandy you pass through a hidden world of intimate villages and quiet byways where you're likely to meet only livestock and farm people. Monmouth is well worth exploring before the long walk down the River Wye's wooded slopes, passing Tintern Abbey, to Chepstow and the end of this superb trail at Sedbury Cliffs.

About this book

This guidebook contains all the information you need; the hard work has been done for you so you can plan your trip from home without the usual pile of books, maps, guides and tourist brochures. It includes:

● All standards of accommodation from campsites to luxurious guesthouses
● Walking companies if you want an organized tour
● A number of suggested itineraries for all types of walkers
● Answers to all your questions: when to go, degree of difficulty, what to pack and the approximate cost of the whole walking holiday

When you're all packed and ready to go, there's detailed information to get you to and from the Offa's Dyke Path and 88 detailed maps (1:20,000) and 12 town plans to help you find your way along it. The route guide section includes:

● Walking times in both directions
● Reviews of accommodation including camping, hostels, B&Bs and guesthouses
● Cafés, pubs, tea-shops, restaurants, and shops for buying supplies
● Rail, bus and taxi information for all the towns and villages on or near the path
● Street maps of the main towns
● Historical, cultural and geographical background information

Minimum impact for maximum insight

Man has suffered in his separation from the soil and from other living creatures ... and as yet he must still, for security, look long at some portion of the earth as it was before he tampered with it. **Gavin Maxwell**

Why is walking in wild and solitary places so satisfying? Partly it is the sheer physical pleasure: sometimes pitting one's strength against the elements and the lie of the land. The beauty and wonder of the natural world and the fresh air restore our sense of proportion and the stresses and strains of everyday life slip away. Whatever the character of the countryside, walking in it benefits us mentally and physically inducing a sense of well-being, an enrichment of life and an enhanced awareness of what lies around us.

All this the countryside gives us and the least we can do is to safeguard it by supporting rural economies, local businesses, low-impact methods of farming and land-management and by using environmentally-sensitive forms of transport – walking being pre-eminent.

In this book there is a detailed and illustrated chapter on the wildlife and conservation of the region and a chapter on minimum impact walking with ideas on how to tread lightly in this fragile environment; by following its principles we can help to preserve our natural heritage for future generations.

The springs of enchantment lie within ourselves; they arise from our sense of wonder, that most precious of gifts. **Eric Shipton**

About the Offa's Dyke Path

'Up, lad, up, 'tis late for lying
Hear the drums of morning play;
Hark the empty highways crying
Who'll beyond the hills away?'
AE Housman

HISTORY

The Offa's Dyke Path is one of 15 National Trails in England and Wales. These are Britain's flagship long-distance paths which grew out of the post-war desire to protect the country's special places, a movement which also gave birth to national parks and Areas of Outstanding Natural Beauty.

An Act of Parliament in 1949 laid down proposals for several routes which included a path to follow the line of Offa's Dyke. The first of these trails, the Pennine Way, was opened in 1965 but it was not until 1971 that Lord Hunt, of Everest fame, officially opened the Offa's Dyke Path.

It was originally the responsibility of the Countryside Commission, but as the path crosses the English/Welsh border many times, two-thirds being in Wales and one third in England, the responsibility for the path passed to the Countryside Council for Wales in 1991. Offa's Dyke Path is managed and maintained by the Offa's Dyke Path Management Service based in Knighton with the close co-operation of the local authorities through whose land it passes.

HOW DIFFICULT IS THE OFFA'S DYKE PATH?

Do not be deceived into thinking this is an easy walk. Although the tourist brochure in Prestatyn declares, 'this now famous walk…meanders up the High Street and climbs the magnificent Prestatyn Hillside ... then wanders its way along the spectacular Clwydian Range and from then on down to Chepstow', this is like leaving out six of the seven ages of man!

A level of fitness and walking competence is required to walk most sections of Offa's Dyke Path. It's 177 miles end to end and assuming you have two weeks available this will require an average of nearly 15 miles a day based on 12 days of walking plus a day to get to the start and a day to get home. This will entail about five to seven hours' walking every day. On at least three days you will probably have to walk 17 miles; quite a tall order. Add to this the fact that there are an estimated 677 stiles to be crossed, an average of nearly four per mile, or on a 17-mile day 68 stiles, you are going to feel a certain amount of tiredness at the end of the walking day. Are you up to it?

There are two severe and testing sections. The first is the crossing of the Clwydian Range (pp75-80) from Bodfari to Clwyd Gate which involves several climbs and descents as well as some incomparable ridge walking. On a fine day you will romp it but in bad weather it can be a severe test of endurance. Luckily there are a number of escape routes which will enable you to arrange a pick-up, possibly by your B&B host for the night. The second challenging section is along Hatterrall Ridge in the Black Mountains (see pp159-71) between Hay-on-Wye and Pandy. It's a distance of $17^1/_2$ miles (28km) through exposed country, the highest point being 703 metres (2307ft), and can take at least $9^1/_2$ hours. There is little shelter and few escape routes although the journey could be broken at Capel-y-Ffin or Llanthony. You will need to think carefully about how you are going to tackle this arduous crossing.

Anyone possessing basic outdoor competence should find themselves coping perfectly well even with these challenging sections but don't underestimate any part of the route; it is not a doddle.

Route finding

The trail is waymarked with scrupulous attention to detail with only a few areas where more work is needed to avoid ambiguity in route-finding. The path was devised and initiated by a band of devotees who were at pains to ensure that

those who came after them could find their way. The waymark throughout is the acorn of the Countryside Commission, supplemented with finger posts and guide posts which are frequently engraved, often in English and Welsh, and many stiles have the symbol of a coin of Offa's reign.

Aided by the waymarks and following the trail maps in this book the walker is unlikely to get lost. A word of advice is not to make assumptions. If the broad inviting path ahead of you looks the obvious route it does not necessarily follow that it is your route. Look for the waymark, especially where the path changes direction.

Waymarker

It also isn't safe to assume the path follows the line of the Dyke in every case. There are places where the right of way diverges from the line of the Dyke; this is true over Baker's Hill between Castle Mill and Racecourse Common (map p103) and on Hawthorn Hill between Knighton and Dolley Green (map p141). Check the trail maps regularly.

HOW LONG DO YOU NEED?

This is the great imponderable. Can the path be walked from end to end in a fortnight's holiday? The answer is yes, probably, but you'll have to get a move on and it won't leave you much time to stop and stare. No time to visit Chirk Castle, see Llangollen, go into Welshpool, call in at the Offa's Dyke Centre in Knighton, shop for second-hand books in Hay-on-Wye, have a pint at the Old Mill Inn at Trefonen or a cup of tea at Bishop's Castle. This is good country and it deserves more than a hurried glance.

To make it easier you could reasonably leave out one or two of the less inspiring sections without losing any of the essential character of the route. Prestatyn to Bodfari (pp68-74), Castle Mill to Llanymynech (pp101-6) and the section along the Severn plain (pp111-12) are all contenders for leaving out if you're in a hurry. However, the walk will be much more enjoyable if you can spare 16 days in all, allowing 14 days for walking and 2 days for travelling to and from home. If you can't spare the time to walk from end to end in one go you could undertake the walk over several shorter trips, gradually accumulating the miles until the great day comes when you have completed it in its entirety. Another option is simply to sample the highlights of the route on day walks and weekend trips; see p27 for a list of recommended sections.

Practical information for the walker

ACCOMMODATION

The path is well served with camping and Bed and Breakfast accommodation allowing for some flexibility in itineraries. A comprehensive selection of places to stay along the full length of the trail is given in the trail guide, Part 4.

Camping

Man is born free under the stars, yet we lock our doors and creep to bed. **Robert Louis Stevenson**

There is a reasonable number of official campsites along the Offa's Dyke Path but it isn't as well served as some of the other popular long-distance footpaths. Don't let this put you off. It is still perfectly possible to backpack the route from end to end, pitching where enterprising B&B owners have made space on their lawn, letting campers use a shower and offering meals as well. Almost every village has at least one place where this is possible although it can occasionally be embarrassing if you have to pitch your tent right outside the family lounge with the family sitting around watching television. The charge is between £2 and £4 per person so this is by far the most economical way to walk the trail.

For those who are never happier than when pitching their tent behind a hedge and striking camp in the morning dew before the world is up, we all salute you, but the Offa's Dyke Path is not ideal for what you want. Farmers used to be more amenable to the odd inconspicuous tent being pitched in a field corner but since the catastrophic foot and mouth epidemic in 2001 attitudes have changed and if you were discovered you would certainly not be made welcome.

Bunkhouses and hostels

Cheap hostel-style accommodation is severely limited along the path. There's a scattering of bunkhouses with dormitory accommodation costing £4–£14 per head, no youth hostels actually on the trail itself and only four within easy reach of the trail. However, if you have the energy to walk the extra distance you are assured of a cheaper night's accommodation than the average B&B. What's more, they all have self-catering facilities and some provide good value evening meals for £5. The cost for staying in a youth hostel varies from £8.50 to £11.50 but you need to be a member of the **Youth Hostels Association** (☎ 0870-870 8808, 🖥 www.yha.org.uk), Trevelyan House, 8 St Stephen's Hill, St Albans, Hertfordshire, AL1 2DY. The cost of membership is currently £15 per year and it's possible to join when you arrive at a hostel.

Bed and breakfast

Staying in B&Bs has its own particular appeal. For anyone unfamiliar with the concept you get a bedroom in someone's home along with a cooked breakfast the following morning. The accommodation is invariably clean and comfortable with the emphasis on floral patterns and chintz but for value for money it has no equal. One night you will be in a bijou bungalow, the next in a working hill farm to be woken by the crowing of a cock. The attraction lies in their variety which gives you a unique insight into the local culture.

What to expect For the long-distance walker tourist board recommendations and star rating systems have little meaning. At the end of a long day you will simply be glad of a place with hot water and a smiling face to welcome you. If they have somewhere to hang your wet and muddy clothes so much the better. It is these criteria that have been used for places recommended in this guide, rather than whether a room has tea- and coffee-making facilities, a shaver point or colour TV.

En suite will often mean a simple shower cunningly built into a recess leaving little space to wield a towel. Some walkers relish the thought of a hot bath rather than a shower at the end of a hard day and hence a non en-suite room where the guest makes use of a shared bathroom might be preferable, although it may mean you have to wait your turn.

Walkers travelling alone may find it hard to find establishments with **single** rooms. Most B&Bs have adopted **family rooms** with enthusiasm since it allows them to pack three or more people into one room, thereby freeing other rooms for further guests. These family rooms can be rather like a dormitory but are perfectly adequate for a group of walkers if you don't mind packing in together.

An **evening meal** is on offer at some of the better establishments but you will have to accept that this is served at a stated time and you will miss it if you are late. Ring ahead if you have been delayed on the trail.

Prices A typical B&B establishment will range in price from £17 to £20 per person for a nice clean room and £21 to £25 per person for a room with en-suite facilities. Lone walkers occupying a twin or double room will be expected to pay a supplement of £5 or sometimes more.

In the off-season it can be worth trying to negotiate a cheaper rate. Not all B&B hosts will respond but some will.

Transport offered by B&B hosts As many of the places offering accommodation are not right on the Offa's Dyke Path it is the custom for B&B owners to collect walkers at an agreed rendezvous and deliver them back to the trail in the morning. This is often regarded as an inclusive service of mutual benefit and one which B&B owners gladly provide. The benefit to the walker is that there is no added mileage at the end of the day to reach the accommodation.

It is important to agree lift arrangements with your host at the time of making the booking. Mobile phone users would find it useful to ring ahead to give their host warning of their impending arrival at the pick-up point.

Booking Always book your accommodation. Not only does this ensure you have a bed for the night but gives you a chance to find out more about the place, check prices and see what's included. If you have to cancel, phone your hosts: it will save a lot of worry and allows them to provide a bed for someone else.

Some walkers opt for booking their accommodation in advance from home during the planning stage of their walk. The key to selecting where to stay lies in anticipating your daily mileage. Many walkers base their average on between twelve and fourteen miles a day and can hence calculate approximately where they are going to end up at the completion of each day's walk. The suggested itineraries on p22 will also be of help.

Pubs and inns
Many rural pubs and inns now offer B&B accommodation and some have seized the challenge enthusiastically, supplying every modern convenience including, in extreme cases, four-poster beds and a pool. At least you do not have far to go to reach the bar. But the idea fails where the proprietor, with every good intention, has nevertheless to mind the bar and restaurant, leaving little time to concern himself with your needs in a busy establishment. Pubs can also be quite noisy for those who retire early so choose carefully if you intend staying on the premises.

Guesthouses
Guesthouses are more impersonal and don't have that private life of their own that is characteristic of good B&Bs, although they can be perfectly acceptable and well run. The best guesthouses are those that 'cater for walkers', which means they understand the way walkers think and are happy to accommodate the problems walkers can bring with them; wet gear, dirty boots, huge rucksacks and a tendency for invading the place like an army on the march. You should expect to pay a bit more for a room in a guesthouse, from £25 per person per night.

Hotels
Many walkers are prejudiced against staying in hotels, reluctant to pay the higher prices and believing, perhaps wrongly, that walkers are unwelcome in more genteel surroundings. You may want to treat yourself to one really luxurious night, possibly to mark the halfway mark or to celebrate at the finish, in which case you may well choose to stay in more up-market accommodation.

The price range is likely to be £35 and upwards per person with some saving for two people sharing a room. Some hotels have adopted the continental system of charging for the room only rather than per person, which for a couple doing the walk together may prove an economical proposition when you consider that two people paying £40 for the room will be the same as £20 each, about the rate of an average B&B. Watch out for the extras though, such as service charge and VAT which will inevitably add to the bottom line when the bill is presented.

Holiday cottages

For the walker intending to cover the mileage end to end self-catering cottages will not be an option but some people will want to walk parts of the route from a fixed base. Under these circumstances self-catering may be an ideal option. Typically these cottages are let on a weekly or fortnightly basis. Prices start at around £150 a week for four people. Holiday cottage accommodation has not been listed in this book. Contact the tourist information centres (see p35) for further details.

FOOD AND DRINK

Drinking water

When walking it is recommended that you drink at least two litres of water a day. On a hot day you will need to increase this to three or four litres to replace the fluids lost through sweating. Though tempting, don't drink from streams or rivers along the trail as they are likely to be laden with harmful chemical contaminants picked up from fields, roads and housing. Either carry enough for the day or fill up at public conveniences or outside taps marked on the trail maps in Part 4. Failing that, farms will usually give you a fill of water if you ask politely; if you go into a pub, shop or café it would be appropriate to buy something first before asking them to fill up your bottle.

Buying camping supplies

There are enough shops along the path to allow you to buy food supplies frequently. You should not need to carry food for longer than one day. Village shops, where they still exist, are open throughout the year and most open seven days a week from 8am to 8pm or even later to take full advantage of casual trade and the sale of alcohol. Fuel for camp stoves may not always be available although Camping Gaz and meths can usually be found.

Breakfast and lunch

A full fry-up of bacon, eggs and sausages is considered de rigueur by many walkers but remember when in Wales to ask for a Full Welsh rather than a Full English breakfast! Others prefer a somewhat lighter continental breakfast which will always be available.

You will probably need a packed lunch which your B&B host will provide you with for a small charge (£3.50 typically) and also fill your flask with coffee or tea. Alternatively you could rely on what you can buy on the trail at village shops or pubs, although in rural areas these are becoming more scarce as people confine their shopping to a visit once a week to the supermarket. Where you get the chance it is always a good idea to give small local retailers the benefit of your custom, even if it is only a pound or two.

Pubs

The Offa's Dyke Path is abundantly supplied with pubs and inns and they are a good choice for your evening meal. Many have restaurants but most walkers will be happy with a bar meal. Some establishments offer a wide and imaginative selection of hot meals including vegetarian options where required.

During licensing hours you can get a pint of beer or any other drink of your choice. The drawback lies in the words 'during licensing hours' which in England and Wales means pubs are permitted to sell alcohol from 11am to 11pm Monday to Saturday and 12 noon to 11pm on Sundays. At present few rural pubs remain open for the full allowed time, often opening for lunch between 11am and 2.30/3pm, closing in the afternoon while the landlord has

---

❏ The perfect pint

Much of the beer found in pubs along the path is pasteurized and manufactured in millions of gallons and distributed throughout Britain. Known as keg beer, it has been reviled by real ale drinkers in its time but is invariably smooth and tastes the same wherever you are.

However, traditional **real ale**, the product of small-scale local breweries, is always in demand. Real ale continues to ferment in the cask and so can be drawn off by hand pump or a simple tap in the cask itself. Keg beer, on the other hand, has the fermentation process stopped by pasteurization and needs the addition of gas to give it fizz and sparkle.

Keep an eye out for pubs with the CAMRA sticker which shows they have been selected by the **Campaign for Real Ale**. This invaluable organization has been largely responsible for the survival of independent brewers in the UK and deserves our plaudits. Keen beer drinkers will be on the lookout for rare or unusual beers only available regionally, some of them even brewed on the premises of the pub where they are served. Examples of this are to be found in Bishop's Castle (see p128), just off-route, where in-house beers are brewed at the Six Bells and at the Three Tuns, whose Offa's Ale, a strong dark bitter of unusual character at 4.9% ABV, is well worth seeking out.

Local brews well distributed in mid-Wales and the Borders are those by Brains of Cardiff and by Hancocks from the West Midlands. Both create good pints but try the brews above 4%ABV for better taste and flavour. Some rarities to add to your list are Bullmastiff Gold Brew, served at the Half Moon Inn in Llanthony (p167), an award-winning independent brewery run by two brothers with a nice sense of humour. Their tongue was firmly in their cheek when they issued Snarlsberg Llager, a cask-conditioned Welsh lager. Their Son of a Bitch at 6% ABV has a bite that is worse than its bark. From the Hereford-based Wye Valley Brewery try Dorothy Goodbody's which has a lovely crisp finish. Lovers of good beer will no doubt sniff out their own choice brews, the Borders area giving plenty of opportunity to keep their love alive. Cheers!

❏ **Welsh specialities**
● **Laver bread** Seaweed with oatmeal fried in bacon fat and served for breakfast
Even supermarkets stock it now.
● **Bara brith** A traditional rich cake made with marmalade, mixed fruit, spices, egg
and flour, not unlike fruit loaf.
● **Welsh cakes** Tasty cakes full of currants and sultanas. You can find them in
supermarkets and in most tea shops and cafés.
● **Welsh rarebit** Melted cheese with a hint of mustard poured over buttered toast.
● **Leek and parsley broth** (*Cawl cennin a phersli*) A traditional broth made from
beef and lamb, root vegetables, herbs and leeks
● **Tregaron granny's broth** (*Cawl mamgu Tregaron*) Another soup full of vegeta-
bles with beef and bacon.
● **Wyau mon** Eggs in cheese sauce with potatoes and leeks.
● **Miner's delight** (*Gorfoledd y glowyr*) A rabbit casserole dish.

---

an afternoon nap before reopening from 6 to 11pm. This means that during the
day hungry and thirsty walkers cannot automatically expect a pub to be open
when they want it to be. The pleasure in discovering a pub open in the middle
of the afternoon just when you are ready for a thirst-quenching pint is one of the
highlights of walking in Britain.

Other places to eat out
In the towns along the path there are good cafés and restaurants as well as the
usual choice of takeaways: Chinese and Indian cuisine has reached even the
remotest outposts of civilization.

MONEY

Plan your money needs carefully. It would be sensible to carry a float of cash
with you for spending on a day-to-day basis although credit cards are accepted
practically everywhere including in the larger pubs and in all but the smallest
village shops. B&Bs are unlikely to have facilities for paying by credit card but
they will usually accept a cheque so you don't need to carry an excessive
amount of cash with you. Start with about £200 and expect to replenish from
cashpoints in the towns you visit along the way. Camping will be most easily
paid for in cash because of the smaller amounts involved.

Supermarkets all offer a cash-back service whereby they charge your debit
card and give you cash from the till. All the towns you pass through have banks,
most of them with cashpoints and cash can also be drawn at post offices but you
will need to have your cheque book or debit card with you. Travellers' cheques
can be exchanged in banks, foreign exchanges and the larger hotels. Foreign
exchange bureaux can often be found in travel agents, such as Thomas Cook, in
the larger towns.

Take a cheque book. Cheques are accepted almost everywhere.

WALKING COMPANIES

For walkers wanting to make their holiday as easy and trouble-free as possible there are several specialist companies offering a range of services from baggage carrying to fully-guided group tours.

Baggage carriers

The thought of carrying a heavy pack puts a lot of people off walking long-distance trails. A baggage-carrying service will deliver your bags to your accommodation each night leaving you free to walk unencumbered during the day. This obviously works out much cheaper if there is a group of you.

● **Byways Breaks** (☎ 0151-722 8050, 💻 www.byways-breaks.co.uk), 25 Mayville Rd, Liverpool, L18 0HG

● **Border Taxis** (☎ 01497-821266, 💻 www.hay-on-wye.co.uk/border) Hay-on-Wye

Some of the **taxi** firms listed in this guide (see Part 4) can provide a similar service within a local area if you are having problems carrying your bags for a day or so. The arrangements are best made with your B&B host. In certain cases he will do the transporting himself but bear in mind that the cost of this service could easily be £15 which may preclude it for lone walkers or pairs. See also below.

Self-guided holidays

The following companies provide customized packages for walkers which usually include detailed advice and notes on itineraries, maps, accommodation booking, daily baggage transfer and transport at the start and end of your walk. If you don't want the whole package some companies can simply arrange **accommodation-booking** or **baggage-carrying** services on their own.

● **Byways Breaks** (see above)

● **Celtic Trails** (☎ 0800-970 7585 or ☎ 01600-860846, 💻 www.walking-w ales.com) PO Box 11, Chepstow, NP16 6DZ

● **Contours Walking Holidays** (☎ 01768-867539, 💻 www.contours.co.uk), Smithy House, Stainton, Penrith, Cumbria, CA11 0ES

● **Discovery Travel** (☎ 01904-766564, 💻 www.discoverytravel.co.uk), 12 Towpath Rd, Haxby, York YO32 3ND

● **Explore Britain** (☎ 01740-650900, 💻 www.xplorebritain.com), 6 George St, Ferryhill, Co Durham, DL17 0DT

● **Footprints of Sussex** (☎ 01903-813381, 💻 www.footprintsofsussex.co.uk), Pear Tree Cottage, Jarvis Lane, Steyning, West Sussex, BN44 3GL

● **InStep Linear Walking Holidays** (☎ 01903-766475, 💻 www.instep hols.co.uk), 35 Cokeham Road, Lancing, West Sussex, BN15 0AE

● **Marches Walks** (☎ 01497-847149, 💻 www.marches-walks.co.uk), Footsteps, Cwmbach, Glasbury-on-Wye, Powys, HR3 5LT

● **Wysk Walks** (☎ 01600-712176), Church Farm, Mitchell Troy, Monmouth NP25 4HZ

Group/guided walking tours

Fully-guided tours are ideal for individuals wanting to travel in the company of others and for groups of friends wanting to be guided. The packages usually include meals, accommodation, transport arrangements, minibus back-up, baggage transfer, as well as a qualified guide. Companies' specialities differ widely with varied sizes of group, standards of accommodation, age range of clients and professionalism of guides, so it's worth checking out several before making a booking.

● **Avalon Trekking** (☎ 01889-575646 or ☎ 0777-596 7644, 🖳 www.avalontrekking.co.uk), 40 Waverley Gardens, Etching Hill, Rugeley, Staffordshire, WS15 2YE

● **Contours Walking Holidays** (☎ 01768-867539, 🖳 www.contours.co.uk), Smithy House, Stainton, Penrith, Cumbria, CA11 0ES

● **Footpath Holidays** (☎ 01985-840049, 🖳 www.footpath-holidays.com), 16 Norton Bavant, Warminster, Wiltshire, BA12 7BB

● **HF Holidays** (☎ 020-8905 9558, 🖳 www.hfholidays.co.uk), Imperial House, Edgware Rd, London NW9 5AL

● **Marches Walks** (see p17)

● **Ramblers Holidays** (☎ 01707-331133, 🖳 www.ramblersholidays.co.uk), Box 43, Welwyn Garden City, Hertfordshire, AL8 6PQ.

● **Wysk Walks** (see p17)

Budgeting

Your trip budget depends largely on the type of accommodation you use and your eating habits. If you camp and cook your own meals, you will be able to keep costs to a minimum. These escalate as you go up the accommodation and eating scales and the extent to which you use the services offered to guests, such as transportation of luggage, packed lunches and other refinements.

CAMPING

You can get by on as little as £8 per person per night pitching your tent at official sites and where B&Bs allow camping in their garden or land and cooking your own food. Typically, camping costs from £2 to £4 per person plus an extra £1 for the use of a shower.

Most walkers will find it hard to live that frugally and will indulge in the occasional cooked breakfast when it's offered (£4–£5.50), the odd pint of beer (£1.80–£2.20) and a pub meal after a long hard day (£5–£8). It's probably more realistic to budget on £10–£12 per day.

B&Bs

You should allow £25 per head for an overnight stay and breakfast plus a further £10–£12 for an evening meal depending on your appetite. If you include your lunchtime needs allow £40–£50 per person per day and you won't be far wrong.

EXTRAS

Don't forget to set some money aside for the inevitable extras: film, batteries, postcards, buses and taxis, beer, snacks, telephone calls, any changes of plan.

When to go

SEASONS

The months when the weather is less likely to be inclement are May to September although April and October often bring days that are bright and breezy when the walking and the surroundings are at their best. Taken in order, the seasons are likely to present the following conditions, detailed overleaf:

❏ **Information for foreign visitors**

● **Currency** The British pound (£) comes in notes of £100, £50, £20, £10, £5 and coins of £2 and £1. The pound is divided into 100 pence (usually referred to as 'p', pronounced 'pee') which comes in silver coins of 50p, 20p, 10p, and 5p and copper coins of 2p and 1p. England and Wales are treated as one and the same place as far as currency is concerned although the design of the pound coin is different in Wales, the Welsh coin carrying a leek.

● **Rates of exchange** Up to date rates can be found on 🖵 www.xe.com/ucc or at any bank or travel agent.

● **Business hours** Most **shops** and main **post offices** are open at least from Monday to Friday 9am–5pm and Saturday 9am–12.30pm but many choose longer hours and some open on Sunday as well. Many **supermarkets** remain open twelve hours a day and the Spar chain usually displays '8 till late' on the door. **Banks** typically open at 9.30am and close at 3.30pm or 4pm Mon–Fri but of course ATM machines are open all the time. **Pub** hours are constantly changing but common opening hours are 11am–2.30pm and 6–11pm Mon–Sat, opening an hour later on Sunday evenings.

● **National holidays** Most business premises close on January 1st, Good Friday and Easter Monday (March/April), first and last Monday in May, the last Monday in August, Christmas Day and Boxing Day (December 25th–26th).

● **Weights and measures** Britain is moving slowly into the metric system but there is resistance. Most food is now displayed and sold in metric (g and kg) but most people still think and talk in the imperial weights of pounds (lb) and ounces (oz). Milk is sold in pints as is beer in the pub, yet most other liquid including petrol (gasoline) is sold in litres. Road distances are shown in miles rather than kilometres and the population remains split between those who still use inches and feet and those who are happy with centimetres and millimetres.

● **Telephone** From outside Britain the international country access code for Britain is ☎ 44 followed by the area code minus the first 0 and then the number you require. Within Britain, to call a number with the same code as the phone you are calling from, the code can be omitted: dial the number only. It is cheaper to ring at weekends, and after 6pm and before 8am on weekdays.

Spring

The weather can be warm and sunny on odd days in **April** but seldom for sustained periods. The conditions are more likely to be changeable with blustery showers and cold spells reminding you that winter has only just passed.

It is worth noting, however, that less rain falls on average in spring than at any other time of the year. This coupled with the milder weather of **May** and **June** make it one of the best times to go walking in Britain.

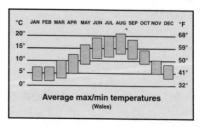

Average max/min temperatures
(Wales)

Summer

July and **August** are the traditional holiday months and the conditions are usually good for walking with long periods of warm settled weather and many hours of daylight.

Unlike many parts of Britain the Border Country is not afflicted by mass tourism. Thankfully there's no need to worry about crowds apart from when passing through the tourist hotspots of Prestatyn, Hay-on-Wye and Llangollen. You can lord it over the daytrippers with your rucksack and big boots which will set you apart as an outdoorsman. Let them look and wonder. Once you're back out among the fields and hills you can leave the hordes behind.

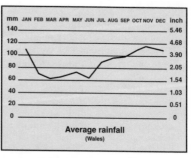

Average rainfall
(Wales)

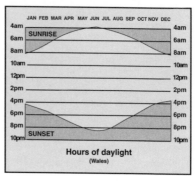

Hours of daylight
(Wales)

Autumn

Late **September** and **October** are a good time to get out on the trail to appreciate the full benefit of the autumn colours in the woodland and the leaves underfoot. Although the air temperature should remain mild, rain is an ever-present threat and showers intensify as the year draws to its close. Nevertheless, many connoisseurs consider autumn, especially early autumn, the best time of year for walking.

Winter

Once the days have shortened you will want to be at your day's end by 4.30–5pm. Colder days, wind and driving rain are not the best accompaniment for a good day on the path although you can hit lulls when the sun comes out and you imagine things are improving.

Some winters (eg 2001) see continuous rain for several months with severe flooding when parts of the path become impassable. Certainly only the very hardiest of souls will attempt the walk in winter.

DAYLIGHT HOURS

If walking in autumn, winter and early spring, you must take account of how far you can walk in the available daylight. It will not be possible to cover as many miles or be out for as long as you would in the summer.

The table opposite gives the sunrise and sunset times for the middle of each month at latitude 52° North which runs through Wales, giving a reasonably accurate picture for daylight for the Offa's Dyke Path. Depending on the weather, you should get a further 30–45 minutes of usable light before sunrise and after sunset.

ANNUAL EVENTS

The following events may need to be considered when planning your walk:

Literary Festival, Hay-on-Wye

Last week in May. The famous book and literary festival with talks and readings all week from top names in the world of writing. It is one of the few opportunities for readers to meet their favourite authors and the town's streets are thronged with visitors. Naturally enough every available room is taken, booked months ahead. You should either book very far in advance or avoid this week altogether.

International Musical Eisteddfod, Llangollen

Second week in July. This is a major festival of music and the performing arts to which groups and individuals come from all over the world. The town and surroundings are booked solid for the whole week.

Royal Welsh Show, Builth Wells

Last week in July. A big date in the farming calendar for the whole of mid and south Wales attracting visitors and competitors from a huge area. This makes big demands on the accommodation locally so it would be best to avoid this week if possible. Kington and Hay-on-Wye are the two centres on the path most likely to be affected.

Knighton Show

Last Saturday in August. An important day for the local community but likely to put pressure on accommodation and pubs for the one day only.

Itineraries

All walkers are individuals. Some like to cover large distances as quickly as possible. Others are happy to amble along, stopping whenever the whim takes them. You may want to walk the Offa's Dyke Path in one go, tackle it in a series of days or weekends or use the trail for a series of linear day walks; the choice is yours. To accommodate these different options, this guide has not been divided up into strict daily sections which can impose too rigid a structure on how you should walk. Instead it has been devised for you to plan an itinerary that suits you.

The **planning map** opposite and **table of facilities** on p24 summarize the essential information for you to make a plan of your own. Alternatively, to make it even easier, have a look at the **suggested itineraries** and simply choose your preferred speed of walking. There are also suggestions on p27 for those who want to experience the best of the trail over a day or a weekend. The **public transport map** (p38) may help at this stage.

Having made a rough plan, turn to **Part 4** where you will find summaries of the route, full descriptions of accommodation, places to eat and other services in each town and village, with detailed trail maps.

ITINERARY FOR STEADY WALKERS

Walking 10-14 miles (16-23km) a day with two longer days of 15-16 miles (24-26km)

Day	Daily schedule	Miles/km	Nearest camping and B&B
1	Prestatyn to Sodom	11/18	Sodom, Bodfari
2	Sodom to Clwyd Gate	13/21	Clwyd Gate, Llanferres, Llanbedr DC
3	Clwyd Gate to Llangollen	14/23	Llangollen
4	Llangollen to Craignant	10.5/17	Craignant
5	Craignant to Llanymynech	11/18	Llanymynech, Four Crosses
6	Llanymynech to Kingswood	16/26	Leighton, Kingswood, Forden
7	Kingswood to Newcastle-on-Clun	13.5/22	Newcastle-on-Clun, Clun
8	Newcastle to Dolley Green (for Presteigne)	12.5/20	Dolley Green, Presteigne
9	Dolley Green to Gladestry	13/21	Gladestry
10	Gladestry to Hay-on-Wye	10/16	Hay-on-Wye
11	Hay-on-Wye to Longtown	12.5/20	Longtown, Capel-y-ffyn, Llanthony
12	Longtown to Caggle Street	10/16	Caggle Street, Llanvertherine
13	Caggle Street to Redbrook	15/24	Redbrook
14	Redbrook to Sedbury Cliffs	14.5/23	Chepstow

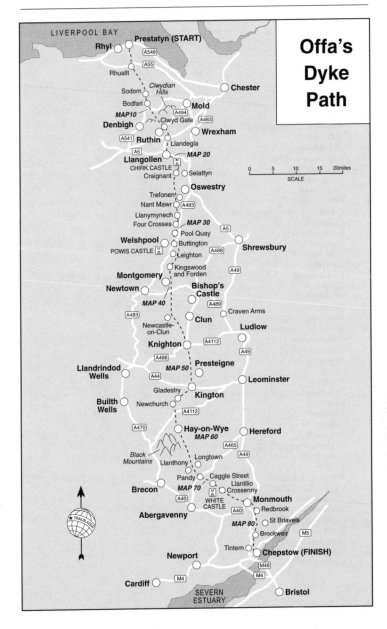

Offa's Dyke Path

Place name Places in (brackets) are a short walk off the path	Distance from previous place approx miles/km	Cash Machine	Post Office	Tourist Information Centre/Point
Prestatyn	Start of ODP	✔	✔	✔
Rhuallt	8/13			
Sodom	3/5			
Bodfari	2/3		✔	
(Llangynhafal)				
(Cilcain)				
(Llanbedr-Dyffryn-Clwyd)				
(Llanferres)				
Clwyd Gate	11/18			
(Llanarmon-yn-Ial)			✔	
Llandegla	6/10		✔	
(Llangollen)		✔	✔	✔
Trevor (and Garth)	11/18		✔	
Froncysyllte	1.5/2		✔	
Castle Mill (and Bronygarth)	4.5/7			
Craignant	2/3			
Racecourse Common	2.5/4			
Trefonen	3.5/5		✔	
Nant Mawr	2/3			
Llanymynech	3/5		✔	
Four Crosses	2.5/4		✔	
Buttington	8/13			
(Welshpool)		✔	✔	✔
Leighton	3/5			
Kingswood and Forden	3/5			
Brompton Crossroads	6.5/10			
(Montgomery)		✔	✔	
(Bishop's Castle)		✔	✔	
Newcastle-on-Clun	7/11			
(Clun)			✔	
Knighton	7.5/12	✔	✔	✔
Dolley Green (for Presteigne)	5/8	✔	✔	✔
Kington	8.5/14	✔	✔	✔
Gladestry	4.5/7		✔	
Newchurch	3.5/6			
Hay-on-Wye	6.5/10	✔	✔	✔
(Capel-y-ffin and Llanthony)				
(Longtown)				
Pandy	17.5/28			
Llangattock-Lingoed	2.5/4			
Caggle St and Llanvetherine	2.5/4		✔	
Monmouth	11.5/18	✔	✔	✔
Redbrook	3.5/6			
(St Riavels)			✔	
Brockweir	7/11			
(Tintern)			✔	
Chepstow	6/10	✔	✔	✔
Sedbury Cliffs	1.5/2			

Note: Distances given are between

TOWN FACILITIES

Eating Place	Food Store	Camp-site	Hostels YHA = Youth Hostel B = Bunkhouse	B&Bs F = a few M = many	Place name Places in (brackets) are a short walk off the path
✔	✔	✔		M	**Prestatyn**
✔					**Rhuallt**
		✔		F	**Sodom**
✔	✔	✔			**Bodfari**
✔				F	**(Llangynhafal)**
✔					**(Cilcain)**
✔		✔		F	**(Llanbedr-Dyffryn-Clwyd)**
✔				F	**(Llanferres)**
✔		✔		F	**Clwyd Gate**
✔			B	F	**(Llanarmon-yn-Ial)**
✔	✔	✔		F	**Llandegla**
✔	✔	✔	YHA	M	**(Llangollen)**
✔	✔			F	**Trevor (and Garth)**
✔		✔	B	F	**Froncysyllte**
				F	**Castle Mill (and Bronygarth)**
		✔		F	**Craignant**
		✔		F	**Racecourse Common**
✔	✔			F	**Trefonen**
		✔	B	F	**Nant Mawr**
✔	✔	✔		F	**Llanymynech**
✔	✔	✔		F	**Four Crosses**
✔	✔	✔		F	**Buttington**
✔	✔	✔		M	**(Welshpool)**
		✔		F	**Leighton**
✔	✔	✔		F	**Kingswood and Forden**
		✔		F	**Brompton Crossroads**
✔	✔			F	**(Montgomery)**
✔	✔			F	**(Bishop's Castle)**
✔		✔		F	**Newcastle-on-Clun**
✔	✔		YHA	F	**(Clun)**
✔	✔	✔		M	**Knighton**
✔	✔	✔		F	**Dolley Green (for Presteigne)**
✔	✔	✔		M	**Kington**
✔		✔		F	**Gladestry**
				F	**Newchurch**
✔	✔	✔		M	**Hay-on-Wye**
✔			YHA	F	**(Capel-y-ffin and Llanthony)**
		✔		F	**(Longtown)**
✔		✔		F	**Pandy**
✔		✔		F	**Llangattock-Lingoed**
		✔		F	**Caggle St and Llanvetherine**
✔	✔	✔		M	**Monmouth**
✔		✔		F	**Redbrook**
✔			YHA	F	**(St Riavels)**
✔				F	**Brockweir**
✔				F	**(Tintern)**
✔	✔	✔		M	**Chepstow**
					Sedbury Cliffs

places *directly on* the Offa's Dyke Path.

ITINERARY FOR FAST WALKERS

Walking 14-16 miles (23-26km) a day with four longer days of up to 18 miles (29km)

Day	Daily schedule	Miles/km	Nearest camping and B&B
1	Prestatyn to Bodfari	13/21	Bodfari
2	Bodfari to Llandegla	17/27	Llandegla
3	Llandegla to Trevor	11/18	Garth, Trevor, Froncysyllte
4	Trevor to Trefonen	14/23	Tyn-y-Coed, Trefonen, Nant Mawr
5	Trefonen to Buttington	15.5/25	Buttington, Welshpool
6	Buttington to Brompton C'roads	12.5/20	Brompton Crossroads, Montgomery
7	Brompton C'roads to Knighton	14.5/23	Knighton
8	Knighton to Kington	13.5/22	Kington
9	Kington to Hay-on-Wye	14.5/23	Hay-on-Wye
10	Hay-on-Wye to Pandy	17.5/28	Pandy
11	Pandy to Monmouth	16.5/27	Monmouth
12	Monmouth to Sedbury Cliffs	18/29	Chepstow

WHICH DIRECTION?

Most of the other guidebooks to the path assume you will walk from south to north but there is no particularly good reason to do this, apart from the slightly spurious view that it is easier with the sun and prevailing wind at your back. There is in fact a good reason for walking the path in the opposite direction, from north to south, namely that the route, without doubt, improves in quality as you move south. This provides a great incentive to spur you ever onward. As you progress south you will get fitter and should be in good fettle by the time you have to tackle the Black Mountains. This direction of travel has been followed in the layout of this book.

But there are good reasons to walk in the other direction, too, and many will chose to do so, especially if walking only part of the route. The maps in Part 4 give timings for both directions and, as route-finding instructions are on the maps rather than in the text, it is straightforward using this guide back to front.

SUGGESTED ITINERARIES

The itineraries on p22 and above are suggestions only and should be adapted to suit your own particular preferences. **Don't forget** to add the travelling time before and after the walk.

TAKING DOGS ALONG THE OFFA'S DYKE PATH

For many walkers a dog is an inseparable companion and there is no reason why yours shouldn't accompany you, provided you act responsibly and are alert to the necessity of keeping man's best friend under control at all times.

❏ HIGHLIGHTS – THE BEST DAY AND WEEKEND WALKS

Day walks

● **Prestatyn to Rhuallt** An exhilarating 8-mile (13km) walk over the escarpment with great views of the North Wales coast, Snowdonia and the Clwydian Range. See pp68-71.

● **Bodfari to Clwyd Gate** A challenging high level walk of 11 miles (18km) through the exposed Clwydian Hills with views on a fine day to Snowdonia and the sea (see pp75-80). Both ends of this walk are relatively well served by buses.

● **Clwyd Gate to Llandegla** Fine hillwalking over the southern outliers of the Clwydian Hills make this 6-mile (10km) walk an excellent one with wide views of the Vale of Denbigh followed by a pleasant stroll through the meadows to the charming village of Llandegla (see pp81-5). Both ends of this walk are served by buses.

● **Llangollen to Trevor via the Panorama route, returning along the canal** A gentle 6-mile (10km) circular walk with varied scenery and much of interest along this bustling stretch of inland waterway. See pp94-7. There are good public transport links to Llangollen.

● **Llanymynech to Pool Quay** Starting with a stretch of the Montgomery Canal, this 8-mile (13km) walk joins the River Severn where the path follows a man-made embankment to Pool Quay (see pp107-12). You can extend this walk with 2½ miles (4km) of canal walking to Buttington Bridge. Llanymynech is well served by buses and Welshpool, a further 1½ miles (2km) on from Buttington Bridge, has both rail and bus connections.

● **Buttington Bridge to Kingswood** Lovely 7-mile (11km) walk over the Iron Age hill-fort of Beacon Ring then through the exotic woodlands of the Leighton Estate to the village of Kingswood. Here you can have lunch at the Cock Inn and catch a bus back to Welshpool. Starting the walk in Welshpool adds 1½ miles to the distance. See pp113-21.

● **The Switchbacks** The 12-mile (19km) section of Dyke between Brompton Crossroads and Selley Cross near Knighton is characterized by a series of ascents and descents to navigate hilly country known as the Switchbacks. It makes a challenging day walk and will involve a lift at the finish to get back to the start, no local transport being available. The distance is made to feel longer by the constant ups and downs but the country is quintessential Borders, secretive, remote and populated by nothing more than cows, sheep and mewing buzzards. See pp125-35.

● **Circular 15-mile walk from Bishop's Castle** Follow the Shropshire Way to its junction with Offa's Dyke Path at the tiny church at Churchtown, an ideal spot for a picnic. Then walk north along the Offa's Dyke Path to where it meets the Kerry Ridgeway then back along quiet lanes to Bishop's Castle. This 15-mile (24km) ramble allows you to experience the real hidden countryside of the Border Country and shows you the Dyke at its best. See pp125-8 in conjunction with Ordnance Survey map Explorer 216. Bishop's Castle is well served by buses.

● **Kington to Gladestry and back** A superb 9-mile (14km) traverse of Hergest Ridge with views to the Shropshire Hills and the Black Mountains. Great walking on springy sheep-cropped turf through bracken and gorse. By doing the return trip after a pint at the pub in Gladestry you get a double helping of a marvellous area. See pp148-52. Kington is on several useful bus routes. *(continued on p28)*

❏ **Highlights – the best day and weekend walks** *(continued from p27)*
● **Hay-on-Wye to Newchurch** North along the Wye at first then through the mysterious glade of Bettws Dingle, this 6½-mile (10km) ramble gives a taste of the countryside which Francis Kilvert writes about in his diary (see p159), including the chance to see Emmeline's Grave at the pretty church of Newchurch (see p154-6). Hay-on-Wye is well served by buses.
● **Monmouth to Redbrook via the Kymin and return along the River Wye** Outstanding 6½-mile (10km) circular walk with a climb to the top of the Kymin with fantastic views over Monmouth and the hidden country beyond, followed by a pint at the unique Boat Inn at Redbrook and return along the silvery Wye. A great walk with loads of variety (see p180-4). Monmouth is well served by buses.
● **Bigsweir Bridge to Chepstow Bridge** This 9-mile (14km) walk includes a visit to the ruins of Tintern Abbey, stunningly located below the heavily wooded slopes of the Wye Valley, a perfect spot for lunch and a chance to visit the abbey. It ends at Chepstow Bridge from where the castle can be seen to dramatic effect before a bus back to Bigsweir. See p187-96.

Weekend walks
● **Bodfari to Llandegla** A spectacular 16-mile (25.7km) traverse of the entire Clwydian Range broken into two easy days by staying overnight at Llanbedr-Dyffryn-Clwyd (see pp75-84).There are bus services at both ends of this walk.
● **Llangollen to Llanymynech** A 24-mile (39km) walk of great variety taking in the aqueduct at Pontcysyllte, Chirk Castle, a pint at the Old Mill Inn in the secretive Morda Valley and the minor summit of Moelydd criss-crossed by mountain-bike trails. See pp94-106. Both ends of the walk are well served by buses.
● **Kington to Pandy** An outstanding 32-mile (52 km) outing in classic Dyke Country. Start by crossing the magnificent Hergest Ridge, stop for the night in the fascinating book town of Hay-on-Wye, then continue along the grand sweep of the Hatterrall Ridge the following day. See pp146-69. Both ends can be reached by bus.
● **Hay-on-Wye to Monmouth** This is a great weekend leg-stretcher of 34 miles (55km) with high-level walking along the spine of the Black Mountains followed by a day wending through the by-ways of the Welsh Marches. On the way you pass lovely villages, country inns and the splendid ruin of the once-mighty White Castle. See p159-81. Hay-on-Wye and Monmouth are well served by buses.
● **Monmouth to Sedbury Cliffs** A stunning walk of 18 miles (28km) following the winding course of the Wye Valley as the river snakes its way to the sea. There are plenty of places for refreshment, a chance to visit the atmospheric ruins of Tintern Abbey and to explore the characterful towns of Chepstow and Monmouth, both of which are well served by public transport. See pp184-97.

It is a legal requirement to keep dogs under control on Rights of Way. It is particularly important to keep your dog on a lead when crossing fields with livestock in them especially around lambing time which can be as early as February or as late as the end of April. Ground nesting birds are active between March and June; dogs can frighten them off and possibly cause them to desert their nests.

Farmers are legally entitled to shoot dogs found worrying sheep and every year there are cases of this happening. Dogs running free in standing crops can also cause damage and this should be actively prevented. Remember also that when walking through farmyards, or past farms, farm dogs may appear and act aggressively towards your dog or even you. They are protecting their territory and you should walk through without offering any threat in return. It is especially important for dogs to be kept on a close lead in these circumstances.

Some enlightened B&Bs positively welcome dogs, others are less keen, but either way, you should let it be known when booking ahead that you have a dog with you. B&Bs don't tend to charge for dogs but hotels often do.

What to take

How much you take with you is a very personal decision which takes experience to get right. For those new to long-distance walking the suggestions below will help you strike a sensible balance between comfort, safety and minimal weight.

I'm facing the wind
And I'm ready to fly
Anywhere my heart takes me tonight
I'm travelling light.
Tom Shapiro and George Teren

KEEP IT LIGHT

In these days of huge material wealth it can be a liberating experience to travel as light as possible to learn how few possessions we really need to be safe and comfortable. It is all too easy to take things along 'just in case' and these little items can soon mount up. If you are in any doubt about anything on your packing list, be ruthless and leave it at home.

HOW TO CARRY IT

The size of your **rucksack** depends on how you plan to walk. If you are camping along the way you will need a pack large enough to hold a tent, sleeping bag, cooking equipment and food; 65 to 75 litres capacity should be ample. This should have a stiffened back system and either be fully adjustable or exactly the right size for your back. If you carry the main part of the load high and close to the body with a large proportion of the weight carried on your hips (not on your shoulders) by means of the padded hip belt you should be able to walk in comfort for days on end. Play around with different ways of packing your gear and adjusting all those straps until you get it just right. It's also handy to have a **bum/waist bag** or a very light **daypack** in which you can carry your camera, guidebook and other essentials when you go off sightseeing.

If you are staying in bunkhouses you may want to carry a sleeping bag for which a 40–60 litre pack should be fine. If you are indulging in the luxury of B&Bs you should be able to get all you need into a 30–40 litre pack. Pack similar things in different coloured **stuff sacks** so they are easier to pull out of the dark recesses of your pack. Put these inside **waterproof rucksack liners**, or tough plastic sacks, that can be slipped inside your pack to protect everything from the inevitable rain.

Of course, if you decide to use a **baggage-carrying service** (see p17) you can pack most of your things in a suitcase and simply carry a small daypack with the essentials you need for the day's walking.

FOOTWEAR

Boots

Your boots are the single most important item of gear that can affect the enjoyment of your walk.

In summer you could get by with a light pair of trail shoes if you're carrying only a small pack, although this is an invitation for wet, cold feet if there is any rain and they don't offer much support for your ankles. Some of the terrain is rough so a good pair of walking boots would be a safer option. They must fit well and be properly broken in. A week's walk is not the time to try out a new pair of boots. Refer to p199 for more blister-avoidance strategies.

If you plan to travel in winter good boots are essential. Fabric boots will soon become saturated and so will your socks unless you adopt the use of Goretex socks which are ideal worn inside fabric boots and will keep your feet completely dry.

Socks

The traditional wearing of a thin liner sock under a thicker wool sock is no longer necessary if you choose a high-quality sock specially designed for walking. A high proportion of natural fibres makes them much more comfortable. Three pairs are ample.

Extra footwear

Some walkers like to have a second pair of shoes to wear when they are not on the trail. Trainers, sport sandals or flip flops are all suitable as long as they are light.

CLOTHES

Wet and cold weather can catch you out even in summer and you should come prepared for the unexpected. Spring and autumn can also be glorious at times so clothes to cope with these wide variations are needed.

Experienced walkers pick their clothes according to the versatile layering system: a base layer to transport sweat away from your skin; a mid-layer or two to keep you warm; and an outer layer or 'shell' to protect you from the wind, rain and, at the worst, snow.

Base layer

Cotton absorbs sweat, trapping it next to the skin which will chill you rapidly when you stop exercising. A thin lightweight **thermal top** made from synthetic material is better as it draws moisture away keeping you dry. It will be cool if worn on its own in hot weather and warm when worn under other clothes in cooler conditions. A spare would be sensible. You may also like to bring a **shirt** for wearing in the evening.

Mid-layers
From May to September a woollen jumper or mid-weight polyester **fleece** will suffice. For the rest of the year you will need an extra layer to keep you warm. Both wool and fleece, unlike cotton, stay reasonably warm when wet.

Outer layer
A **waterproof jacket** is essential year-round and will be much more comfortable (but also more expensive) if it's also 'breathable' to prevent the build-up of condensation on the inside. This layer can also be worn to keep the wind off.

Leg wear
Whatever you wear on your legs it should be light, quick-drying and not restricting. Many British walkers find polyester tracksuit bottoms comfortable. Poly-cotton or microfibre trousers are excellent. Denim jeans should never be worn; if they get wet they become heavy, cold and bind to your legs. A pair of **shorts** should be carried for sunny days.

Thermal **longjohns** or thick tights are cosy if you're camping and necessary for winter walking. **Waterproof trousers** are necessary most of the year but in summer could be left behind if your main pair of trousers is reasonably wind-proof and quick-drying. **Gaiters** are not needed but in very wet and muddy conditions can protect your boots and socks.

Underwear
Three changes of what you normally wear should suffice. Women may find a **sports bra** more comfortable because pack straps can cause bra straps to dig into your shoulders.

Other clothes
A **warm hat** and **gloves** should be carried at any time of the year. Take two pairs of gloves in winter. In summer you should carry a **sunhat** and possibly a **swimsuit**; there are a few swimming pools along the route which can be nice at the end of a hot day. A small **towel** will be needed if you are not staying in B&Bs.

❑ **Outdoor clothing – cheaper alternatives**
Modern, synthetic outdoor clothing is light and quick-drying but doesn't come cheap. If you are new to walking and feel the expense of equipping yourself properly is prohibitive then of course you can get by with 'normal' cotton clothing under a good waterproof layer, especially in summer. However, if this is the case, you must carry a complete spare set of clothes that you should always keep dry. If this means pulling on the damp clothes you wore the day before then do so.

TOILETRIES

Only take the minimum: a small bar of **soap** in a plastic container (unless staying in B&Bs) which can also be used instead of shaving cream and for washing clothes; a tiny tube of **toothpaste** and a **toothbrush**; one roll of **loo paper** in a plastic bag. If you are planning to defecate outdoors you will also need a lightweight **trowel** for burying the evidence (see p43 for further tips). A **razor**, **deodorant, tampons/sanitary towels** and a high-factor **sunscreen** should cover all your needs.

FIRST-AID KIT

Medical facilities in Britain are excellent so you only need a small kit to cover common problems and emergencies; pack it in a waterproof container. A basic kit will contain **aspirin** or **paracetamol** for treating mild to moderate pain and fever; **plasters/Band Aids** for minor cuts; '**moleskin**', '**Compeed**', or '**Second Skin**' for blisters; a **bandage** for holding dressings, splints, or limbs in place and for supporting a sprained ankle; **elastic knee support** for a weak knee; a small selection of different sized **sterile dressings** for wounds; **porous adhesive tape**; **antiseptic wipes**; **antiseptic cream**; **safety pins**; **tweezers**; and **scissors**.

GENERAL ITEMS

Essential

A **compass** should be carried but it will be of no use to you without some familiarity with its use. You won't need it constantly but on the occasions when you do it can be invaluable especially in poor visibility. An emergency **whistle** for summoning assistance; a one- or two-litre **water bottle**; a **torch** (flashlight) with spare bulb and batteries in case you end up walking after it's got dark; **emergency food** which your body can quickly convert into energy (see p198); a **penknife**; a **watch** with an alarm; and several **plastic bags** for packing out any rubbish you accumulate (see p42 for further information). If you're not carrying a sleeping bag or tent you should also carry an emergency plastic **bivvy-bag**.

Useful

Many would list a **camera** as essential but it can be liberating to travel without one once in a while; a **notebook** can be a more accurate way of recording your impressions; a **book** to pass the time on train and bus journeys, or in the tent; a pair of **sunglasses** in summer; **binoculars** for observing wildlife; a **walking stick** or pole to take the shock off your knees (some walkers use two poles but this leaves no free hand); a **vacuum flask** for carrying hot drinks – your B&B host will probably be happy to fill it for you; and a **mobile phone**. Many walkers carry mobile phones but it is important to remember that the network may not provide full coverage of the area through which you are walking due to the terrain. Mid Wales is poorly served by the networks and it is quite likely that you will be unable to make your call. Take the mobile by all means but don't rely on it.

SLEEPING BAG

Unless you are camping there is no need to carry a sleeping bag. Youth hostels provide linen and do not allow you to use sleeping bags. Bunkhouses vary in their policy, some requiring you to bring your own bag, others providing linen. If you intend to stay in them it would be worth telephoning to check whether a sleeping bag is necessary.

CAMPING GEAR

If you're camping you will need a decent **tent** (or bivvy bag if you enjoy travelling light) able to withstand wet and windy weather; a two- or three-season **sleeping bag**; a **sleeping mat**; a **stove** and **fuel** (there is special mention in Part 4 of which shops stock which fuel; bottles of meths and the various gas cylinders are readily available, Coleman fuel is sometimes harder to find); a **pan** with frying pan that can double as a lid/plate is fine for two people; a **pan handle**; a **mug**; **cutlery**; and a wire/plastic **scrubber** for washing up.

MONEY

There are numerous banks in the towns along the path but you'll need to have an adequate supply of ready **cash**. A **debit card** is the easiest way to draw money either from banks or cash machines and can be used to pay in larger shops, restaurants and hotels. A **cheque book** is very useful for walkers with accounts in British banks as a cheque will often be accepted where a card is not. Supermarkets all provide a **cash-back** facility at the check-out for which you will need a debit card (or a credit card if you don't mind paying some interest).

TRAVEL INSURANCE

Visitors from other countries within the EU should complete form E111 which entitles you to medical treatment under the National Health Service. This is no substitute, however, for proper medical cover on your travel insurance for unforeseen bills and getting you home should that be necessary.

All walkers should consider insurance cover for loss or theft of personal belongings, especially if you are camping or staying in hostels, as there will be times when you'll have to leave your belongings unattended.

MAPS

The hand-drawn maps in this book cover the trail at a scale of 1:20,000; plenty of detail and information to keep you on the right track. **Ordnance Survey** (☎ 0845-200 2712, 🖳 www.ordsvy.gov.uk) cover the whole route at a scale of 1:25,000 on the following seven maps: Explorer series (the ones with the orange cover) numbers 265, 256, 240, 216, 201, and Outdoor Leisure series (yellow cover) 13 and 14. Not all of these are strictly necessary if you pay careful attention to the maps in this guide. This will come as a relief as all seven weigh about 2lb (1kg) and are expensive at £6.75 each. For the sake of safety you should carry the maps of the Clwydian Range (Explorer 265 and 256) and Brecon Beacons National Park (Outdoor Leisure Map 13) as the path crosses rugged and hilly terrain where visibility could be restricted. In such conditions a map from which you can take compass bearings is essential.

Enthusiastic map buyers can reduce the often considerable expense of purchasing them: members of the **Ramblers' Association** (see opposite) can borrow up to 10 maps for a period of six weeks at 30p per map from their library; members of the **Backpackers' Club** (see opposite) can purchase maps at a significant discount through their map service.

RECOMMENDED READING

General guidebooks

There's the comprehensive *Wales: The Rough Guide;* Lonely Planet's *Wales* is also good.

Flora and fauna field guides

Any good guide will do; the Collins Pocket Guide series is unfailingly practical:
● *Birds of Britain and Europe* by Herman Heinzl, Richard Fitter, and John Parslow (Collins, 1991)
● *Wild Flowers of Britain and Northern Europe* by Richard Fitter, Alastair Fitter and Marjorie Blamey (Collins, 1996)
● *Insects of Britain and Western Europe* by Michael Chinery (Collins, 1986)
● *The Mammals of Britain and Europe* by David MacDonald and Priscilla Barrett (Collins, 1993)
● *Trees of Britain and Northern Europe* by Alan Mitchell and John Wilkinson (Collins, 1988)

General reading

● *Wild Wales* by George Borrow (Everyman Library). Quirky, opinionated yet irrepressible account of the author's visit to Wales in the mid-19th century. Not much about the areas you pass through though.
● *Kilvert's Diary* edited by William Plomer (Penguin, 1978). Lovely man, curate of Clyro Church near Hay-on-Wye in the Victorian era. Well worth dipping into.
● *On the Black Hill* by Bruce Chatwin (Vintage Paperback, 1998). Atmospheric, gives a good idea of what it was like to be a Welsh hill farmer after WWII.
● *Welsh Border Country* by Maxwell Fraser (Batsford, 1972). Sadly no longer in print but worth hunting for if you want a taste of this beautiful, secret area.
● *A History of Wales* by John Davies (Penguin, 1994). The best book on Welsh history from the ice age to the present. Honest, objective and packed with detail.
● *The Ladies of Llangollen* by Elizabeth Mavor (Penguin, 2001). Intriguing account of the unconventional lives of the two devoted friends who set up home in Plas Newydd, attracting the greatest figures of the early 19th century to their door. The question remains unanswered – were they or weren't they?
● *The Keys to Avalon* by Steve Blake and Scott Lloyd (Harper Collins, 2001). If you thought Avalon was in Cornwall or Glastonbury, here's another theory; Arthur was Welsh! This closely argued account also suggests the Romans built

❏ FURTHER INFORMATION

Trail information

● **Offa's Dyke Association** (☎ 01547-528753, 🖳 www.offasdyke.demon.co.uk), West St, Knighton, Powys, LD7 1EN. This independent, voluntary organization looks after the interests of walkers on the Offa's Dyke Path. Full membership is £12 a year. They publish a rather esoteric newsletter three times a year, an annual accommodation guide and *Route Notes*, a detailed step-by-step description of the route in both directions; accurate but dull. Much of this information is available on their excellent website. They are based at the tourist information centre in Knighton and are unfailingly helpful and informative about every aspect of the path.

● **Offa's Dyke Path Management Service** (☎ 01547-528192, 🖳 odp@offasdyke. demon.co.uk) look after the running of this National Trail, fixing broken stiles and bridges, dealing with erosion and making sure the route is well signposted. Any problems encountered along the way should be reported to them at their headquarters in the Offa's Dyke Centre in Knighton.

Tourist information centres

Tourist information centres (TICs) provide all manner of locally specific information for visitors and an accommodation booking service (for which there is usually a charge). There are TICs on or near the path in **Prestatyn** (☎ 01745-889092), **Mold** (☎ 01352-759331), **Ruthin** (☎ 01824-703992), **Llangollen** (☎ 01978-860828), **Oswestry** (☎ 01691-662753), **Welshpool** (☎ 01938-552043), **Knighton** (☎ 01547-529424), **Presteigne** (☎ 01544-260650), **Kington** (☎ 01544-230778), **Hay-on-Wye** (☎ 01497-820144), **Monmouth** (☎ 01600-713899), **Chepstow** (☎ 01291-623772).

Tourist boards

The tourist boards produce glossy brochures on their region and can be a good source for general information.

● **Heart of England Tourist Board** (☎ 01905-761100, 🖳 www.hetb.co.uk), Woodside, Larkhill Rd, Worcester, WR5 2EF

● **Wales Tourist Board** (☎ 029-2049 9909, 🖳 www.visitwales.com), Brunel House, 2 Fitzalan Rd, Cardiff, CF24 0UY

Organizations for walkers

● **The Backpackers' Club** (🖳 www.backpackersclub.co.uk), 29 Lynton Drive, High Lane, Stockport, Cheshire, SK6 8JE. A club aimed at people who are involved or interested in lightweight camping through walking, cycling, skiing, canoeing, etc. They produce a quarterly magazine, provide members with a comprehensive advisory and information service on all aspects of backpacking, organize weekend trips and also publish a farm-pitch directory. Membership is £12 per year.

● **The Long Distance Walkers' Association** (🖳 www.ldwa.org.uk). Membership includes a journal three times per year giving details of challenge events and local group walks as well as articles on the subject. Information on over 500 Long Distance Paths is presented in the LDWA's Long Distance Walkers' Handbook. Membership is currently £7 per year.

● **The Ramblers' Association** (☎ 020-7339 8500, 🖳 www.ramblers.org.uk), 2nd Floor, Camelford House, 87–89 Albert Embankment, London, SE1 7BR. Looks after the interests of walkers throughout Britain. They publish a large amount of useful information including their *Yearbook* (£4.99 to non-members), a full directory of services for walkers. Membership is £20 per year.

the Dyke; another one of those ideas akin to spacemen building Stonehenge.

● *The Making of the English Landscape* by WG Hoskins (Hodder and Stoughton, 1956). A classic work on how our countryside came to be as it is today and a provocative and eye-opening account which suggests that every change we have made to it has been for the worse.

● *Journey through Britain* by John Hillaby (Constable, 1968). The author's classic account of his walk from Land's End to John O'Groats in 1968, a vanished age sadly. Some parts of Offa's Dyke are described.

● The Brother Cadfael books by Ellis Peters are a fictional account of a monk/sleuth who solves medieval mysteries in and around the abbey of Shrewsbury. You either love them or hate them but they are a good read, true to their time and place and specific to the area. Try *The First Cadfael Omnibus* (Time Warner Paperbacks, 1990).

Poetry

The poets that have relevance for visitors to the Border Country and North and South Wales include RS Thomas, AE Housman, John Ceiriog Hughes and Gerard Manley Hopkins, all of whose works will be found in anthologies. In Hay-on-Wye the works of all these poets can be found in the Poetry Bookshop (☎ 01497-821812, Brook St).

❑ GETTING TO BRITAIN

● **Air** Most international airlines serve London Heathrow and London Gatwick. A number of budget airlines fly from many of Europe's major cities to the other London terminals at Stansted and Luton. From London it takes about three hours to get to Prestatyn or Chepstow by train. There are a few flights from Europe to Bristol, Cardiff and Birmingham which are closer to the Offa's Dyke Path than London.

● **From Europe by train** Eurostar (☎ 020-7928 5163, 💻 www.eurostar.com) operates a high-speed passenger service via the Channel Tunnel between Paris and London (2 hours 45 minutes) and Brussels and London (2 hours 30 minutes). Trains arrive and depart London from the international terminal at Waterloo station. Waterloo has connections to the London Underground and to all other main railway stations in London. There are also various rail/ferry services between Britain and Europe; for more information contact Rail Europe (☎ 08705 848848, 💻 www.rail europe.co.uk).

● **From Europe by bus** Eurolines (☎ 08705-143219, 💻 www.eurolines.co.uk) has a huge network of long-distance bus services connecting over 500 cities in 25 European countries to London.

● **From Europe by car** P&O Ferries (☎ 08705 202020, 💻 www.POferries.com) and Hoverspeed (☎ 08702 408070, 💻 www.hoverspeed.co.uk) run frequent ferries between Calais and Dover. The journey takes about 75 minutes. Eurotunnel (☎ 08 705-353535, 💻 www.eurotunnel.com) operates the shuttle train service for vehicles via the Channel Tunnel between Calais and Folkestone taking one hour between the motorway in France and the motorway in Britain. There are also countless other ferries plying routes between all the major North Sea and Channel ports of mainland Europe and the ports on Britain's eastern and southern coasts.

Getting to and from the Offa's Dyke Path

Both Prestatyn at the northern end of the trail and Chepstow, at the southern end, are easily reached by train, bus, National Express coach or car. In addition, several of the towns along the trail are also on the rail and coach networks. Where towns are not directly served by train or coach there will always be local buses to link you to the rail network. This makes getting to any of the major points along the Offa's Dyke Path by public transport relatively straightforward and this should always be the preferred mode of travel for walkers keen to put as much back into the countryside as they take out.

The local bus network between villages is good in some areas and non-existent in others. However, with careful planning it is possible to make use of these services for linear day, or multi-day, walks.

NATIONAL TRANSPORT

By rail
There are six principal rail routes along the length of the walk. These are as follows with the towns closest to the path highlighted:
● Chester–**Prestatyn** (see p66)–Bangor
● Birmingham–Shrewsbury–Gobowen–**Chirk** (2 miles from Castle Mill p101; or regular bus to Llangollen p86)–Ruabon–Chester
● Shrewsbury–**Welshpool** (about $1^1/_2$ miles off route, see p114)–Aberystwyth
● Shrewsbury–**Knighton** (p133)–Llanelli–Swansea
● Cardiff–Newport–**Abergavenny** (6 miles from Pandy, see p169, regular buses)–Hereford–Shrewsbury–Crewe
● Cardiff–Newport–**Chepstow** (p190)–Gloucester–Worcester–Birmingham

To get to Prestatyn from Chepstow, or vice versa, having completed the walk, the route would be: Chepstow–Gloucester; Gloucester–Birmingham; Birmingham–Crewe; Crewe–Prestatyn.

All timetable and fare information can be found at **National Rail Enquiries** (☎ 08457-484950; 🖳 www.nationalrail.co.uk).

By coach
National Express (☎ 08705-808080, lines open 8am–10pm daily, 🖳 www.goby coach.com) is the principal long-distance bus operator in Britain. Services of use to Offa's Dyke walkers include those to Prestatyn, Llangollen, Chirk (2 miles from Castle Mill), Welshpool, Monmouth, Abergavenny (6 miles from Pandy, regular buses) and Chepstow.

Travel by coach is usually cheaper than train but takes rather longer. Advance bookings can carry discounts so try to book at least a week ahead.

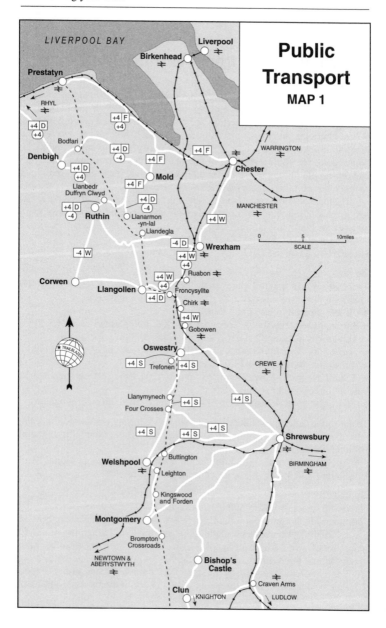

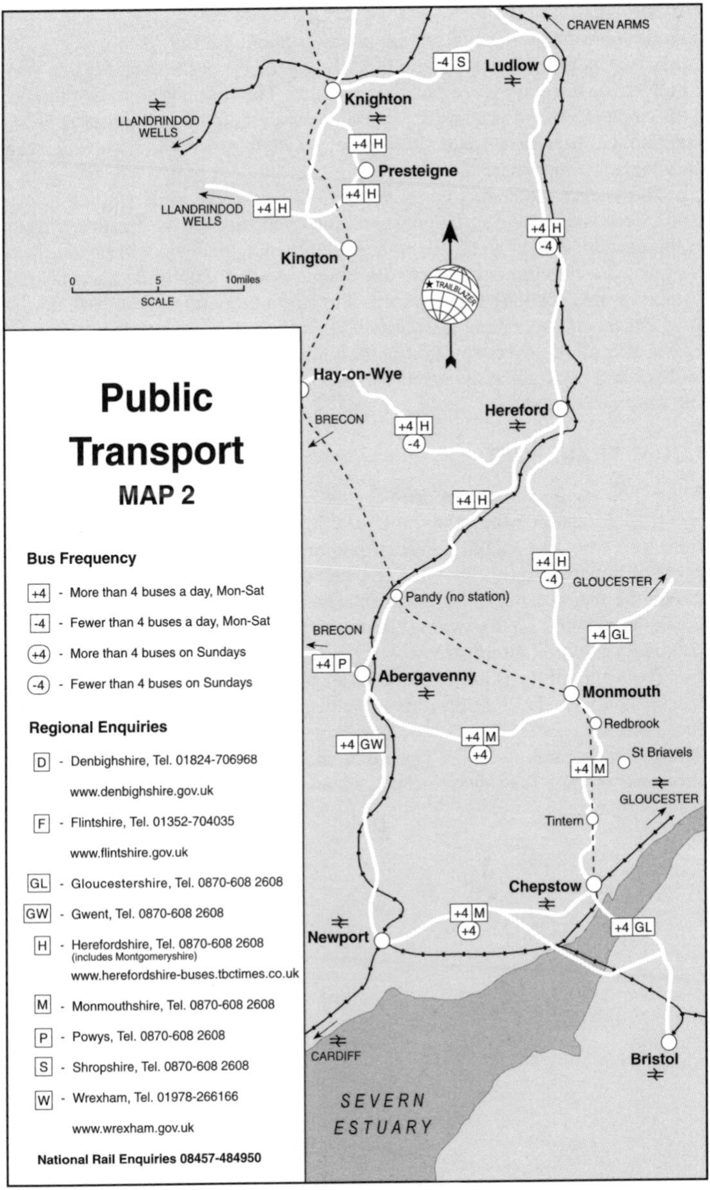

CRAVEN ARMS

-4 S Ludlow

LLANDRINDOD WELLS

Knighton

+4 H

Presteigne

+4 H

LLANDRINDOD WELLS +4 H

Kington

+4 H
-4

0   5   10miles
SCALE

TRAILBLAZER

Hay-on-Wye

BRECON

Hereford

+4 H
-4

Public
Transport
MAP 2

+4 H

+4 H
-4   GLOUCESTER

Pandy (no station)

Bus Frequency

+4 - More than 4 buses a day, Mon-Sat

-4 - Fewer than 4 buses a day, Mon-Sat

(+4) - More than 4 buses on Sundays

(-4) - Fewer than 4 buses on Sundays

BRECON

+4 P   Abergavenny

+4 GL

+4 M
(+4)

Monmouth

Redbrook

St Briavels

+4 M

GLOUCESTER

Regional Enquiries

D - Denbighshire, Tel. 01824-706968

www.denbighshire.gov.uk

F - Flintshire, Tel. 01352-704035

www.flintshire.gov.uk

GL - Gloucestershire, Tel. 0870-608 2608

GW - Gwent, Tel. 0870-608 2608

H - Herefordshire, Tel. 0870-608 2608
(includes Montgomeryshire)
www.herefordshire-buses.tbctimes.co.uk

M - Monmouthshire, Tel. 0870-608 2608

P - Powys, Tel. 0870-608 2608

S - Shropshire, Tel. 0870-608 2608

W - Wrexham, Tel. 01978-266166

www.wrexham.gov.uk

National Rail Enquiries 08457-484950

+4 GW

Tintern

Chepstow

+4 GL

Newport

+4 M
(+4)

CARDIFF

Bristol

SEVER
ESTUARY

By car

Prestatyn has quick links to the motorway network via the A548 to the M56. Likewise Chepstow is just off the M48. Using the car is the most flexible way to travel but there are some notable problems. The first is how to get back to your car at the end of your walk. Unless you can arrange to leave a car at either end you will have to use a combination of public transport and taxis which can be a logistical nightmare.

The second problem is where to park the car safely while you are on the trail. Some B&Bs have sufficient space to let you park for the duration of your walk, usually without a charge on the understanding that you will favour them with your custom for a night or two's accommodation. Public car parks are not usually geared for long-stay parking. The only other option is to park on the road but this means taking a security risk and is not recommended. It may be easier after all, to leave the car at home and use public transport. You can then sit back and congratulate yourself on supporting local rural services and helping the environment.

LOCAL TRANSPORT

The public transport maps on pp38-9 give an overview of the most useful bus and train routes for walkers, approximate frequency of services in both directions and who you should contact for detailed timetable information. If the regional county enquiry lines for bus information prove unsatisfactory, telephone the national public transport information line, **Traveline** (☎ 0870-608 2608, 7am–9pm; 🖳 www.traveline-cymru.org.uk). Timetables can also be picked up at tourist information centres along the trail.

The nature of the Border Country is such that bus services tend to be rather fragmented with different operators establishing routes on their own patch as local demand, particularly school bus services and shopping needs, dictates. Timetables in rural areas can change at short notice and summer and winter services can vary. It's safest to check ahead to make sure that the service you want is running.

PART 2: MINIMUM IMPACT WALKING

Walk as if you are kissing the Earth with your feet **Thich Nhat Hanh** *Peace is every step*

The countryside through which you pass when walking the Offa's Dyke Path holds a fascination and an appeal that has attracted visitors since tourism first began. Perhaps its juxtaposition of attractive towns and easily accessible countryside makes it an ideal area for a short or long visit to re-charge your batteries and call a temporary halt to the pace of life.

Visitors have come in large numbers for over a century to sample the healing balm that comes from walking in these less touched places and as the world gets increasingly faster, more polluted and urbanized there is an even greater need for unspoiled countryside where you can go for recreation in the true sense of the word.

Inevitably this too brings its problems. As more and more people enjoy the freedom of open country so the land comes under increasing pressure and the potential for conflict with other land-users is heightened. Everyone has a right to this natural heritage but with it comes a responsibility to care for it too.

By following some simple guidelines while walking you can have a positive impact, not just on your own well-being but also on local communities and the environment, thereby becoming part of the solution.

ECONOMIC IMPACT

Rural businesses and communities in Britain have been hit hard in recent years by a seemingly endless series of crises.

The countryside through which Offa's Dyke Path passes was hit as hard as any by the foot and mouth crisis of 2001 and indeed was closed to walkers for practically all the spring and summer months. Walkers showed that they were ready to help in any way possible: this was mainly manifested in staying away.

In normal circumstances, playing your part involves much more than simply observing the country code. Although this is important, the new watchword is 'local' and with it comes huge social, environmental and psychological benefits.

Buy local

Look and ask for local produce to buy and eat. Not only does this cut down on the amount of pollution and congestion that the transportation of food creates, so-called 'food miles', but also ensures that you are supporting local farmers and producers; the very people who have moulded the countryside you have come to see and who are in the best position to protect it. If you can find local food which is also organic so much the better.

Support local businesses

If you spend £1 in a local business 80p of that pound stays within the local economy where it can be spent again and again to do the most good for that community and landscape. If, on the other hand, you spend your money in a branch of a national or multinational chain store, restaurant or hotel the situation is reversed; only 20% (mainly the staff wages) stays within the local economy and the other 80% is effectively lost to that community as it's siphoned off to pay for goods, transport and profit. The more money which circulates locally and is spent on local labour and materials the more power the community has to effect the change it wants to see; a world of difference from the 'corporatization' of the countryside which we are currently witnessing.

Encourage local cultural traditions and skills

No part of the countryside looks the same. Buildings, food, skills and language evolve out of the landscape and are moulded over hundreds of years to suit the locality. Discovering these cultural differences is part of the pleasure of walking in new places. Visitors' enthusiasm for local traditions and skills brings awareness and pride, nurturing a sense of place; an increasingly important role in a world where economic globalization continues to undermine the very things that provide security and a feeling of belonging.

ENVIRONMENTAL IMPACT

By choosing a walking holiday you have already made a positive step towards minimizing your impact on the wider environment. By following these suggestions you can also tread lightly along the Offa's Dyke Path.

Use public transport whenever possible

With a little research (see p40) you can find local buses that service many of the villages through which you pass and it's possible to use them for getting back to where you started after a day or several days on the trail. Public transport is always preferable to using private cars as it benefits everyone; visitors, locals and the environment. Also of use are the local taxi firms who are only too happy to ferry walkers or their luggage around. Using this service boosts the local economy too.

Never leave litter

Leaving litter shows a total disrespect for the natural world and others coming after you. As well as being unsightly, litter kills wildlife, pollutes the environment and can be dangerous to farm animals. **Please** carry a plastic bag so you can dispose of your rubbish in a bin in the next village. It would be very helpful if you could pick up litter left by other people too.

● **Is it OK if it's biodegradable?** Not really. Apple cores, banana skins, orange peel and the like are unsightly, encourage flies, ants and wasps and ruin a picnic spot for others.

● **The lasting impact of litter** A piece of orange peel left on the ground takes six months to decompose; silver foil 18 months; a plastic bag 10 years; clothes 15 years; and an aluminium drinks can 85 years.

Erosion

● **Stay on the waymarked trail** The effect of your footsteps may seem minuscule but when they are multiplied by several thousand walkers each year they become rather more significant. Avoid taking shortcuts, widening the trail or creating more than one path; your boots will be followed by many others.

The principal causes of erosion to the Offa's Dyke earthwork are agriculture, burrowing animals and tourism and these have to be balanced against its practical purposes, namely as a boundary, a wildlife corridor, a local landmark and a lane or footpath.

There are conflicting demands made on Offa's Dyke and conservationists and those responsible for its preservation have a difficult task in steering the most appropriate course to ensure that future generations will be able to experience the same degree of interest and enjoyment from it as we do today.

● **Consider walking out of season** Maximum disturbance by walkers coincides with the time of year when nature wants to do most of its growth and repair. In high use areas, like that along much of the path, the trail is often prevented from recovering. Walking at less busy times eases this pressure while also generating year-round income for the local economy.

Not only that, but it may make the walk a more relaxing experience for you as there are fewer people on the path and there's less competition for accommodation.

Respect all wildlife

Care for all wildlife you come across on the path; it has just as much of a right to be there as you. Tempting as it may be to pick wild flowers, leave them so the next person who passes can enjoy them too. Don't break branches off or damage trees in any way.

If you come across wildlife keep your distance and don't watch for too long. Your presence can cause considerable stress particularly if the adults are with young or in winter when the weather is harsh and food scarce. Young animals are rarely abandoned. If you come across deer calves or young birds keep away so that their mother can return.

The code of the outdoor loo

'Going' in the outdoors is a lost art worth re-learning, for your sake and everyone else's. As more and more people discover the joys of the outdoors this is becoming an important issue. In some parts of the world where visitor pressure is higher than in Britain walkers are required to pack out their excrement. This could soon be necessary here. Human excrement is not only offensive to our senses but, more importantly, can infect water sources.

● **Where to go** Wherever possible wait until you can **use a toilet**. Public toilets are marked on the trail maps in this guide and you will also find facilities in pubs, cafés and campsites.

If you do have to go outdoors choose a site at least **30 metres away from running water**. Carry a small trowel and **dig a small hole** about 15cm (6") deep in which to bury your excrement. It decomposes quicker when in contact with the top layer of soil or leaf mould. Use a stick to stir loose soil into your deposit as well as this speeds up decomposition even more. Do not squash it under rocks as this slows down the composting process. If you have to use rocks to hide it make sure they are not in contact with your faeces.

● **Toilet paper and sanitary towels** Toilet paper takes a long time to decompose whether buried or not. It is easily dug up by animals and could then blow into water sources or onto the trail. The best method for dealing with it is to **pack it out**. Put the used paper inside a paper bag which you place inside a plastic bag (or two). Then simply empty the contents of the paper bag at the next toilet you come across and throw the bag away. You should also pack out **tampons** and **sanitary towels** in a similar way; they take years to decompose and will be dug up and scattered about by animals.

Wild camping
Wild camping is not permitted anywhere along the Offa's Dyke Path. Carrying a tent is no problem since there are many campsites, both purpose-built and those in the gardens of B&Bs where you can camp on the lawn, using the washing facilities in the house. It goes without saying that you should leave your pitch exactly as you found it: unmarked, without litter and without any obvious signs that you have been there.

ACCESS

Right to roam
Walkers can be forgiven for being confused by all the talk recently about where they can and can't go in the countryside. What is meant by 'The Right to Roam'? Where do we stand with the new legislation? Has anything changed?

The answer is not yet, but change is coming. The Countryside and Rights of Way Act 2000 is relevant to England and Wales and covers Access to Open Country, Public Rights of Way, Nature Conservation and Areas of Outstanding Natural Beauty(AONBs).

❏ **Nourishing facts to ponder while walking**
● A supermarket provides one job for every £250,000 spent, compared with a village shop which provides one job for every £50,000 spent.
● Sheep can be bought for as little as 25p a head.
● Farm incomes have fallen 90% in the last 5 years.
● BSE has cost every household in the UK £200.
● Britain imports 125,000 tonnes of lamb and exports 102,000 tonnes of lamb.
● The UK earns £630 million a year from meat and dairy exports yet the cost of the foot and mouth epidemic in terms of lost tourism, government compensation etc is estimated to be over £9 billion.

The purpose of the Act is to:
- Create a new statutory right of access to certain types of land
- Bring the public rights-of-way system up to date
- Strengthen legislation on nature conservation
- Facilitate better management of AONBs

The perception had taken hold that we the public were being denied access to land that people felt should be available to all. More extreme views held that we should be allowed to go wherever we chose, after all 'it's a free country' but this conflicted strongly with the interests of private land ownership which did not want their land trampled on willy-nilly by all and sundry. After all, would you want your garden thrown open to access by all? It's partly about challenging the fencing-off of tempting looking moorland for shooting. Why should wealthy fat-cats keep hundreds of acres for their own private amusement when we might want to walk across it for ours?

At bottom it's a 'them and us' situation. Somewhere in between is a reasonable compromise that allows areas previously closed to us to be open. After all, it is argued, if it hadn't been for the protesters on Kinder Scout in the 1930s, we wouldn't have the freedom we have today.

The Act will only come into full effect once the country has been mapped to designate what areas fall within its scope, which includes mountainous land, moorland, heath, downland and registered common land. This, it is estimated, will be some time in 2004. Altogether this is a complicated piece of legislation that is going to mean money has to be found from somewhere.

It doesn't take a genius to divine that we will ourselves finish up paying for it through our local council tax bill. Will we see the benefit? I doubt it, but perhaps generations to come will praise the foresight of our existing legislators to enshrine basic human rights in the new Act. We shall see.

Rights of way

In the meantime, it helps to understand the meaning of terms like 'rights of way', footpath, bridle way and by-way. Briefly these are defined as follows:
- A **right of way** is a path that anyone has the right to use on foot provided they stay on the path and do not cause damage or obstruct it in any way
- A **footpath** is open to walkers only, not to cyclists, horse-riders or vehicles
- A **bridleway** is open to walkers, horse-riders and cyclists
- A **by-way** is open to motorized traffic as well as to walkers, riders and cyclists.

Not all footpaths are necessarily rights of way. For instance some canal tow-paths aren't official rights of way but their use for this purpose is more or less taken for granted.

Sometimes a landowner will allow a path across his land to be used for the convenience of walkers although it may not be recognized as a right of way. This is known as a **permissive path**. The maintenance of rights of way is down to the landowner in conjunction with the county council through whose area it passes and sometimes the local authority.

Waymarking

There is a national standard for waymarks, as follows:

- **Yellow** Public footpaths
- **Blue** Bridleways
- **Red** By-ways

National Trails are waymarked by the acorn symbol. This waymark appears along the length of the Offa's Dyke Path but sometimes, such as around Hay-on-Wye, upside down. One can only assume this was an error on the part of those installing them.

The Country Code

Much of the route which walkers on the Offa's Dyke Path follow is through farmland, frequently passing farm buildings and grazing livestock to the point that it is impossible to be unaware of the business of farming. Farmers are faced with a harsh environment, a short grazing season and severe weather conditions; so let's not add the nuisance of long-distance walkers to their problems.

The landscape of the countryside and its wildlife has been created to a large extent by farming. Centuries of grazing by sheep has created the close-cropped grassy hillsides characteristic of the Clwydian Hills and the Black Mountains and hill farming has shaped the land and made for us the special identity which is so appealing to walkers and visitors. But farmers draw only minor benefit from tourism unless they can supplement their income with bed and breakfast or self-catering accommodation in the summer months.

The hill farm helps sustain a service and supply industry, from feed suppliers to transport, fuel, machinery, farm labour, fencing and walling, vets and auction marts. It should be seen as a part of the vital rural infrastructure rather than an isolated farmstead at the end of a long and winding road. Let's try to tread lightly through this landscape. We are only passing through whilst the farmer remains, summer and winter. If we can try to understand the life they live, perhaps they will look favourably on us.

> *I am the farmer, stripped of love*
> *And thought and grace by the land's hardness:*
> *But what I am saying over the fields'*
> *Desolate acres, rough with dew,*
> *Is, listen, listen, I am a man like you.*
> **RS Thomas** *The Hill Farmer Speaks*

- **Enjoy the countryside and respect its life and work** Access to the countryside depends on being sensitive to the needs and wishes of those who live and work there. Being courteous and friendly to those you meet will ensure a healthy future for all based on partnership and co-operation.
- **Guard against all risk of fire** Accidental fire is a great fear for farmers and foresters. Never make a camp fire and take matches and cigarette butts out with you to dispose of safely.
- **Leave all gates as you found them** If in doubt close a gate to avoid farm animals straying.

● **Keep your dogs under control** You must keep your dog on a lead whenever you cross enclosed land or go near livestock so that the farmer knows it is under control. See p26 for more advice on walking with dogs.

● **Keep to paths across farmland** Avoid damaging crops by sticking to the waymarked route whenever you are crossing arable or pasture land.

● **Use gates and stiles to cross fences, hedges and walls** All along the Offa's Dyke Path there are stiles and kissing gates through boundaries. You should not have to climb over a gate. If you find yourself doing so, check your route. You'll probably have gone wrong. Often stiles will be beside gates and if you choose to spare your muscles by going through the gate, always close it behind you.

● **Leave livestock, crops and machinery alone** Help farmers by not interfering with their means of livelihood.

● **Take your litter home** (see p42).

● **Help keep all water clean** Many properties along the path depend on streams for their domestic water supply. Take care with your personal hygiene to avoid causing pollution (see p43).

● **Protect wildlife, plants and trees** (see p43).

● **Take special care on country roads** If you travel by car, drive with care and reduce speed on country roads. Park your car with consideration for others' needs; never block a gateway. Walkers should take special care on country roads. Cars travel dangerously fast on narrow winding lanes. To be safe, walk facing the oncoming traffic and carry a torch or wear highly visible clothing when it's getting dark.

● **Make no unnecessary noise** Enjoy the peace and solitude of the outdoors by staying in small groups and acting unobtrusively. Avoid noisy and disruptive behaviour which might annoy residents and other visitors and cause alarm to farm animals and wildlife.

Lambing

This takes place from mid-March to mid-May and is a critical economic time for the hard-pressed hill farmers. Please do not interfere with livestock farming in any way. If a ewe or lamb seems to be in distress contact the nearest farmer. Dogs should be kept off land where sheep are grazing throughout this season so that pregnant ewes are not disturbed.

❏ **Beware of the bull!**
Sometimes a field full of cows will be accompanied by their lord and master, a bull. This is in fact in contravention of the law, especially if they endanger the public. In theory, bulls aged more than 10 months must not be allowed in a field through which a public footpath passes. In practice, if the farmer decides to let his bull out in a field there's not much you can do about it. The best thing you can do if you spot one is give it a wide berth. Keep to the edge of the field and keep a healthy distance between it and you. If it seems to be taking notice of you, quicken your exit from the field without delay.

PART 3: THE ENVIRONMENT & NATURE

Conserving the Anglo-Welsh Border Country

It's the business of government to see that the countryside is preserved for the pleasure and sanity of all of us. The fatal mistake has been to imagine that the interests of the countryside are in some way different from the interests of farmers. The countryside can only be maintained by a healthy agriculture. If farming dies, a most precious part of Britain dies with it. **John Mortimer**

The countryside has become a political football since the Labour Government seized on the Right to Roam and the banning of fox hunting as two issues they thought would receive overwhelming popular support. Unexpectedly they found that the people of the countryside had a voice that demanded to be heard, the Countryside Alliance attracting a groundswell of support from country people who saw their interests being disregarded. At the time of writing, the Right to Roam will become enshrined in law within five years and hunting with dogs will soon take its place with cock fighting and bear baiting as a quaint activity no longer relevant in the modern world.

These milestones could be interpreted as examples of how individual freedoms are being eroded. Is our countryside under threat? Frequently we are made aware that hostile interests from construction, development and the transport infrastructure make demands on our woods and fields, replacing them with concrete and brick. In the words of Joni Mitchell, 'they paved paradise and put up a parking lot'. But are we losing our natural environment? Are we allowing it to slip through our fingers while we stand and do nothing?

There are plenty of organizations who are determined not to let it happen, some of them listed on p52. Environmental issues are of major interest worldwide and thanks to the efforts of these largely voluntary bodies, the fight-back is gaining ground. The need to build new housing for the families of the future is directed first to so-called 'brown-field' sites, disused industrial areas in cities no longer needed for factories, rather than eroding our green-belt areas.

There is reason to be optimistic but the struggle cannot be sustained without the active participation of people who care. This is where walkers can play their part. We are the ones who can see what's going on. We are the spies, the fifth column, the silent majority. We can go into the countryside with our eyes open and report back on what we see happening. If you see obvious examples of despoliation or threat to an area, let somebody know.

(Opposite) The ruins of 13th-century Llanthony Abbey (see p167), wonderfully-located near Hatterrall Ridge. Some of the surviving buildings now house the Abbey Hotel.

You cannot alone stop industrial blight and pollution but there are plenty of ways of making your feelings known through local councillors, your MP or MEP, or by joining one of the voluntary bodies. The countryside needs our help – it's the only one we've got.

GOVERNMENT AGENCIES AND SCHEMES

Government responsibility for the countryside is handled in England by the **Countryside Agency** and in Wales by the **Countryside Council for Wales** (CCW). Their efforts are delegated to a bewildering array of bodies, each with its mnemonic which is supposed to be easy to remember but usually simply confuses and alarms. Many visitors will not be greatly concerned about who is responsible for what but it is worth being aware of the part played by central government in dealing with countryside issues.

❑ **Government agencies**
● **Brecon Beacons National Park** (☎ 01874-624437, 🖥 www.breconbeacons.org), 7 Glamorgan St, Brecon, Powys, LD3 7DP. Covers the Black Mountains area through which the Offa's Dyke Path runs.
● **CADW: Welsh Historic Monuments** (☎ 029-2050 0200, 🖥 www.cadw.wales. gov.uk), National Assembly for Wales, Cathays Park, Cardiff, CF10 3NQ. Protects, conserves and promotes an appreciation of the built heritage of Wales.
● **Clwyd-Powys Archaeological Trust** (CPAT) (☎ 01938-553670, 🖥 www .cpat.org. uk), 7a Church St, Welshpool, Powys, SY21 7DL. This organization, in partnership with English Heritage, has formed the Offa's Dyke Initiative to raise the profile of Offa's Dyke, to conserve it as a site of major archaeological interest and to encourage a more integrated long-term approach to the management of the Dyke as a whole monument.
● **Countryside Agency** (☎ 01242-521381, 🖥 www.countryside.gov.uk), John Dower House, Crescent Place, Cheltenham, Gloucestershire, GL50 3RA. Resulted from a merger between the Countryside Commission and the Rural Development Commission, its aims are to conserve and enhance the countryside and to help everyone to enjoy it.
● **Countryside Council for Wales** (☎ 08451-306229, 🖥 www.ccw.gov.uk), Maes-y-Ffynnon, Penrhosgarnedd, Bangor, Gwynedd, LL57 2DW. The statutory advisor to government on sustaining natural beauty, wildlife and the opportunity for outdoor enjoyment in rural Wales.
● **English Heritage** (☎ 0870-333 1181, 🖥 www.english-heritage.org.uk) Customer Services Dept, PO Box 569, Swindon, SN2 2YP. Government body responsible for the care and preservation of ancient monuments in England.
● **Forestry Commission,** (☎ 0131-334 0303, 🖥 www.forestry.gov.uk) 231 Corstophine Road, Edinburgh, EH12 7AT. Government department for establishing and managing forests for a variety of uses.

(Opposite) Top: Part of Offa's Dyke near Neath Bridge (see p109). **Bottom**: Cantilever bridge over the Montgomery Canal (see p113).

National parks

The Offa's Dyke Path touches only one national park, the Brecon Beacons, into which area the Black Mountains between Hay-on-Wye and Pandy fall. National park status is the highest level of landscape protection available in Britain and recognizes the importance of the area in terms of landscape, biodiversity and as a recreational resource. Although the Brecon Beacons is one of the lesser-known national parks, bank holidays and summer weekends can see the area choked with traffic and practically full to bursting with picnickers and trippers. Conservation in national parks is always a knife-edge balance between protecting the environment, the rights and livelihoods of those who live in the park and the needs of visitors.

The existence of the national parks raises the question of what is being done to conserve and protect the countryside outside their boundaries? The policy of giving special protection to certain areas suggests that those areas not protected tend to be ignored when funding comes to be allocated. Since only 7% of the British Isles has national park status, the conclusion to be drawn is that vast areas remain neglected.

Areas of Outstanding Natural Beauty (AONBs)

Land which falls outside the remit of a national park but which is nonetheless deemed special enough for protection may be designated as an AONB, the second level of protection after national park status. The Offa's Dyke Path crosses three AONBs; the Clwydian Range, administered by Denbighshire Countryside Service (☎ 01352-810614); the Shropshire Hills, under the care of the Shropshire Hills Countryside Unit (☎ 01694-781588); and the Wye Valley, controlled by the Wye Valley AONB (☎ 01600-713977).

Sites of Special Scientific Interest (SSSIs)

SSSI is an important designation which affords extra protection to unique areas against anything that threatens the habitat or environment. Although they are not widely known, they range in size from small sites where orchids grow, or

❏ **Sustainability websites**

For lovers of the natural world who have ever asked 'but what can I do', the following websites are a good place to start.

● *The Ecologist Magazine* (🖥 www.theecologist.org) Britain's longest-running environmental magazine.

● **Friends of the Earth** (🖥 www.foe.co.uk) International network of environmental groups campaigning for a better environment.

● **International Society for Ecology and Culture** (🖥 www.isec.org.uk) Promoting locally-based alternatives to the global consumer culture to protect biological and cultural diversity.

● **Permaculture Magazine** (🖥 www.permaculture.co.uk) Explains the principles and practice of sustainable living.

● **Resurgence Magazine** (🖥 www.gn.apc.org/resurgence) 'The flagship of the green movement'.

birds nest, to vast swathes of upland, moorland and wetland. The country of the Offa's Dyke Path has its share but they are not given a high profile for the very reason that this would draw unwanted attention when what is wanted is for them to be left undisturbed. 'Triple S Is' are managed in partnership with the owners and occupiers of the land who must give written notice of any operations likely to damage the site and who cannot proceed until consent is given.

The England Rural Development Programme (ERDP)

This was introduced in 2001 by the **Department of Environment, Food and Rural Affairs (DEFRA)** to underpin the Government's New Direction for Agriculture with the intention of making farmers more environmentally responsible. Funding to the tune of £1.6bn will be made available over the next seven years for environmental protection and rural development.

Environmentally Sensitive Areas (ESAs)

The ESA scheme was first introduced in 1987. The crucial difference is that this is a voluntary scheme through which farmers are enticed to adopt low-impact agricultural practices by being offered grants. Clun (see p130) and the Shropshire Hills are areas in the scheme through which the Offa's Dyke Path passes.

Tir Gofal: the new agri-environment scheme for Wales

In Wales, the CCW has an equivalent scheme to ESAs known as Tir Gofal meaning 'Land Care', the latest in a series of schemes designed to promote farm management and conservation. In the language of the bureaucrat the purpose is:

'to provide support to the farming community as custodians of the diverse historical, cultural and wildlife heritage of Wales, helping them maintain the fabric of the countryside, and reflect public aspirations for environmental benefits and greater opportunities for enjoyment.'

The scheme is open to anyone farming more than three hectares. If they become part of the scheme they must sign up for ten years, promising to maintain habitat, trees, streams and rivers, protect all historic sites, not remove rocky outcrops, not introduce non-native plant species and follow all recommendations of good practice.

Less Favoured Areas

Much of the route which walkers on the Offa's Dyke Path will follow is through farmland, frequently passing farm buildings and grazing livestock to the point

❏ **Staying and going**
The mighty mountains changeless stand
Tireless the winds across them blow,
The shepherd's song across the land
Sounds with the dawn so long ago.
Still around with rocks each day
The bright white daisies nod and climb
Only the shepherds cannot stay
Upon those hills till end of time
Old Welsh customs need must change
As years progress from age to age.
The generations each arrange
Their own brief patterns of the page
After his long watch on the hill
Alun Mabon too had gone.
Yet lives the ancient language still,
And still the melodies play on.

John Ceiriog Hughes 1832-1887

that it is impossible to be unaware of the business of farming in what the European Union defines as Less Favoured Areas (LFAs). Two-thirds of our beef cows and breeding ewes are farmed in these LFAs and their owners are faced with a harsh environment, a short grazing season and severe weather conditions and all for scant reward. The average income for dairy and livestock farmers in Wales during the year 2000 was £4100. People ask why farmers continue to eke out a living under these conditions but there are few options agriculturally, other than cattle and sheep. In 1997 they were hit by BSE and in 2000 by foot and mouth disease (FMD), two further body blows to this beleaguered group.

VOLUNTARY ORGANIZATIONS (see p205)

Voluntary organizations started the conservation movement back in the mid 1800s and are still at the forefront of developments. Independent of government but reliant on public support, they can concentrate their resources either on acquiring land which can then be managed purely for conservation purposes, or on influencing political decision-makers by lobbying and campaigning.

Managers and owners of land include the well-known bodies such as the **Royal Society for the Protection of Birds** (RSPB) with their 150 nature reserves and nearly a million members and the **Council for the Protection of Rural England** (CPRE) which exists to promote the beauty and diversity of rural England by encouraging the sustainable use of land and other natural resources in town and country. Their Welsh equivalent is the **Campaign for the Protection of Rural Wales** (see box on p205).

Action groups such as **Friends of the Earth**, **Greenpeace** and the **World Wide Fund for Nature** (WWF) also play a vital role in environmental protection by raising public awareness with government agencies when policy needs to be formulated. A huge increase in public interest and support during the last 20 years indicates that people are more conscious of environmental issues and believe that it cannot be left to our political representatives to take care of them for us without our voice. We are becoming the most powerful lobbying group of all: an informed electorate.

BEYOND CONSERVATION

When we read about the work of the numerous voluntary and statutory bodies responsible for conservation it is easy to conclude that the countryside is in good hands and that we don't have to worry. But each day we read reports of how threatened the countryside really is. Walkers are supposed to be environmentally friendly people, the kind who take their newspapers to the paper bank and recycle their plastic bottles, carefully removing the caps. Yet there is not one among us who cannot examine their own commitment to environmental issues and find himself or herself wanting.

What is called for is a total change in attitude so that care for our environment is our first consideration, not the last. We all need to take a long, hard look at the way we live now and ask ourselves if we are not contributing to the gradual destruction of the natural world. Who has not seen the contents of a car ash-tray deposited on a car park, the filter tips affronting the very tarmac itself? Who has not walked along a canal and seen plastic wrappers stuffed into the hedgerow, or seen plastic bags festooning the hawthorn bushes alongside roads? We are all guilty. Because for every person who has seen these horrors, how many have cleared them away? Is other people's litter our problem? I think it is.

❏ Timber growing

Trees have been grown to provide timber for as long as records have been kept, whether for building, burning for fuel and warmth, to supply power, make charcoal or for industrial manufacture. One thinks of wheels for carts, barrels, pit props and furniture, fencing, and for the making of paper.

Originally oak and ash dominated but with the growth of coal mining, pit props were in much demand leading to the introduction of fast-growing conifers from America, adaptable to poor upland soils unsuitable for growing crops.

The mechanization of extracting timber brought about changes to the landscape and in Wales gave rise to a massive softwood-processing industry creating thousands of jobs. However, the downside was the desecration of a vast acreage of moorland, blanketed with regimented rows of trees that became a familiar sight in Britain under the auspices of the Forestry Commission. The impact of hundreds of square kilometres of identical trees was made worse by the policy of making tax advantages available which allowed many wealthy investors a safe haven for their surplus cash. These short-sighted policies produced the eyesores that defaced many a lovely valley, the effect of which is still felt today.

The negative impression caused by the visual impact of this phenomenon is as nothing compared with the ecological impact. Thousands of acres of species-rich moorland have been ploughed up and replaced by a monoculture of conifers. With it go birds like the merlin and the golden plover. Once mature the trees cannot support much wildlife as the close canopy allows little light to penetrate to the forest floor. Nothing else can grow and as a consequence few animals venture into this sterile environment. As with all monocultures, pests easily thrive and have to be controlled with chemical pesticides. The deep ploughing and use of heavy machinery damages soil structure and also leads to a higher risk of flash floods as drainage patterns are altered. It has also been found that acid rain gets trapped in the trees and is released into the streams during heavy rain to the detriment of fish and invertebrates.

Finally, the end product from this environmental disaster is a low-grade timber used mainly for paper making, a hideous waste of raw materials. Perversely and misleadingly this is often trumpeted as 'paper from sustainable forestry'.

In future a better balance between conifer and broadleafed trees is desirable, as well as better felling management to avoid huge areas of plantation being laid waste. Wales has devised a woodland strategy for improved management and control in future which will, it is hoped, lead to multi-purpose woodlands with a contribution to make to tourism, agriculture and the environment. Mixed varieties of trees can be planted to cover areas blighted by previous despoilation due to industry and mining and to bring back an appropriate habitat where it has previously been absent.

Forest and woodland areas make up 14% of the land area of Wales, 70% of it coniferous but the policy is in place to reverse this trend in favour of broadleaved trees in future.

For if there are people irresponsible enough to scatter their waste across the countryside, doesn't it need a balance of people who are willing to pick it up?

Yet this is just the tip of the iceberg. As our materialistic society expands, so the demand for affluence and acquisition increases. Put simply, the more we buy, the more nature we destroy. Consumerism means profligacy and waste, all exerting pressure on the world around us.

Why should we, individually, do more than we are doing to slow down this massive consumption of our natural resources on a global scale? Because, quite simply, we can do more. And we must do more if the world we know is going to be here for our descendants, our great, great grandchildren, not just our children. When we return a book borrowed from a friend, would we send it back tattered and torn and defaced with every evidence of our carelessness and indifference? Of course not. The countryside is the book we borrowed. Let us pass it on in even better condition than we found it so that future generations will say that we knew what it meant to take care.

❏ Sheep

Since sheep are the one animal you are likely to see every single day of your walk it is worth trying to recognize the diverse breeds that graze in the Borders. Because of the widespread crossing of breeds most animals you will see will be cross-breeds, usually referred to as mules, and reared for their meat. Fleeces no longer command a price in today's markets and sheep reared solely for their wool are a rarity.

Among the different varieties which may be noticed look out for the following:

● **Welsh Black Mountain** Small, black sheep with no wool on the face or legs below the knee and hock. Rams are typically horned and ewes hornless. The meat obtained is of premium quality and much prized.

● **Balwen Welsh Mountain** The Balwen has a white blaze on the face, four white feet and a white tail and is said to have been used over the years as landmarks on the hills as a means of recognizing one's flock. It is a small, hardy breed which can get by on very little at peak times of the year.

● **Welsh Mountain Badger Faced** Ancient breed, once common, it has a distinctive broad stripe on the face with a black band from its jaw extending under the belly to the tail. The fleece is used mainly for the carpet industry.

● **Kerry Hill** A well-balanced, sturdy sheep with ears set high and free from wool, a black nose and sharply-defined black and white markings on head and legs. The ewe is a perfect mother, adaptable and a good forager producing strong, lean lambs.

● **Shropshire** A sheep with a gentle disposition, the Shropshire has a white fleece and black face with wool on the head. The lambs are hardy, vigorous and meaty and the ewes make wonderful mothers.

● **Hill Radnor** A hill or mountain breed found in Powys and Gwent; a hardy sheep with a grey aquiline nose and a tan face and legs. Rams have long curved horns and ewes hornless.

● **Clun Forest** A hardy animal that breeds well; many flocks have been kept for years in the hills of the Clun Forest area. It has a long clean dark brown face, free from wrinkles with bold, bright eyes. The head is wool-covered and the ears set well to the top of the head.

The Offa's Dyke Path embraces an entire landscape along the England/Wales border passing from wooded hillside to canal towpath, from the swooping ridges of the Clwydian Hills to the Severn plain. It offers opportunities for seeing a wide range of wildlife and wild flowers, both familiar and unfamiliar.

> ❏ *I turned and looked at the hills I had come across. There they stood, darkly blue, a rain cloud, like ink, hanging over their summits. Oh, the wild hills of Wales, the land of old renown and of wonder, the land of Arthur and Merlin!*
> **George Borrow**
> *Wild Wales,* (1861)

Unfortunately, areas of natural and semi-natural habitat are being lost at an alarming rate to developments of all kinds and particularly to agricultural 'improvement'. For example, in the last 40 years between one-third and half of all ancient woodlands have been felled, approximately 50% of all lowland heath has been ploughed, planted or built upon and a similar proportion of coastal grazing marsh has been converted to arable fields. Increasingly, wildlife is being confined to nature reserves leaving the open countryside sparsely populated by species that were once commonplace.

Flora and fauna

MAMMALS

The **rabbit** (*Oryctolagus cuniculis*) is abundant along the Dyke and is indeed responsible in part for the erosion of the earthwork in which it makes its burrows. Rabbits are responsible for an estimated £100,000,000 damage a year to crops and in spite of being prey to buzzards, foxes, feral cats, stoats and man, they are able to replenish their numbers, bucks mating at four months old and does at three and a half months. For townsfolk rabbits are delightful creatures but for the countryman they are a pest to be exterminated.

The **brown hare** (*Lepus europaeus*) is larger than the rabbit with large powerful hind legs and very long black-tipped ears. They are locally common on farmland and rough grazing and rely for escape on their great acceleration, being capable of attaining speeds of up to 45mph (70km/h). In upland areas the **mountain hare** (*Lepus timidus*) replaces the brown, being distinguishable by its slightly blue colour that blends more easily with rocky terrain. In winter in mountain country they adopt a white coat, supposedly for camouflage in the snow, although it has been suggested that the white fur offers a thermal advantage, creating a greenhouse effect on the outer layers of the skin.

Badgers (*Meles meles*) are nocturnal animals and rarely seen during the day, lying up in their underground burrows known as setts. Litters of cubs are born in February. There are thought to be around 300,000 badgers in England and Wales and they are a protected species. There is some suggestion that cattle can catch

---

❏ **Cattle**

Apart from the breeds common to the British Isles generally, you will almost certainly come across the **Welsh Black** when walking in the Border Country. A native British breed descended from cattle of pre-Roman origin, they are ideally suited to the rough upland country characteristic of the area. Bred for beef production, they are hardy and adapted to a rough environment and can be out-wintered. Prolific milkers, they thrive on poor pasture. They make excellent mothers and grow quicker and heavier than most other British breeds.

Elsewhere on the trail you may come across unusual breeds such as **Red Poll**, a breed of brown cattle without horns; an excellent cheese is made from their milk. There is a herd which grazes near the church at Llanfihangel-Ystern-Llewern (p176).

In the same area but a little further south around the site of the vanished Grace Dieu Abbey (p176) is a herd of rare **White Park** cattle, said to have similarities to the famed wild white Chillingham herd, the oldest breed still surviving. They look like the Texas Longhorns from cowboy films, with wide horns that you wouldn't want to get too near. Beautiful looking beasts as they are, give them a wide berth.

---

the TB virus through contact with badgers which has led to them being culled in some areas. It is estimated that each year 50,000 badgers are killed on the roads.

Red foxes (*Vulpes vulpes*) are becoming common in spite of occasional persecution by man, and our murderous roads. Readily identifiable by their colour and bushy tail, foxes are shy animals that come out mainly at night to hunt for food. Their supposed habit of killing all the hens in a coop and taking only one is apparently not the result of vicious rage but done to take advantage of abundance while it is available to compensate for times when food is scarce. There are still about 190 fox hunts in England and Wales but these account for only a small proportion of foxes killed. The law regarding hunting may be changed during the life of this book.

The **red squirrel** (*Sciurus vulgaris*) is the only squirrel indigenous to the British Isles and is protected by law. There is concern that in the next 20 years the red squirrel will become extinct due to a combination of disease, loss of habitat and the dominance of the grey squirrel. Active during the day mainly in coniferous and deciduous woodland, the red squirrel is recognized by its colour which varies from deep brown to chestnut to grey brown but its smaller size and tufted ears easily distinguish it from the much larger grey. There are only a few thousand left in Wales. The **grey squirrel** (*Sciurus carolinensis*) was introduced to this country from North America in the 19th century and is an altogether more robust species than the red, adaptable to the changing habitat of our woodland and perfectly at home in parks and domestic gardens.

The **weasel** (*Mustela nivalis*) is one of our smaller carnivores, found in a wide range of habitats and not a protected species. It is considered an enemy of gamebirds and is sometimes trapped and killed by gamekeepers. Mainly nocturnal and preferring dry areas, the weasel is smaller than the **stoat** (*Mustela erminea*) and the tip of the stoat's tail is always black.

It is possible that you may sight an **otter** (*Lutra lutra*) along one of the riverbanks, where they live their secretive semi-acquatic life, as the species is increasing in numbers. They mainly eat fish but will take moorhens and their chicks and in spring frogs are an important food item. Litters of cubs can be born at any time of the year. Their dens are called holts and are usually in holes in riverbanks or under a pile of rocks.

The species of deer you are most likely to see is the **roe deer** (*Capreolus capreolus*) which are quite small with an average height of 60–70cm at the shoulder. They are reddish brown in summer, grey in winter and have a distinctive white rear end which is conspicuous when the deer is alarmed. Males have short antlers with no more than three points. Abundant in mixed coniferous and deciduous woodland, they are active at dawn and dusk and can sometimes be heard barking. If you come across a young kid apparently abandoned, leave it alone and go away; it's normal behaviour for the mother to leave her kid concealed while she goes off to feed.

REPTILES

The **adder** (*Vipera berus*) is the only poisonous snake in Britain but poses very little risk to walkers and will not bite unless provoked, doing its best to hide. The venom is designed to kill small mammals such as mice and shrews so human deaths are rare. You are most likely to encounter them in spring when they come out of hibernation and during the summer when pregnant females warm themselves in the sun. They are easily identified by the striking zigzag pattern on their back and a 'V' on the top of their head behind the eyes. Adders are beautiful and should be left undisturbed.

Grass snakes (*Natrix natrix*) are Britain's largest reptile, growing up to a metre in length. They prefer rough ground with plentiful long grass in which to conceal themselves, laying their eggs in warm, rotting vegetation such as garden compost heaps, the young hatching in August. They are sometimes killed by people mistaking them for adders but are neither venomous nor aggressive and should be left alone. The body has vertical black bars and spots running along the sides and usually has a prominent yellow collar round the neck.

The **slow worm** (*Anguis fragilis*) looks like a snake but is actually a legless lizard. It has no identifying marks on the body varying in colour from coppery brown to lead grey and is usually quite shiny in appearance. Like lizards, they have eyelids and are able to blink; snakes have no eyelids. They are completely harmless, love to sun themselves and are found in old buildings under stones or discarded roofing sheets.

BIRDS

Streams, canals, rivers

The familiar sight of a **swan** (*Cygnus olor*), **mallard** (*Anas platyrhynchos*), **coot** (*Fulica atra*) or **moorhen** (*Gallinula chloropus*) may be all that is immediately apparent to the walker following the path along water courses but there

SWALLOW
L: 190MM/7¹/₂"

HOUSE MARTIN
L: 140MM/5¹/₂"

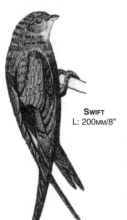

SWIFT
L: 200MM/8"

will be occasional surprises to add to your enjoyment of the natural environment. The **grey heron** (*Ardea cinerea*) is a striking sight as it takes off on its ungainly and unhurried flight or is spotted standing sentinel at the water's edge, as Dylan Thomas says, like a priest.

A rare sighting of a **kingfisher** (*Alcedo atthis*) would be exciting since they are quite hard to see as they fly at great speed and are often simply a flash of blue, there one minute and gone the next. The **grey wagtail** (*Motacilla cinerea*) and the **dipper** (*Cinclus cinclus*) are two delightful birds which can be seen year-round bobbing up and down on boulders in fast-flowing streams. With blue-grey head and yellow underside the grey wagtail is the most striking of the wagtails. The dipper's flight is unmistakable, with its rapid wingbeat, white bib and tail held upright all helping in identification. They are joined in summer by the **common sandpiper** (*Tringa hypoleucos*) a long-legged long-billed wader whose characteristic stance is with the body tilted forward, head lowered and the tail bobbing up and down almost continuously.

Swallows (*Hirundo rustica*), **house martins** (*Delichon urbica*) and **swifts** (*Apus apus*) love to swoop low over water to drink or take flies. The swift cannot perch like the swallow and martin: its legs are mere hooks and it is unable to walk. The less common **sand martin** (*Riparia riparia*) nests in colonies in holes in steep riverbanks and has a curious low buzz for its call.

The **reed bunting** (*Emberiza schoeniclus*) frequents reed beds and is recognizable by its white collar, black hood and bib.

Woodland

The familiar woodland residents such as **chaffinches** (*Fringilla coelebs*), **robin** (*Erithacus rubecula*), **blue tit** (*Parus caeruleus*) and **great tit** (*Parus* *major*), **song thrush** (*Turdus philomelos*) and **blackbird** (*Turdus merula*) are joined by birds that we seldom see in our gardens including the **coal tit** (*Parus ater*) which has a black head with white on the cheeks and nape of the neck; it's seen in coniferous woodland. Its relative, the **long-tailed tit** (*Aegithalos caudatus*), is smaller in size and has a very long tail which distinguishes it from other tits.

The **willow warbler** (*Phylloscopus trochilus*) and **chiffchaff** (*Phylloscopus collybita*) will keep you guessing since distinguishing between them is quite difficult. The chiffchaff is generally rather browner than the willow warbler and its legs are blackish. The **whitethroat** (*Sylvia communis*) is easier to identify since its characteristic behaviour is its constant activity, never keeping still. You may also see the **pied flycatcher** (*Ficedula hypoleuca*) which prefers deciduous woods, especially oak, and darts after insects in the air, seldom returning to the same perch after an aerial sally.

The **green woodpecker** (*Picus viridis*) is a striking bird with its bright green body and red head and its curious call, a kind of laughing cry that carries a long way. Its near kindred the **great spotted woodpecker** (*Dendrocopos major*) with its striking black and white plumage and the smaller **lesser spotted woodpecker** (*Dendrocopos minor*) both habitually drum on trees, usually to mark their territory and extract insects rather than to bore holes for a nest site.

Of the finches, the **greenfinch**, **goldfinch** and **linnet** are relatively common but you might spot the **siskin** (*Carduelis spinus*) which has similar greenish plumage to the greenfinch but is much smaller and more streaked, and the **brambling** (*Fringilla montifringilla*) which often mixes with chaffinches in winter but is easily distinguished from them by its distinct white upper rump. The **bullfinch** (*Pyrrhula pyrrhula*) has a slow and deliberate movement and a rosy red underside as it feeds on berries, buds and seeds in the trees and bushes. A much smaller bird is the **goldcrest** (*Regulus regulus*) which is the smallest European bird, recognized by its yellow crown with black edges.

A darting movement on the trunks of trees may reveal the **treecreeper** (*Certhia familiaris*), a small brown bird with a curved bill which creeps spirally up trees searching for insects, dropping down to the bottom of another one when one is explored, or the **nuthatch** (*Sitta europaea*) which has a bluish-grey upper side and is very acrobatic, often climbing down tree trunks head first which woodpeckers cannot do.

It is highly likely that the **magpie** (*Pica pica*) will be seen and the **jay** (*Garrulus glandarius*) is becoming more common everywhere; both are highly efficient at cleaning eggs out of birds' nests and even taking young birds. Less often seen and not heard as much now is the **cuckoo** (*Cuculus canorus*) which is grey or very occasionally brown in colour which makes it easy to confuse with birds of prey such as kestrels and sparrowhawks.

Among the dove family, **wood pigeons** (*Columba palumbus*) and **collared doves** (*Streptopelia decaocto*) are seen everywhere but you may try to distinguish the **stock dove** (*Columba oenas*) which is a darker, smaller bird than the wood pigeon, nesting in holes.

❏ The Red Kite

Red kites were common throughout Britain centuries ago and were known to scavenge the streets of London but they have since been shot, trapped or poisoned to the extent that by the end of the 19th century they had retreated to a tiny colony in Wales. They were saved from extinction by a dedicated group of conservationists and, with the help of the Nature Conservancy Council, the Joint Nature Conservation Committee and the RSPB, they were re-introduced from 1989 onwards. The project has been a great success and by the year 2000 there were as many as 500 birds in Wales alone, besides healthy numbers elsewhere in England and Scotland, introduced from Spain and Sweden and released into the wild.

Although the common belief has been that kites feed on lambs, this has proved to be a misconception. They do not have the strength to tear the carcass of a lamb, let alone kill a live animal. They will feed on scraps left by crows and buzzards but wait their turn, knowing better than to get involved with these fiercer birds. The main prey of kites is small mammals, insects and earthworms and it has been estimated that a growing kite consumes the equivalent each day of a small rabbit.

RED KITE
L: 650MM/25"

Offa's Dyke walkers might with luck spot a kite, although their main territory is further west among the hills and valleys of West Wales. There is a useful website – 🖳 www.kitecountry.co.uk – for further information on where to see kites and learn more about them.

Open farmland and upland areas

The two birds you're most likely to see are the **wheatear** (*Oenanthe oenanthe*), the male of which has a steel grey back and crown and often bows and flicks its tail and perches on walls or rocks, and the **stonechat** (*Saxicola torquata*), much smaller and darker in plumage and identifiable by its call, a single sharp 'teck'.

Among the smaller birds seen on open moorland are the **meadow pipit** (*Anthus pratensis*) and the **skylark** (*Alauda arvensis*). You may also see the **ring ouzel** (*Turdus torquatus*) which looks like a blackbird but with a white bib. In autumn huge flocks of **redwings** (*Turdus iliatus*) and **fieldfares** (*Turdus pilaris*) fly over from Scandinavia to feed on the berries.

Pheasants (*Phasianus colchicus*), **partridges** (*Perdix perdix*) and **lapwings** (*Vanellus vanellus*) are likely to be seen practically everywhere. In summer in upland areas the bird whose bubbling call will first alert you before you spot its characteristic flight is Britain's largest wader the **curlew** (*Numenius arquata*), a large brown bird with a long down-curved bill. The **oyster catcher** (*Haematopus ostralegus*) is also quite common in the breeding season and is distinctive in its black and white plumage and orange pointed bill and legs. You may also put up a **snipe** (*Gallinago gallinago*) which has a zig-zag flight when

❏ The Raven

RAVEN
L: 650MM/25"

There are said to be about 7000 breeding pairs of ravens in the British Isles and Wales is home to the largest population, supposedly thanks to upland farmers leaving their sheep out all winter. Ravens feed mainly on carrion and they seem to be partial to sheep carrion, which gets them through the winter, whilst elsewhere they have a hard time of it.

Ravens are territorial and having once adopted a territory they stick to it. They can be seen year-round in many of the areas through which the Offa's Dyke Path passes, particularly where crags are in evidence, their favourite nesting places.

Ravens when fully grown measure two feet from beak to tail, much larger than their cousin the carrion crow with which they are sometimes confused, although seeing them together leaves you in no doubt which is which. Their call is a deep-throated croak, once heard, never forgotten or mistaken for the lightweight crow.

Ravens breed early in the year making a flimsy nest of twigs lined with moss and sheep wool usually high on a ledge on a cliff face or quarry wall. The birds are often seen in pairs although they can sometimes gather in quite large numbers, with first-year birds usually flocking together. In the early months of the year ravens perform aerial acrobatics, swooping and diving and looping the loop in an extraordinary display which is part of their courting ritual.

flushed, or in wooded areas the **woodcock** (*Scolopax rusticola*), easily distinguished from the snipe by its larger size and more rounded wings. Its camouflage makes it difficult to observe during the day.

CARRION CROW
L: 480MM/19"

The birds of prey which you will be likely to see are the **kestrel** (*Falco tinnunculus*), the **sparrowhawk** (*Accipiter nisus*) and the much larger **buzzard** (*Buteo buteo*). **Red kites** (*Milvus milvus* – see box opposite) can now be seen once again in mid-Wales and have been successfully re-introduced in the Midlands. You may be lucky to spot the **merlin** (*Falco columbarius*) which has a darkish bluish back and tail and flies fast and low over the ground chasing pipits and larks.

Much larger than the **carrion crow** (*Corvus corone corone*), the **raven** (*Corvus corax*) is now quite common in upland areas; see the box above.

BUTTERFLIES [see colour plate opposite p65]

Given the numerous factors that militate against the survival of butterflies including high winds and heavy rain throughout the year, the use of pesticides and loss of habitat and the removal of hedgerows and intensive farming, it is surprising how often one does see butterflies whilst on the trail during the summer months.

Breeding in nettle patches left alone by most grazing animals, the nettle feeders include **peacock** (*Inachis io*), **tortoiseshell** (*Aglais urticae*), **red admiral** (*Vanessa atalanta*) and **painted lady** (*Cynthia cadui*). They are in colourful contrast to the **meadow brown** (*Maniola jurtina*), **wall** (*Lasiommata megera*) and **small heath** (*Coenonympha pamphilus*), all of which are likely to be seen on warm, sunny days. **Large whites** (*Pieris brassicae*) and **small whites** (*Artogeia rapae*) are common everywhere but should not be disregarded, having their own place in the ecological chain. Although rarer nowadays you could still see the **common blue** (*Polyommatus icarus*), the **orange tip** (*Anthocaris cardamines*) and the **green-veined white** (*Artogeia napi*), especially in areas like the disused quarries on Llanymynech Hill and along Montgomery Canal.

DRAGONFLIES

The commoner dragonflies fall into two groups, the hawkers and the darters. The **hawkers** restlessly patrol their territory by a river, lake or canal which the male, much more brightly coloured than the female, defends against intruders. Most common is the **brown aeshna**, the wingspan of which is 10cm (4in). **Darters** are less restless than hawkers and have a sturdier body, spending time clinging to vegetation and making occasional darts after prey. The males have a blue bloom on their bodies.

TREES

Deciduous

Trees are abundant along the Borders and all the common indigenous species are evident in large numbers. These include the oak, both **English oak** (*Quercus robur*) and **sessile oak** (*Quercus petraea*), the difference between them being that the leaves of the sessile have stalks and the acorns unstalked; **sycamore** (*Acer pseudoplatanus*), **ash** (*Fraxinus excelsior*), **beech** (*Fagus sylvatica*), **birch** (*Betula pubescens*), **lime** or **linden** (*Tiliax vulgaris*), **horse chestnut** (*Aesculus hippocastanum*) and **hornbeam** (*Carpinus betulus*).

Amongst mixed woodland you will also see trees such as **rowan** or **mountain ash** (*Sorbus aucuparia*) with its bright red berries from August, a favourite food for birds, **silver birch** (*Betula pendula*), **aspen** (*Populus tremula*), **alder** (*Alnus glutinosa*), **wych elm** (*Ulmus glabra*), **poplar** (*Populus alba*) and **hazel** (*Corylus avellana*). The **English elm** (*Ulmus procera*) has been virtually wiped out by Dutch elm disease.

The willow most commonly seen along riverbanks and streams is the **crack willow** (*Salix fragilis*) which is often pollarded to encourage growth. The tree on which catkins appear is the **goat** or **pussy willow** (*Salix caprea*).

Conifers

The Borders are not afflicted by mass planting of conifers to anything like the same extent as Scotland, the Lake District and Northumberland although there are some stretches of the trail where the dark, silent environment of closely planted conifers is likely to cause some discouragement. The trouble with such plantations is that they are devoid of other life. Birds don't go there, flowers won't grow due to the lack of light and the sun does not reach the forest floor. Fortunately the policy of blanket planting of conifers has fallen out of favour as environmental issues have been taken on board and a more responsible approach has been adopted (see p53).

The commoner plantation trees are the **sitka spruce** (*Picea sitchensis*) introduced from North America and capable of 1.5m growth a year, **Norway spruce** (*Picea abies*) which can reach a height of 40m, the **European larch** (*Larix decidua*) and the **Scots pine** (*Pinus sylvestris*).

Walkers on the Offa's Dyke Path will be encouraged by the wide diversity of trees growing in the areas through which they pass and the efforts being made to replant cleared plantations by introducing local broadleafed species. Felling is still apparent in areas like World's End near Llangollen and Kings Wood near Monmouth and this can have the effect of the path becoming obscured and waymarks displaced.

WILD FLOWERS

Hedgerows and field boundaries

In spring and early summer the variety of wild flowers in the hedgerows and along the verges of the minor roads and lanes which you will walk along will be rich indeed.

Even those with no knowledge will soon learn to recognize the commoner species such as **red campion** (*Silene dioica*), **cowslip** (*Primula veris*), **primrose** (*Primula vulgaris*), **birdsfoot trefoil** (*Lotus corniculatus*) or 'bacon and eggs', **common speedwell** (*Veronica officinalis*) which can cure indigestion, gout and liver complaints, **bugle** (*Ajuga repans*), **bluebell** (*Endymion nonscriptus*), **tufted vetch** (*Vicia cracca*) and **common dog violet** (*Viola riviniana*), all of which are familiar.

Later on from May to September they will be joined by **buttercup** (*Ranunculus acris*), the flowers of which when rubbed on a cow's udders were said to improve the milk, **yellow pimpernel** (*Lysimacia nemorum*), **golden-rod** (*Solidago virgaurea*) once used in folk medicine to treat wounds, **viper's bugloss** (*Echium vulgare*), **harebell** (*Campanula rotundifolia*), **herb robert** (*Geranium robertianum*), **foxglove** (*Digitalis purpurea*) which is poisonous and from which the drug Digitalin is extracted to treat heart disease, **field poppy** (*Papaver rhoeas*) and **ox-eye daisy** (*Leucanthemum vulgare*), also known as dog daisy or marguerite.

Honeysuckle (*Lonicera periclymenum*), also known as woodbine, makes its appearance growing through hedges from June to September, the fruits ripening to red in the autumn. **Bindweed** (*Convolvulus arvensis*) with its white trumpet-shaped flowers is also a common sight during the summer months.

Other hedgerow regulars are the common **bramble** (*Rubus fruticosus*) known to us for its blackberry fruit and the **common dog rose** (*Rosa canina*), which produces rosehips, an excellent source of vitamin C when taken as a syrup.

The tall white flowering heads of members of the carrot family such as **cow parsley** (*Anthrisus sylvestris*), **yarrow** (*Achillea millefolium*), the use of which in the treatment of wounds goes back to Achilles, and upright **hedge parsley** (*Torilis japonica*) will be obvious along with, occasionally, **hogweed** (*Heracleum sphondylium*) which can grow to 1.75m (6ft) high.

Woodland

It is always a pleasure to see wild fruit growing and **wild strawberry** (*Fragaria vesca*) and **wild raspberry** (*Rubus idaeus*) will certainly be spotted in wooded areas. Other berries will be sloes on the **blackthorn** (*Prunus spinosa*) bushes and occasionally **bilberry** (*Vaccinium myrtilis*) flowering from April to June.

Other woodland flowers include **wood anemone** (*Anemone nemorosa*), **wood-sorrel** (*Oxalis acetosella*), the flowers of which close at night and in bad weather, **crow garlic** (*Allium vineale*), distinctive by its smell, **bluebell** (*Endymiom non-scriptus*) and the poisonous **bittersweet** or **woody nightshade** (*Solanum dulcamara*). **Early purple orchids** (*Orchis mascula*) are seen in some areas from April to June, often growing with bluebells.

Moorland

Bracken and **gorse** (*Ulex europaeus*) are everywhere on the trail especially over the exposed open moorland of the Clwydian Hills, Hergest Ridge and the Black Mountains where you will also see **heather** or **ling** (*Calluna vulgaris*) and the gentle **broom** (*Cytisus scoparius*) with its characteristic seed-pods in the autumn.

Riverbanks and wet areas

Lady's smock (*Cardamine pratensis*) and **ragged robin** (*Lychnis flos-cuculi*) are two pink flowers that are often seen in damp areas. **Watermint** (*Mentha aquatica*), **meadowsweet** (*Filipendula ulmaria*), which medicinally has the same properties as aspirin, and the poisonous **water-crowfoot** (*Ranunculus aquatilis*) make canals and ponds their habitat. Sometimes the prolific **policeman's helmet** (*Impatiens glandulifera*), distinctive by the shape of its flowers, will be found colonizing riverbanks.

Rough ground and waste land

Uncultivated areas such as land that has been cleared of buildings or disturbed by construction seems to attract certain plants which move in and sometimes take over the whole area. These include the ubiquitous **rosebay willowherb** (*Epilobium angustifolium*), **ragwort** (*Senecio jacobaea*) which is poisonous to horses, **dandelion** (*Taraxacum officinale*) and **groundsel** (*Senecio vulgaris*). You will also see **Aaron's rod** (*Verbascum thapsus*) which used to be smoked like tobacco in a pipe, **rape** (*Brassica napus*), **knotgrass** (*Polygonum aviculare*), **field scabious** (*Knautia arvensis*) and **valerian** (*Valeriana officinalis*), the smell of which cats are said to love.

Meadow Buttercup
Ranunculis acris

Common Ragwort
Senecio jacobaea

Gorse
Ulex europaeus

Birdsfoot-trefoil
Lotus corniculatus

Primrose
Primula vulgaris

Ox-eye Daisy
Leucanthemum vulgare

Daffodil
Narcissus pseudo-narcissus

Foxglove
Digitalis purpurea

Red Campion
Silene dioica

Rosebay Willowherb
Chamerion angustifolium

Common Vetch
Vicia sativa

Bell Heather
Erica cinerea

Heather (Ling)
Calluna vulgaris

Yarrow
Achillea millefolium

Violet
Viola riviniana

Honeysuckle
Lonicera periclymemum

Holly (this impressive tree seen near Llangollen)
Ilex aquifolium

Rowan tree
Sorbus aucuparia

Herb-Robert
Geranium robertianum

Germander Speedwell
Veronica chamaedrys

Common Poppy
Papaver rhoeas

Devil's-bit Scabious
Succisa pratensis

Harebell
Campanula rotundifolia

Blackthorn
Prunus spinosa

Small Tortoiseshell
Aglais urticae

Large Garden/Cabbage White
Pieris brassicae

Peacock
Inachis io

Small Garden/
Cabbage White
Artogeia rapae

Small Heath
Coenonympha pamphilus

Common Blue
Polyommatus icarus

Painted Lady
Cynthia cadui

Red Admiral
Vanessa atalanta

PART 4: ROUTE GUIDE & MAPS

The route guide and maps have not been divided into rigid daily stages since people walk at different speeds and have different interests. Some sections fall naturally into full days such as Knighton to Kington but more often the choice is up to the walker.

The **route summaries** below describe the trail between significant places and are written as if walking the path from north to south. To enable you to plan your own itinerary **practical information** is presented clearly on the trail maps. This includes walking times, places to stay, camp and eat, as well as shops where you can buy supplies. Further service details are given in the text under the entry for each place. For an overview of this information, see pp22-9.

TRAIL MAPS

Scale and walking times
The trail maps are to a scale of 1:20,000 (1cm = 200m; 3^1/8 inches = one mile). Walking times are given along the side of each map and the arrow shows the direction to which the time refers. Black triangles indicate the points between which the times have been taken. **See note below on walking times**.

The time-bars are a tool and are not there to judge your walking ability. There are so many variables that affect walking speed, from the weather conditions to how many beers you drank the previous evening. After the first hour or two of walking you will be able to see how your speed relates to the timings on the maps.

Up or down?
The trail is shown as a dotted line. An arrow across the trail indicates the slope; two arrows show that it is steep. Note that the arrow points towards the higher part of the trail. If, for example, you are walking from A (at 80m) to B (at 200m) and the trail between the two is short and steep it would be shown thus: A— — — >> — — – B. Reversed arrow heads indicate downward gradient.

Accommodation
Accommodation marked on the map is either on or within easy reach of the trail. It is normal for B&B proprietors to collect walkers from the nearest point on the trail and deliver them back again next morning. Details of each place are given in the accompanying text. Unless otherwise specified, B&B prices are

---

❏ **Important note – walking times**
Unless otherwise specified, **all times in this book refer only to the time spent walking**. You will need to add 20-30% to allow for rests, photography, checking the map, drinking water etc. When planning the day's hike count on 5-7 hours actual walking.

summer high-season prices per person, assuming two people sharing a room. The number of rooms of each type is given after each entry: S=Single, T= Twin room, D=Double room, F= Family room (sleeps at least 3 people).

Other features
Features are marked on the map when pertinent to navigation. In order to avoid cluttering the maps and making them unusable, not all features have been marked each time they occur.

The route guide

PRESTATYN   MAP 1
Prestatyn came to prominence in the 19th century with its combined attractions of sea bathing and the supposed abundant sunshine, although what became of the sunshine is anybody's guess.

Today it is home, in common with most of the North Wales coastal resorts, to thousands of caravans, which is fine for enthusiasts but rather detrimental to the landscape.

The Offa's Dyke Path starts, or ends, at Prestatyn, on the seafront at one of three alternative plaques claiming to be the official start. Traditionally walkers remove their boots and paddle in the sea, a symbolic introduction, or conclusion, to their walk. Since the act is only a token, no need to go barefoot: go down to the water's edge, that'll do. If you need a token, pick up a pebble and carry it with you to the trail's end and toss it into the Bristol Channel. In ten thousand years there'll be quite a mound of these pebbles, each one representing a private triumph.

Transport
The town is very accessible by road and rail. The M56 motorway gives easy access to the A548, and Prestatyn is on the Chester to Holyhead line. Frequent **trains** run through the day. **Buses** connect to Chester and Wrexham (see public transport map, p38).

A reliable local **taxi** firm is Roberts Bros (☎ 01745-853746) located just over the footbridge from the railway station, across the road from Offa's Tavern.

Services
The **tourist information centre** (☎ 01745-889092, open Easter–Sept) also houses the **Offa's Dyke Centre**, a small sound and vision exhibition spreading the word about both the famous earthwork and the walk. If you require tourist information in the off-season contact the TIC in Rhyl (☎ 01745-355068) which is open all year.

High St contains the major **banks**, all with cashpoints, and the **post office** is on King's Ave. Provisions for the trail can be picked up at **Spar** (Mon–Sat 8am–11pm, Sun 8am–10.30pm) on the High St, or at **Aldi** (Mon–Wed 9am–6pm, Thu–Fri 9am–7pm, Sat 8.30am–5.30pm) on Meliden Rd.

There is a lively **outdoor market** on Tuesday, Friday and Sunday between the bus station and railway station. The main **doctors' surgery** (☎ 01745-886444) is on Ffordd Pendyffryn which runs parallel with the High St.

Where to stay
Both **campsites** near Prestatyn are over a mile out of town on Gronant Rd; *Nant Mill Touring Site*, (☎ 01745-852360, Easter–Sept) and *St Mary's Touring Site*, (☎ 01745-853951, Easter–Sept).

Being a seaside town, **B&B** accommodation is widely available. The best place is *Traeth Ganol* (☎ 01745-853594, 41 Beach Rd West, 1S/1T/1D/6F) on the seafront, run with a high standard of consideration by Chris and Jo Groves who love walkers. The rooms are very nicely furnished. Rates are a

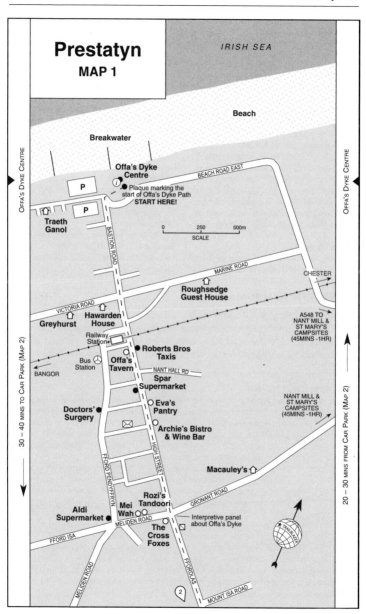

Prestatyn
MAP 1

IRISH SEA

Beach

Breakwater

BEACH ROAD EAST

Offa's Dyke Centre

OFFA'S DYKE CENTRE

P

P

Plaque marking the start of Offa's Dyke Path **START HERE!**

Traeth Ganol

BASTION ROAD

0   250   500m
SCALE

MARINE ROAD

OFFA'S DYKE CENTRE

CHESTER

Roughsedge Guest House

A548 TO NANT MILL & ST MARY'S CAMPSITES (45MINS -1HR)

VICTORIA ROAD

Greyhurst   **Hawarden House**

Railway Station

BANGOR

Bus Station

Offa's Tavern

Roberts Bros Taxis

NANT HALL RD

Spar Supermarket

Doctors' Surgery

Eva's Pantry

Archie's Bistro & Wine Bar

NANT MILL & ST MARY'S CAMPSITES (45MINS -1HR)

HIGH STREET

FFORD PENYOTFFRYN

Macauley's

GRONANT ROAD

Rozi's Tandoori

Aldi Supermarket

Mei Wah

MELIDEN ROAD

Interpretive panel about Offa's Dyke

The Cross Foxes

FFORD ISA

FFORDLAS

MELIDEN ROAD

2

MOUNT ISA ROAD

30 – 40 MINS TO CAR PARK (MAP 2)

20 – 30 MINS FROM CAR PARK (MAP 2)

little more than the average at £42 single and £31 per person double and the evening meal for those who have pre-booked is £11, or £13.50 for those who haven't.

Other B&Bs include two close together on Victoria Rd, *Hawarden House* (☎ 01745-855395, 1S/3D/2F) and *Greyhurst*, (☎ 01745-852812, 2T/1D/1F) both charging £38 for a double en suite. A twin room let as a single is £25 per night.

Also worth trying is *Roughsedge Guest House*, (☎ 01745-887359, 26–28 Marine Rd, 2S/2T/3D/2F) charging £19.50 per person, or £22.50 for an en-suite room.

Macauley's Café Bar (☎ 01745-852442, 17 Gronant Rd, 1T/1D) has B&B at £42 per room. Meals are taken in the bar. They have parking and you could negotiate to leave your car here whilst off on the trail.

Where to eat

The High St has an abundance of small sandwich shops and cafés, either for a quick coffee or to stock up for a packed lunch. The best is *Eva's Pantry* (☎ 01745-857 484, 93 High St) with a wide choice of freshly-made sandwiches. Of the restaurants, *Archie's Bistro and Wine Bar* (☎ 01745-855 106, 147–151 High St) is the most upmarket, offering a varied three-course menu for £19.95.

Offa's Tavern (☎ 01745-886046, 2–10 High St) is a typical renovated pub with plenty of choice for food and drink. *The Cross Foxes* (☎ 01745-854984, Pendre Sq) is an appropriate watering hole to mark the beginning or end of your adventure with a celebratory drink. The beer is undistinguished but sometimes a guest beer can be found. Meals are the usual pub fare, including steak and kidney pie, chicken curry and sweet and sour chicken.

In close proximity there's also *Rozi's Tandoori* (☎ 01745-856310, 16–18 Meliden Rd) and a Chinese restaurant, *Mei Wah* (☎ 01745-853533, 34 Meliden Rd).

PRESTATYN TO RHUALLT   MAPS 1–4

This **8-mile (13km, 3$^{1}/_{2}$–4$^{1}/_{4}$hrs)** stretch of farmland involves navigating a network of fields, tracks and lanes and with numerous stiles to cross should not be underestimated. The waymarking is good and route-finding is unlikely to be a problem but, be warned, there are no places for refreshment along the way so

---

❏ **King Offa (757-96)**
The Anglo-Saxon period (between the 5th and 11th centuries AD) was a turbulent time in an England divided into virtual armed camps which were in a state of almost permanent war. Into this chaos came a member of an ancient Mercian family, Offa, who came to prominence in the civil war that followed the murder of his cousin King Aethelbald in AD757.

By the ruthless suppression of his enemies, Offa was able to seize overall power and establish a state that covered most of England from the Humber to the South Coast and rule it as a single

Coin (c790) entity. He used other methods besides those of the sword to maintain his sovereignty including a trade treaty with the Emperor Charlemagne and a religious agreement with the Pope. He forged links with Northumbria and Wessex by marrying his daughters to their rulers and struck a coinage for the first time that was in use throughout his lands.

The Dyke that bears his name is his lasting memorial. Built to control the Borders between England and the plundering tribes to the west, it was as much a defining boundary as a fortification. For walkers it offers a unique opportunity to explore a landscape not greatly changed from the days when the broadsword and the axe held sway.

you will need to carry your own water and food. In the wet it will be slippery in places, particularly crossing the **Bryn Prestatyn** hillside, a gorse and bracken covered escarpment with fine views to the sea, Snowdonia and ahead to the Clwydian Hills which are a challenge to come.

Marian Cwm (Tai-Marian) is a scattered group of houses with a telephone kiosk and nothing else but you could always send for a taxi from Prestatyn if you suddenly change your mind about the whole idea. This somewhat agricultural introduction to the trail is not untypical of what you are going to meet as you move south. Field paths, woodland, enclosed lanes, heathland and deep countryside are all encountered, relatively easy terrain for the first day but sufficiently taxing to ensure that you will have tired legs by teatime.

RHUALLT   MAP 4

The *Smithy Arms* (☎ 01745-582298) does meals but not accommodation. The landlord, a former trawler skipper with a good choice in fish, is strict in observing the licensing hours and after 2pm there will be no lingering. Last orders means what it says.

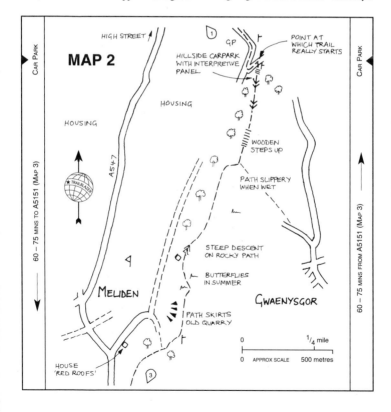

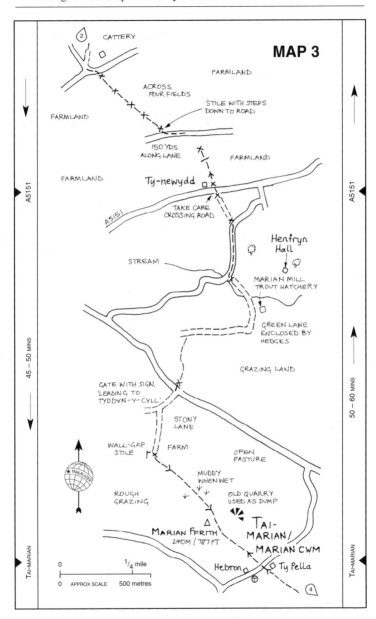

MAP 3

CATTERY

FARMLAND

ACROSS
FOUR FIELDS

STILE WITH STEPS
DOWN TO ROAD

FARMLAND

FARMLAND

150 YDS
ALONG LANE

FARMLAND

Ty-newydd

FARMLAND

A5151

TAKE CARE
CROSSING ROAD

Henfryn
Hall

STREAM

MARIAN MILL
TROUT HATCHERY

GREEN LANE
ENCLOSED BY
HEDGES

GRAZING LAND

GATE WITH SIGN,
'LEADING TO
TYDDYN-Y-CYLL'

STONY
LANE

WALL-GAP
STILE

FARM

OPEN
PASTURE

ROUGH
GRAZING

MUDDY
WHEN WET

OLD QUARRY
USED AS DUMP

TAI-
MARIAN/
MARIAN CWM

MARIAN FFRITH
240M / 787 FT

Hebron

Ty Pella

★ TRAILBLAZER

0   1/4 mile
0   APPROX SCALE   500 metres

A5151

45 – 50 MINS

TAI-MARIAN

A5151

50 – 60 MINS

TAI-MARIAN

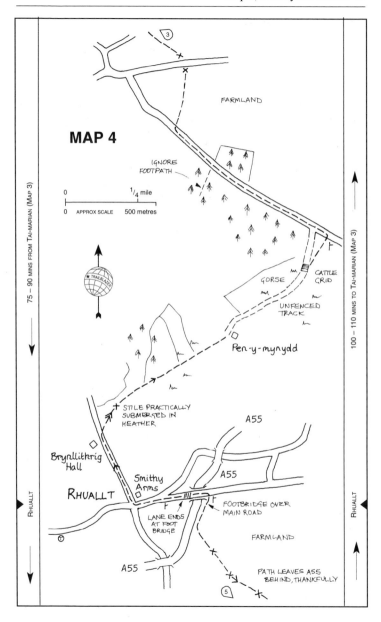

MAP 4

FARMLAND

IGNORE
FOOTPATH

0   ¼ mile

0   APPROX SCALE   500 metres

★ TRAILBLAZER

GORSE   CATTLE
GRID

UNFENCED
TRACK

Pen-y-mynydd

STILE PRACTICALLY
SUBMERGED IN
HEATHER

A55

Brynllithrig
Hall

A55

RHUALLT   Smithy
Arms

FOOTBRIDGE OVER
MAIN ROAD

LANE ENDS
AT FOOT
BRIDGE

FARMLAND

A55

PATH LEAVES A55
BEHIND, THANKFULLY

75 – 90 MINS FROM TAI-MARIAN (MAP 3)

100 – 110 MINS TO TAI-MARIAN (MAP 3)

RHUALLT

RHUALLT

RHUALLT TO BODFARI   MAPS 4–6

As the road climbs
You will pause for breath and the far sea's
Signal will flash, till you turn again
To the steep track, buttressed with cloud.
RS Thomas

This **5-mile (8km, 2–2¹/₂hrs)** stretch leaves the crossroads in Rhuallt, crosses the
footbridge over the busy A55 and for the next hour climbs through a succession
of rough grazed fields, each one with its obligatory stiles. This is farming country and you will almost certainly be walking through stock. Leave cows and
sheep alone and they will ignore you. Look back for glimpses of the sea.

You are entering the foothills of the **Clwydian Range** and have plenty of
work to do before reaching Bodfari, including a steep pull up to **Cefn Du** before
you descend to the scattered hamlet of **Sodom**, a tiny outpost of **Bodfari** which
is 40–50 minutes further on.

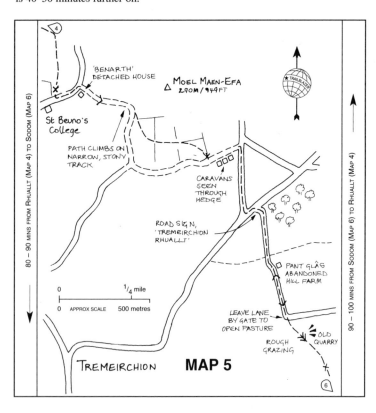

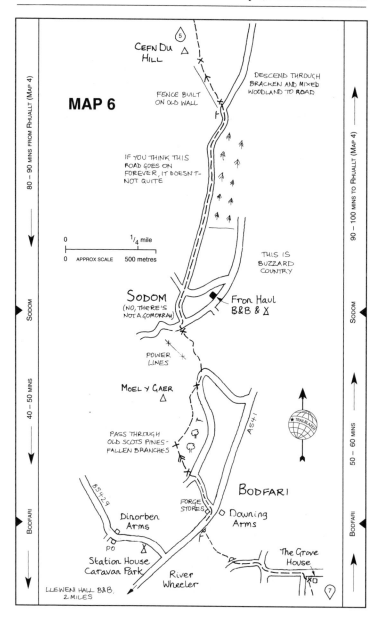

MAP 6

CEFN DU HILL △ ⑤

DESCEND THROUGH BRACKEN AND MIXED WOODLAND TO ROAD

FENCE BUILT ON OLD WALL

IF YOU THINK THIS ROAD GOES ON FOREVER, IT DOESN'T - NOT QUITE

80 – 90 MINS FROM RHUALLT (MAP 4)

90 – 100 MINS TO RHUALLT (MAP 4)

0   1/4 mile
0   APPROX SCALE   500 metres

THIS IS BUZZARD COUNTRY

SODOM (NO, THERE'S NOT A GOMORRAH)

Fron Haul B&B & ☒

SODOM

SODOM

POWER LINES

MOEL Y GAER △

40 – 50 MINS

50 – 60 MINS

A541

★ TRAILBLAZER

PASS THROUGH OLD SCOTS PINES - FALLEN BRANCHES

BODFARI

FORGE STORES

Downing Arms

B5429

Dinorben Arms

Station House Caravan Park

PO

River Wheeler

The Grove House

⑦

BODFARI

BODFARI

LLEWENI HALL B&B, 2 MILES

❏ **St Beuno's College**

The best-known student of this theological college was the poet and Jesuit priest Gerard Manley Hopkins (1844–1889) who studied here as a young man. He loved the natural world and took delight in its infinite variety. It is said that he composed one of his most celebrated poems, *Pied Beauty*, on a walk through open meadows to a nearby chapel, the very surroundings which the walker on the Offa's Dyke Path experiences, and you can imagine the poet absorbing the impressions vying for his attention, from sky and clouds, trees, fields to the animals and birds around him.

Glory be to God for dappled things –
For skies of couple-colour as a brinded cow,
For rose-moles all in stipple upon trout that swim:
Fresh firecoal chestnut falls, finches wings:
Landscape plotted and pierced – fold, fallow and plough:

Hopkins learned the Welsh language and drew from its tonal qualities the inspiration for his own innovative 'sprung rhythm', based on the Welsh *cynghanedd*, the 'chiming of consonants'.

SODOM MAP 6

Fron Haul (☎ 01745-710301, 1S/1T/2D/ 1F) is an isolated oasis where Mrs Edwards charges £25 for B&B and £4 for **camping** including the use of a shower in the converted outhouse. There is limited space and booking is advisable. The pub is too far to walk to unless you're desperate. It's 50 minutes to the village each way.

BODFARI MAP 6

The village is really nothing more than a staging post on the Denbigh to Ruthin road but it has good amenities including the **Forge Stores** (Mon–Fri 7am–8pm, Sat and Sun 7.30am–8pm), for all basic supplies as well as offering cash-back, and a **post office** just back from the main road. The Denbigh–Mold **bus** stops here eight times a day and twice on Sundays (see public transport map, p38).

You have a choice of two pubs. *The Downing Arms* (☎ 01745-710265) has Bass and Worthington E on draught and a fairly formal restaurant where diners speak in hushed whispers. All the meat is Welsh blackface from Daniel Jones in St Asaph and the fish comes from the fish farm next door. *The Dinorben Arms* (☎ 01745-710309) keeps some choice real ale including such specials as Old Speckled Hen and Bateman's SB, both really excellent brews. Generous bar meals are available including the challenging farmhouse buffet at £10. When the weather is fine you can sit in a pleasant outdoor terrace area.

There's camping at *Station House Caravan Park* (☎ 01745-710372) at £3 for a single camper and £4 for a two-person tent. Showers are free.

❏ **Important note – walking times**

Unless otherwise specified, **all times in this book refer only to the time spent walking**. You will need to add 20-30% to allow for rests, photography, checking the map, drinking water etc. When planning the day's hike count on 5-7 hours actual walking.

BODFARI TO CLWYD GATE (A494) MAPS 6–12

This is a challenging **11-mile (18km, $5^3/4$–$6^1/2$hrs)** section which involves the crossing of the **Clwydian Hills**. Leaving Bodfari, the first landmark of the day is **Moel-y-Parc**, the hill with the radio mast on top, which remains in sight throughout this section although your route takes you over the shoulder without visiting the summit.

You do top out on the next hill, **Pen-y-Cloddiau**, an Iron Age hill-fort with a flat top surrounded by earthwork defences, the first of several hill-forts which you come across in this stage.

The tops follow each other in succession, **Moel Arthur**, **Moel Dywyll**, **Moel Fammau** and **Foel Fenlli** before reaching **Clwyd Gate**, where the A494 Mold to Ruthin road cuts through the range.

Where to stay and eat: Bodfari to Clwyd Gate (A494)

The section along the spine of the Clwydian Hills has a few escape routes so you can retreat to the safety of a village pub if the weather closes in.

Between Pen-y-Cloddiau and Moel Arthur the village of **Llandyrnog** can be reached by heading west down the road for about 2 miles (3km, $^3/4$–1hr).

From the cattle grid between Moel Arthur and Moel Llys-y-coed you could walk west then south down the lane to **Llangynhafal**, $2^1/2$ miles away (4km, 1–$1^1/4$ hrs). Llangynhafal can also be reached from the summit of Moel Dywyll where there is a path descending west to the village, $1^1/4$ miles away (2km, 30–40mins). There is a cosy local pub here, the *Golden Lion* (☎ 01824-790451), and a B&B, *Esgairlygain* (☎ 01824-704047, 1D/1F) charging £22. It's tricky to find; their drive is next to a house called Wylan.

From Moel Dywyll there is a path descending east via the reservoir to **Cilcain**, 2 miles (3km, $^3/4$ –1hr) away, where you'll find the *White Horse* (☎ 01352 -740142, Mon–Sat 12–3pm, 6.30–11pm, Sun 12–3pm, 7–10.30pm) which does meals but not accommodation.

The quickest way off Moel Fammau is to stay on the Offa's Dyke Path until Bwlch Penbarra, then head west down the road for $1^1/4$ miles (2km, 25–30mins) to **Llanbedr-Dyffryn-Clwyd**. It's well worth visiting the village if only for its gem of a pub, *The Griffin* (☎ 01824-702792, 2T/1D), one of

the top ten places along the entire route. B&B is from £27 for single occupancy, or there's **camping** in the garden from £2.50. The meals are a credit to the imaginative chef, the menu changes regularly and the beer is Robinsons from Stockport. The landlord will collect you from Bwlch Penbarra or Clwyd Gate if you are staying overnight and deliver you back the next morning, thoroughly refreshed.

If you head east down the lane at Bwlch Penbarra you'll reach **Llanferres** where the welcoming *Druid Inn* (☎ 01352-810898, 1S/2T/2D/1F) does B&B from £26.50 and bar meals from around £10.

The last thing you would expect to find on a long distance trail is a motel so to discover the *Clwyd Gate Inn and Motel* (☎ 01824-704444, 1S/3T/4D/3F) where the Offa's Dyke Path meets the A494 may come as a surprise. Don't be put off, it serves a purpose, but one that's perhaps more suited to the motorized traveller than the pedestrian. It's a busy place charging £42 for a single room and £60 for a double room including the use of their Jacuzzi, sauna and pool, a welcome relief after a hard day on the trail. For those who prefer a less cosmopolitan ambience, there is welcoming B&B at *Ffynnon-y-Berth* (☎ 01824-780298, 1T/1D/1F) charging from £17.50 per person, although you may be discouraged by the unavoidable walk of nearly a mile east along the verge of the busy A494. You can also **camp** here for £2.50.

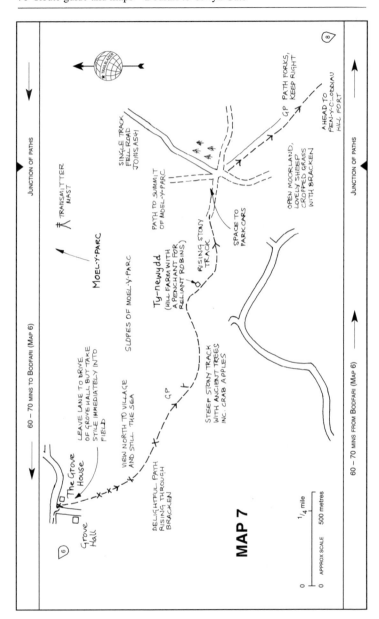

60 – 70 MINS TO BODFARI (MAP 6)

JUNCTION OF PATHS

JUNCTION OF PATHS

60 – 70 MINS FROM BODFARI (MAP 6)

TRANSMITTER MAST

MOEL-Y-PARC

SINGLE TRACK FELL ROAD JOINS (ASH)

PATH TO SUMMIT OF MOEL-Y-PARC

SLOPES OF MOEL-Y-PARC

GP PATH FORKS, KEEP RIGHT

AHEAD TO PEN-Y-CLODDIAU HILL FORT

OPEN MOORLAND, LOVELY SHEEP CROPPED GRASS WITH BRACKEN

SPACE TO PARK CARS

RISING STONY TRACK

Ty-newydd (HILL FARM WITH A PENCHANT FOR RELIANT ROBINS)

STEEP STONY TRACK WITH ANCIENT TREES INC. CRAB APPLES

GP

LEAVE LANE TO DRIVE OF GROVE HALL BUT TAKE STILE IMMEDIATELY INTO FIELD

VIEW NORTH TO VILLAGE AND STILL THE SEA

The Grove House

Grove Hall

DELIGHTFUL PATH RISING THROUGH BRACKEN

MAP 7

1/4 mile

500 metres

0   APPROX SCALE

6

8

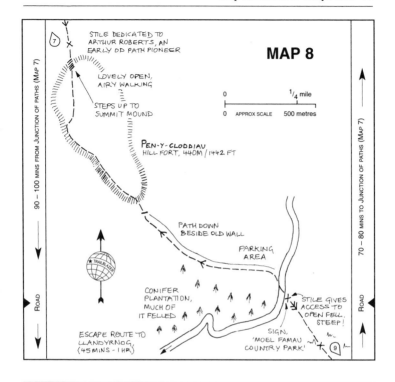

STILE DEDICATED TO
ARTHUR ROBERTS, AN
EARLY OD PATH PIONEER

MAP 8

LOVELY OPEN,
AIRY WALKING

STEPS UP TO
SUMMIT MOUND

0   ¹/₄ mile

0   APPROX SCALE   500 metres

PEN-Y-CLODDIAU
HILL FORT, 440M / 1442 FT

PATH DOWN
BESIDE OLD WALL

PARKING
AREA

TRAILBLAZER

CONIFER
PLANTATION,
MUCH OF
IT FELLED

STILE GIVES
ACCESS TO
OPEN FELL.
STEEP!

SIGN,
'MOEL FAMAU
COUNTRY PARK'

ESCAPE ROUTE TO
LLANDYRNOG,
(45 MINS - 1 HR)

90 – 100 MINS FROM JUNCTION OF PATHS (MAP 7)

ROAD

70 – 80 MINS TO JUNCTION OF PATHS (MAP 7)

ROAD

❏ The Clwydian Hills

Stretching for 20 miles (32km) in a series of whaleback ridges, the narrow line of the Clwydian Hills marks the boundary between the industrial landscape of Deeside and the gentle Vale of Clwyd, a lush area of trees and fields interspersed with small settlements and a few compact towns like Ruthin and Denbigh.

The highest point is **Moel Fammau**, the mother mountain, which at 555m (1820ft) is crowned with the squat blockhouse of Jubilee Tower, built in 1810 to mark the jubilee of George III but re-built many times since, being no match for the fierce winds.

The walking is on springy turf and the views splendid. There are two dramatic losses in height either side of **Moel Arthur** at 455m (1494ft) a striking, conical hill surmounted by another hill-fort which you'll miss unless you divert from the path to visit the summit.

Foel Fenlli and **Moel Eithinen** are the next hills before another gap allows the road to cut through, then you climb again to **Moel Gyw**, **Moel Llanfair** and **Moel y Plas**, the southernmost outliers in the range which peters out in the valley of the River Alun and Llandegla.

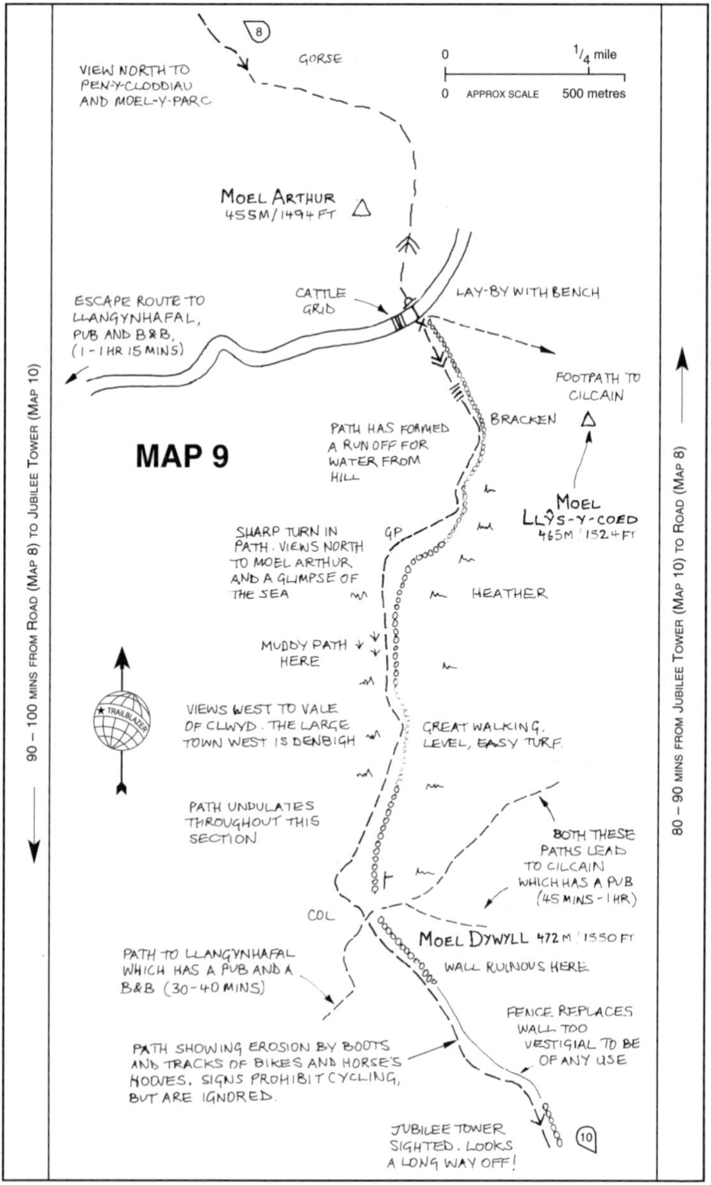

VIEW NORTH TO
PEN-Y-CLODDIAU
AND MOEL-Y-PARC

GORSE

8

0   1/4 mile

0   APPROX SCALE   500 metres

MOEL ARTHUR
455M/1494 FT

ESCAPE ROUTE TO
LLANGYNHAFAL,
PUB AND B&B,
(1 – 1HR 15 MINS)

CATTLE
GRID

LAY-BY WITH BENCH

FOOTPATH TO
CILCAIN

MAP 9

PATH HAS FORMED
A RUN OFF FOR
WATER FROM
HILL

BRACKEN

MOEL
LLŶS-Y-COED
465M / 1524 FT

SHARP TURN IN
PATH. VIEWS NORTH
TO MOEL ARTHUR
AND A GLIMPSE OF
THE SEA

GP

HEATHER

MUDDY PATH
HERE

VIEWS WEST TO VALE
OF CLWYD. THE LARGE
TOWN WEST IS DENBIGH

GREAT WALKING.
LEVEL, EASY TURF.

PATH UNDULATES
THROUGHOUT THIS
SECTION

BOTH THESE
PATHS LEAD
TO CILCAIN
WHICH HAS A PUB
(45 MINS – 1 HR)

COL

MOEL DYWYLL 472M / 1550 FT

PATH TO LLANGYNHAFAL
WHICH HAS A PUB AND A
B&B (30–40 MINS)

WALL RUINOUS HERE

FENCE REPLACES
WALL TOO
VESTIGIAL TO BE
OF ANY USE

PATH SHOWING EROSION BY BOOTS
AND TRACKS OF BIKES AND HORSE'S
HOOVES. SIGNS PROHIBIT CYCLING,
BUT ARE IGNORED.

JUBILEE TOWER
SIGHTED. LOOKS
A LONG WAY OFF!

10

★ TRAILBLAZER

90 – 100 MINS FROM ROAD (MAP 8) TO JUBILEE TOWER (MAP 10)

80 – 90 MINS FROM JUBILEE TOWER (MAP 10) TO ROAD (MAP 8)

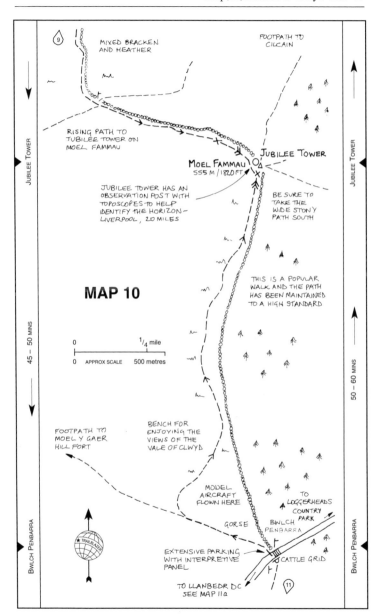

9

MIXED BRACKEN
AND HEATHER

FOOTPATH TO
CILCAIN

JUBILEE TOWER

RISING PATH TO
JUBILEE TOWER ON
MOEL FAMMAU

JUBILEE TOWER

MOEL FAMMAU
555 M / 1820 FT

JUBILEE TOWER HAS AN
OBSERVATION POST WITH
TOPOSCOPES TO HELP
IDENTIFY THE HORIZON –
LIVERPOOL, 20 MILES

BE SURE TO
TAKE THE
WIDE STONY
PATH SOUTH

THIS IS A POPULAR
WALK AND THE PATH
HAS BEEN MAINTAINED
TO A HIGH STANDARD

MAP 10

0   1/4 mile

0   APPROX SCALE   500 metres

45 – 50 MINS

50 – 60 MINS

JUBILEE TOWER

FOOTPATH TO
MOEL Y GAER
HILL FORT

BENCH FOR
ENJOYING THE
VIEWS OF THE
VALE OF CLWYD

MODEL
AIRCRAFT
FLOWN HERE

TO
LOGGERHEADS
COUNTRY
PARK

GORSE

BWLCH
PENBARRA

TRAILBLAZER

EXTENSIVE PARKING
WITH INTERPRETIVE
PANEL

CATTLE GRID

11

TO LLANBEDR DC
SEE MAP 11a

BWLCH PENBARRA

BWLCH PENBARRA

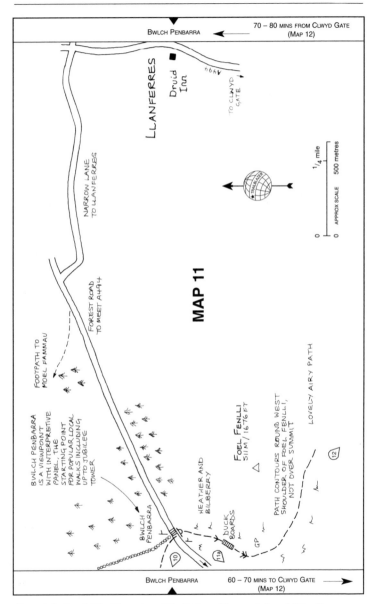

BWLCH PENBARRA

70 – 80 MINS FROM CLWYD GATE
(MAP 12)

BWLCH PENBARRA ▼

LLANFERRES

Druid Inn

A494

TO CLWYD GATE

NARROW LANE TO LLANFERRES

¼ mile

0   500 metres
0   APPROX SCALE

TRAILBLAZER ★

MAP 11

FOREST ROAD TO MEET A494

FOOTPATH TO MOEL FAMMAU

BWLCH PENBARRA IS A VIEWPOINT WITH INTERPRETIVE PANEL, THE STARTING POINT FOR POPULAR LOCAL WALKS INCLUDING UP TO JUBILEE TOWER.

BWLCH PENBARRA

FOEL FENLLI 511M / 1676 FT

HEATHER AND BILBERRY

DUCK BOARDS

GP

PATH CONTOURS ROUND WEST SHOULDER OF FOEL FENLLI, NOT OVER SUMMIT

LOVELY AIRY PATH

10   11a   12

BWLCH PENBARRA

60 – 70 MINS TO CLWYD GATE ⟶
(MAP 12)

(Opposite) Top: Jubilee Tower (see p79). **Bottom:** View south from Jubilee Tower.

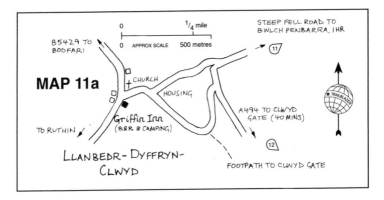

MAP 11a

STEEP FELL ROAD TO
BWLCH PENBARRA, 1HR

B5429 TO
BODFARI

0   APPROX SCALE   500 metres

+ CHURCH

HOUSING

Griffin Inn
(B&B & CAMPING)

TO RUTHIN

A494 TO CLWYD
GATE (40 MINS)

LLANBEDR - DYFFRYN -
CLWYD

FOOTPATH TO CLWYD GATE

TRAILBLAZER

CLWYD GATE TO LLANDEGLA   MAPS 12–15

The next **6 miles (10km, 2³/₄–3¹/₄hrs)** continue through the Clwydian Hills, contouring round the broad shoulders of **Moel Gyw** and **Moel Llanfair** to the col between **Moel Llanfair** and **Moel y Plas** where the road comes up from the peaceful village of **Llanarmon-yn-Ial**. You leave the hills behind and follow field paths with some road walking until, at the **River Alun**, you find yourself among water meadows on the approach to the unassuming village of **Llandegla**, arriving beside the church dedicated to St Tegla after whom the village is named.

❑ Hill-forts
As many as 30 hill-forts have been identified in the county of Clwyd and some of the best are on your path. These fortified settlements date from the 600–800 years before the Roman invasion of Britain (AD43), the Iron Age. They were inhabited by tribes who lived by hunting and farming but who tried to guarantee their security by fortifying hilltops for their protection. There was usually a double rampart and ditch; the inner rampart would carry a timber stockade from which attackers could be repulsed. The coming of the Romans meant that the superior discipline and power of the fighting troops was able to overwhelm them and they were abandoned.

Perhaps viewed to best effect from the air, the walker can usually make out the ring of former ramparts but for the most part it is in the imagination that you can best appreciate them.

(Opposite) **Top**: Plas Newydd, Llangollen (see p90), former home of the 'Ladies of Llangollen'. (Photo © Bryn Thomas). **Bottom**: Crossing the screes below the Eglwyseg Crags (see p89).

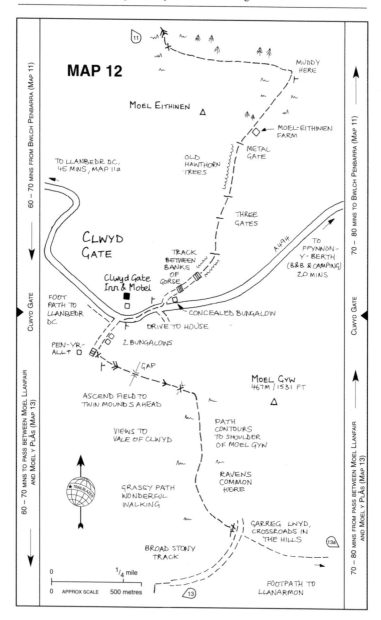

MAP 12

MUDDY HERE

MOEL EITHINEN △

MOEL-EITHINEN FARM

METAL GATE

OLD HAWTHORN TREES

TO LLANBEDR DC, 45 MINS, MAP 11a

THREE GATES

CLWYD GATE

A494

TO FFYNNON-Y-BERTH (B&B & CAMPING) 20 MINS

TRACK BETWEEN BANKS OF GORSE

Clwyd Gate Inn & Motel

FOOT PATH TO LLANBEDR DC

CONCEALED BUNGALOW

DRIVE TO HOUSE

PEN-YR-ALLT □

2 BUNGALOWS

GAP

MOEL GYW 467M / 1531 FT △

ASCEND FIELD TO TWIN MOUNDS AHEAD

PATH CONTOURS TO SHOULDER OF MOEL GYW

VIEWS TO VALE OF CLWYD

★ TRAILBLAZER

RAVENS COMMON HERE

GRASSY PATH WONDERFUL WALKING

GARREG LWYD, CROSSROADS IN THE HILLS

13a

BROAD STONY TRACK

0   1/4 mile

0   APPROX SCALE   500 metres

13

FOOTPATH TO LLANARMON

60 – 70 MINS FROM BWLCH PENBARRA (MAP 11)

CLWYD GATE

60 – 70 MINS TO PASS BETWEEN MOEL LLANFAIR AND MOEL Y PLÂS (MAP 13)

70 – 80 MINS TO BWLCH PENBARRA (MAP 11)

CLWYD GATE

70 – 80 MINS FROM PASS BETWEEN MOEL LLANFAIR AND MOEL Y PLÂS (MAP 13)

11

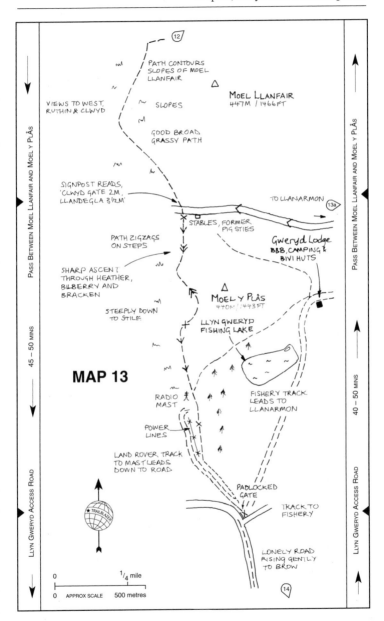

MAP 13

12

PATH CONTOURS
SLOPES OF MOEL
LLANFAIR

△ MOEL LLANFAIR
447M / 1466FT

VIEWS TO WEST,
RUTHIN & CLWYD

~ SLOPES

GOOD BROAD
GRASSY PATH

SIGNPOST READS,
'CLWYD GATE 2M,
LLANDEGLA 3½M'

TO LLANARMON

13a

STABLES, FORMER
PIG STIES

PATH ZIGZAGS
ON STEPS

Gweryd Lodge
B&B, CAMPING &
BIVI HUTS

SHARP ASCENT
THROUGH HEATHER,
BILBERRY AND
BRACKEN

△ MOEL Y PLÀS
440M / 1443FT

STEEPLY DOWN
TO STILE

LLYN GWERYD
FISHING LAKE

RADIO
MAST

FISHERY TRACK
LEADS TO
LLANARMON

POWER
LINES

LAND ROVER TRACK
TO MAST LEADS
DOWN TO ROAD

PADLOCKED
GATE

TRACK TO
FISHERY

LONELY ROAD
RISING GENTLY
TO BROW

14

★ TRAILBLAZER

0   ¼ mile

0   APPROX SCALE   500 metres

PASS BETWEEN MOEL LLANFAIR AND MOEL Y PLÀS

45 – 50 MINS

LLYN GWERYD ACCESS ROAD

PASS BETWEEN MOEL LLANFAIR AND MOEL Y PLÀS

40 – 50 MINS

LLYN GWERYD ACCESS ROAD

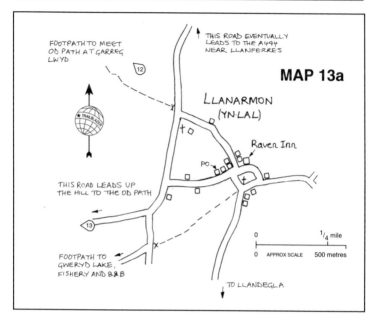

LLANARMON-YN-LAL   MAP 13a

The village is 20 minutes east of the path and has a **post office** and a pub, the ***Raven Inn*** (☎ 01824-780787), which does excellent bar meals. The Ruthin–Mold **bus** calls at two-hourly intervals on weekdays (see public transport map, p38).

If you need accommodation try ***Gweryd Lodge*** (☎ 01824-780230, 1T/1D), or use their bivvy huts for **bunkhouse**-style accommodation at £5 single or £3.75 double occupancy. It's also possible to **camp** for £2 each. This establishment caters mainly for fishermen using the lake but is close to the path and near enough to the village to make a walk to the pub for a meal a reasonable proposition.

LLANDEGLA   MAPS 14-15

The highest settlement you visit along the way, Llandegla has a **post office** and general **store** and that's about it. The ***Crown Inn*** (☎ 01978-790228) on the main road, the A525, may be your only prospect for a meal unless ***The Willows Restaurant*** (☎ 01978-790237), a more formal establishment, appeals to you. B&B accommodation is conveniently available right on the path at ***Hand House*** (☎ 01978-790570, 1S/2T/2D), a former inn and a very nice, clean and hospitable establishment where you will pay £23 for a night's rest and be welcomed with a tray of tea. Further afield is ***Llainwen Uchaf*** (☎ 01978-790253, 1S/1D/1F) where Mrs Parry charges £20 for the room, £10 for an evening meal; Welsh hospitality at its best! It's two miles (3km) of road walking to the pub so you'd better pick up a four-pack at the shop if the idea of an evening without a drink cannot be entertained. ***Raven Farm*** (☎ 01978-790224, 2S/2T/2D), situated conveniently close to the path, is a reasonably-priced B&B. There's a **campsite** behind the Memorial Hall in the village which costs an economical £2.

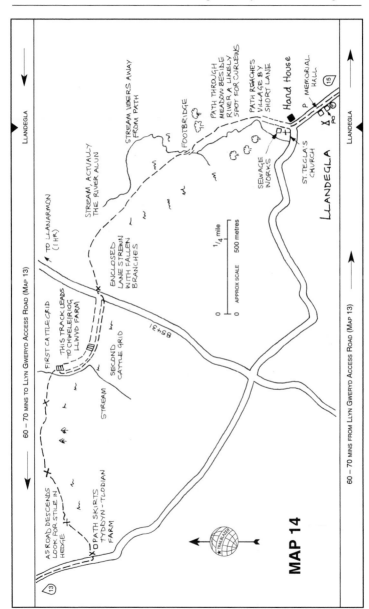

60 – 70 MINS TO LLYN GWERYD ACCESS ROAD (MAP 13)

LLANDEGLA

TO LLANARMON (1 HR)

STREAM VEERS AWAY FROM PATH

STREAM, ACTUALLY THE RIVER ALUN

FOOTBRIDGE

PATH THROUGH MEADOW BESIDE RIVER A LIKELY SPOT FOR CURLEWS

PATH REACHES VILLAGE BY SHORT LANE

Hand House

P MEMORIAL HALL

15

PO

ST. TEGLA'S CHURCH

SEWAGE WORKS

LLANDEGLA

FIRST CATTLEGRID

THIS TRACK LEADS TO CHWELEIRIOG LLWYD FARM

ENCLOSED LANE STREAM WITH FALLEN BRANCHES

SECOND CATTLE GRID

STREAM

B5431

¼ mile

0

0   500 metres

APPROX SCALE

13

AS ROAD DESCENDS LOOK FOR STILE IN HEDGE

PATH SKIRTS TYDDYN-TLODIAN FARM

MAP 14

TRAILBLAZER

60 – 70 MINS FROM LLYN GWERYD ACCESS ROAD (MAP 13)

LLANDEGLA

❏ **Did the Romans build Offa's Dyke?**

According to *The Keys to Avalon* (2001) by Steve Blake and Scott Lloyd, there is compelling evidence to support this theory. Ancient texts refer to a wall running north to south for 130 miles, constructed of an earth bank surmounted by turves with a timber palisade running along the top. It is claimed that this wall was built by the Emperor Septimius Serverus around AD200, 600 years before Offa, King of Mercia.

Excavations of the nearby Wat's Dyke, known to be 200 years younger than Offa's and supposedly built to reinforce weaker areas, revealed a Roman hearth containing pottery sherds which carbon dating placed somewhere between 411 and AD561. This reasoning indicates that Offa's Dyke was contemporary with Serverus who built it to put down an uprising of certain tribes in the area.

The contrary argument says that there is no supporting evidence on the ground such as roads, remains or other finds that normally go with Roman occupation. Unless of course the Dyke was built in a great hurry to regain control of an overrun area, in which case there would not have been the time to build the complex infrastructure that went along with Hadrian's Wall for example.

Ultimately there is no proof that conclusively dates the Dyke to Roman times. The key questions, such as why and how the Dyke was built, remain unanswered. Does it matter? For the walker, ruminating as he or she plods beside, or in places along, the very mound itself, it fuels speculation and the chance to come up with theories which can never be proved conclusively. This did not discourage von Daniken from proposing that spacemen built Stonehenge, which nobody can disprove, unlikely as it seems. So let's leave the Dyke to the credit of King Offa.

LLANDEGLA TO LLANGOLLEN   MAPS 15–18

This **8-mile (13km)** section takes about **3³/₄ to 4¹/₄ hours**. Leaving Llandegla, you are soon in the dense conifer forest managed by the Shotton Paper Company. According to an interpretive panel we need trees like these for newspapers. The path leads through the trees and across open moorland to the unfenced road between **Minera** and **World's End**, in other words between nowhere and nowhere. World's End may not be the end of the world but it is certainly no comfort station. Once a popular spot for picnics, it is now suffering from the effects of forestry clearance and the path becomes indistinct. Once past this confusing area you begin the fine traverse of the screes below **Eglwyseg Crags**, a haunt for hawks and ravens.

Ahead the forbidding outline of **Castell Dinas Bran** (see box, p94) looms into view and you know that you will soon be within reach of the comfortable borough of **Llangollen** nestling in the valley; worth the short detour as it's a haven for travellers with its many services and attractions.

LLANGOLLEN   MAP 17b

The Offa's Dyke Path does not actually pass through Llangollen (pronounced 'clangoth-len') but if there is time in your schedule it is well worth the mile detour. It is a

charming small town with a unique character which attracts an element of the alternative society who have found a haven here. In summer it also attracts the holiday hordes

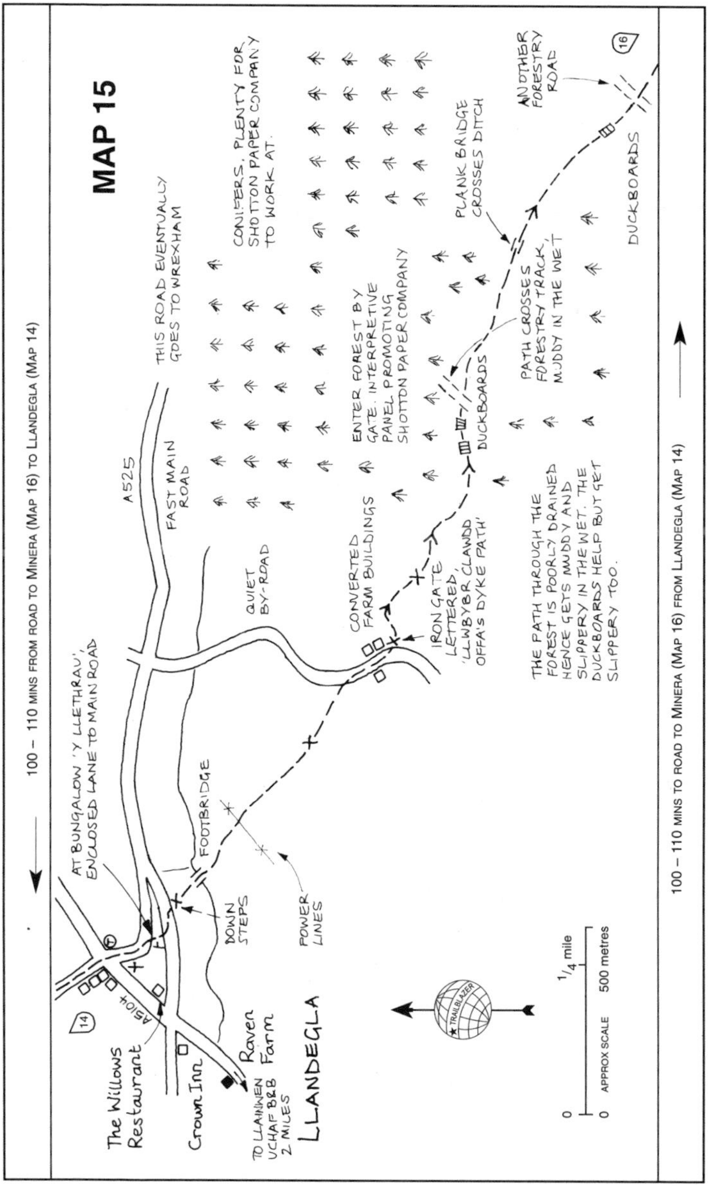

MAP 15

100 – 110 MINS FROM ROAD TO MINERA (MAP 16) TO LLANDEGLA (MAP 14)

100 – 110 MINS TO ROAD TO MINERA (MAP 16) FROM LLANDEGLA (MAP 14)

THIS ROAD EVENTUALLY GOES TO WREXHAM

CONIFERS, PLENTY FOR SHOTTON PAPER COMPANY TO WORK AT.

ANOTHER FORESTRY ROAD

PLANK BRIDGE CROSSES DITCH

DUCKBOARDS

PATH CROSSES FORESTRY TRACK, MUDDY IN THE WET

ENTER FOREST BY GATE. INTERPRETIVE PANEL PROMOTING SHOTTON PAPER COMPANY

DUCKBOARDS

THE PATH THROUGH THE FOREST IS POORLY DRAINED HENCE GETS MUDDY AND SLIPPERY IN THE WET. THE DUCKBOARDS HELP BUT GET SLIPPERY TOO.

A525 FAST MAIN ROAD

QUIET BY-ROAD

CONVERTED FARM BUILDINGS

IRON GATE LETTERED 'LLWYBYR CLAWDD OFFA'S DYKE PATH'

DUCKBOARDS

AT BUNGALOW 'Y LLETHRAU', ENCLOSED LANE TO MAIN ROAD

FOOTBRIDGE

DOWN STEPS

POWER LINES

The Willows Restaurant

Crown Inn

Raven Farm

TO LLANVIHEN UCHAF B&B 2 MILES

LLANDEGLA

¼ mile

APPROX SCALE

500 metres

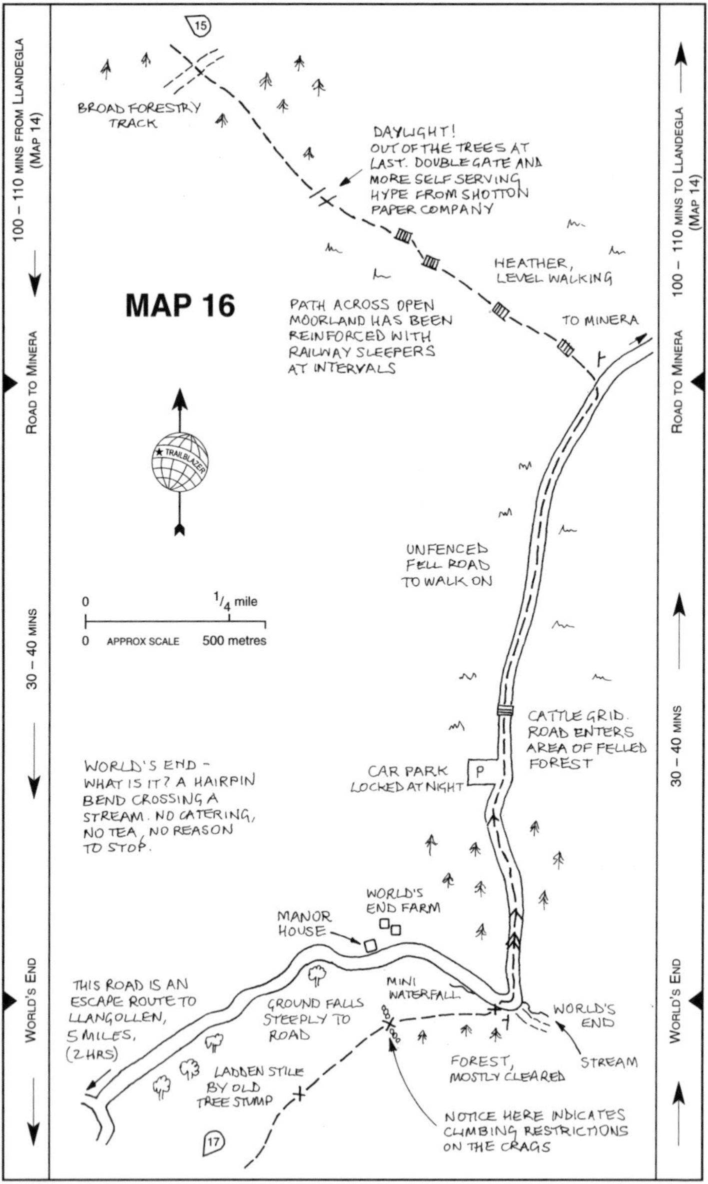

15

BROAD FORESTRY TRACK

DAYLIGHT!
OUT OF THE TREES AT LAST. DOUBLE GATE AND MORE SELF SERVING HYPE FROM SHOTTON PAPER COMPANY

HEATHER, LEVEL WALKING

TO MINERA

MAP 16

PATH ACROSS OPEN MOORLAND HAS BEEN REINFORCED WITH RAILWAY SLEEPERS AT INTERVALS

★ TRAILBLAZER

0   1/4 mile
0   APPROX SCALE   500 metres

UNFENCED FELL ROAD TO WALK ON

WORLD'S END – WHAT IS IT? A HAIRPIN BEND CROSSING A STREAM. NO CATERING, NO TEA, NO REASON TO STOP.

CATTLE GRID. ROAD ENTERS AREA OF FELLED FOREST

CAR PARK LOCKED AT NIGHT   P

WORLD'S END FARM

MANOR HOUSE

THIS ROAD IS AN ESCAPE ROUTE TO LLANGOLLEN, 5 MILES, (2 HRS)

GROUND FALLS STEEPLY TO ROAD

MINI WATERFALL

WORLD'S END

STREAM

LADDER STILE BY OLD TREE STUMP

FOREST, MOSTLY CLEARED

NOTICE HERE INDICATES CLIMBING RESTRICTIONS ON THE CRAGS

17

Left margin (top to bottom): 100 – 110 MINS FROM LLANDEGLA (MAP 14) · ROAD TO MINERA · 30 – 40 MINS · WORLD'S END

Right margin (top to bottom): 100 – 110 MINS TO LLANDEGLA (MAP 14) · ROAD TO MINERA · 30 – 40 MINS · WORLD'S END

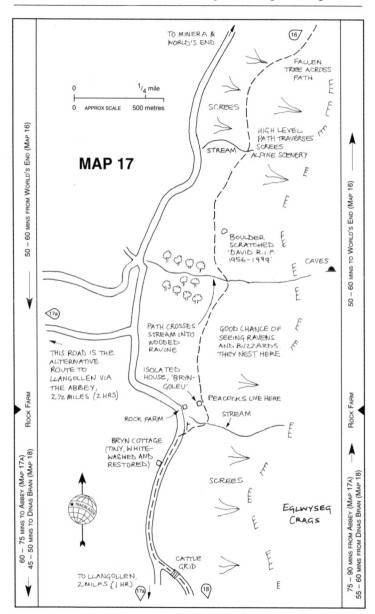

TO MINERA &
WORLD'S END

16

FALLEN TREE ACROSS PATH

SCREES

HIGH LEVEL PATH TRAVERSES SCREES
ALPINE SCENERY

STREAM

MAP 17

0   ¼ mile
0   APPROX SCALE   500 metres

BOULDER SCRATCHED 'DAVID R.I.P. 1956-1999'

CAVES

50 – 60 MINS FROM WORLD'S END (MAP 16)

50 – 60 MINS TO WORLD'S END (MAP 16)

17a

THIS ROAD IS THE ALTERNATIVE ROUTE TO LLANGOLLEN VIA THE ABBEY, 2½ MILES (2 HRS)

PATH CROSSES STREAM INTO WOODED RAVINE

GOOD CHANCE OF SEEING RAVENS AND BUZZARDS THEY NEST HERE

ISOLATED HOUSE, 'BRYN-GOLEU'

PEACOCKS LIVE HERE

ROCK FARM

STREAM

BRYN COTTAGE (TINY, WHITE-WASHED AND RESTORED)

SCREES

EGLWYSEG CRAGS

ROCK FARM

ROCK FARM

TRAILBLAZER

60 – 75 MINS TO ABBEY (MAP 17A)
45 – 50 MINS TO DINAS BRAN (MAP 18)

75 – 90 MINS FROM ABBEY (MAP 17A)
55 – 60 MINS FROM DINAS BRAN (MAP 18)

CATTLE GRID

TO LLANGOLLEN, 2 MILES (1 HR)

17a

18

❏ **Alternative route to Llangollen via Valle Crucis Abbey   Map 17a**

For those with the time or a thirst for ruins, there is another way down to Llangollen that takes in both the Abbey of Valle Crucis and Eliseg's Pillar (see box, p94), whilst also offering a choice of two pubs, one of which does accommodation.

After the traverse of the screes below the Eglwyseg Crags, the path reaches the lane close to Rock Farm. From here it takes over an hour to reach the so-called Dinas Bran turn where the lane takes you down to Llangollen. Instead, turn right past Rock Farm and follow the quiet by-roads to meet the busy A542 where in half a mile you will come to the *Britannia Inn*, good for bar food but closed Monday and Tuesday. A better option is to stay on the main road and walk to *Abbey Grange Hotel* (☎ 01978-860753, 4S/2T/3D/1F) where B&B is £23-25 per person. The ancient Eliseg's Pillar is in a field by the main road and the ruins of Valle Crucis Abbey stand serene, indifferent to the ugly static caravans nearby.

A path follows the river through farmland to soon join the canal. The canal towpath takes you directly to Llangollen Wharf past the futuristic structure put up for the International Musical Eisteddfod.

with plenty of things for them to do from a sedate steam railway and canal-barge trip to adrenaline-pumping whitewater rafting down the River Dee. If these appeal a rest day might be in order especially as there are also a number of interesting historical monuments within easy reach.

Plas Newydd, home of the 'Ladies of Langollen' (see p34) from 1780 to 1829 and decorated in an eclectic mix of Tudor and Gothic styles, is open daily from Easter to October (£3, 10-5pm, last entry 4.15pm). It's well worth visiting.

If you are planning to walk in July be warned that for seven days during the first or second week in this month Llangollen becomes the venue for the massive **International Musical Eisteddfod**, which fills the Royal Pavilion with musicians, singers and dancers from all over the world. Every room in town gets booked up at this time so book well in advance or try to miss this hectic week altogether. For festival dates contact the tourist information centre.

Transport

There are regular **buses** throughout the week to Wrexham, Chirk and Oswestry. The nearest **railway stations** are Chirk and Ruabon (see public transport map, p38). For a **taxi** contact Premier Cars (☎ 01978-861999) near the Dee Bridge.

Services

The **tourist information centre** (☎ 01978-860828), on Castle St, is open 9.30am to 5pm everyday except Wednesday. There are three **banks** in town, Barclays and NatWest on Castle St and HSBC on Bridge St, all with cash machines. Tuesday is **market day**, worth catching if you are in town as the centre comes alive.

The best place to stock up with food is at the Londis **supermarket** (daily, 7am–10pm) on Abbey Rd which has conveniently long opening hours.

There are two good **bakers** in the centre of town for buying lunch for the trail, a **laundrette** on Regent St where you will also find Regent **Pharmacy** (☎ 01978-860657) and opposite, the **health centre** (☎ 01978-860657). The nearest **accident and emergency hospital** is in Wrexham (☎ 01978-291100).

Where to stay

Due to its prominence as a tourist destination there are many excellent B&Bs in Llangollen. As long as you avoid the weekdays in July around the time of the Eisteddfod you shouldn't have any problems finding somewhere to stay.

Those **camping** will find a quiet site on a working farm just a quarter of a mile off the route at *Wern Isaf* (☎ 01978-

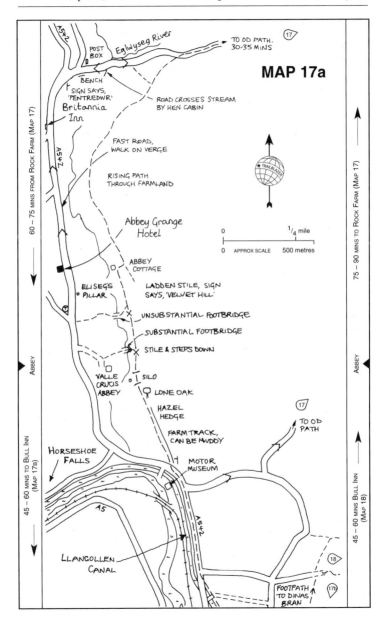

MAP 17a

TO OD PATH.
30-35 MINS

17

POST BOX

Eglwyseg River

BENCH
SIGN SAYS,
'PENTREDWR'
Britannia Inn

ROAD CROSSES STREAM
BY HEN CABIN

FAST ROAD,
WALK ON VERGE

RISING PATH
THROUGH FARMLAND

Abbey Grange Hotel

ABBEY COTTAGE

ELISEGS PILLAR

LADDEN STILE, SIGN
SAYS, 'VELVET HILL'

UNSUBSTANTIAL FOOTBRIDGE

SUBSTANTIAL FOOTBRIDGE

STILE & STEPS DOWN

VALLE CRUCIS ABBEY

SILO

LONE OAK

HAZEL HEDGE

FARM TRACK,
CAN BE MUDDY

HORSESHOE FALLS

MOTOR MUSEUM

TO OD PATH

17

A5

A542

LLANGOLLEN CANAL

18

FOOTPATH TO DINAS BRAN

17b

A542

60 – 75 MINS FROM ROCK FARM (MAP 17)

45 – 60 MINS TO BULL INN (MAP 17b)

ABBEY

75 – 90 MINS TO ROCK FARM (MAP 17)

ABBEY

45 – 60 MINS BULL INN (MAP 18)

0   ¼ mile
0   APPROX SCALE   500 metres

TRAILBLAZER

860632, Wern Rd). The charge per person is a very reasonable £2.50.

There is a top of the range and very busy *youth hostel* (☎ 01978-860632, 134 beds) 20 minutes' walk east of the town centre, which does B&B from £11.75 and has a fully licensed restaurant with evening meals for £5. It is, however, located three miles (5km, 1hr each way) from the trail so you may be better off choosing one of the lower-priced B&Bs in town, which are nearer the path. To reach the hostel from the town centre follow the A5 east towards Shrewsbury, after the fire station bear right up Birch Hill and then bear right at the next 'Y' junction; the hostel is half a mile further on.

For B&B, *4 Bishops Walk* (☎ 01978-860529, 2T) is one of the cheapest places in town at £18 per person, but it's open from March to November only. Only slightly more expensive is *Walton House* (☎ 01978-860825, 1 Queen St, 2D/2F) where you are assured a warm welcome from Mrs James. She charges £16.50 per person or £18.50 for en suite. Also good value if you're not on your own is *River Lodge* (☎ 01978-869019, Mill St) which has 16 en-suite rooms sleeping one, two or three people for £35-39 per room. It is popular with canoeists so can be rather rowdy and festooned with wetsuits.

Bridge St is close to the centre of town, handy for an evening meal and has a wide range of accommodation. One of the gems of Llangollen is the intimate and friendly *Cornerstones* (☎ 01978-861569, 15 Bridge St, 2S/2D) where B&B costs £25 per person en suite (£35 in a single room). They can provide an evening meal for £10 and smokers and small dogs are welcome; it's nice to see special needs catered for in some places!

Two established guesthouses, both offering a fair standard of accommodation, are *Cambrian Guest House* (☎ 01978-861418, 1S/2T/2D/1F, Berwyn St) which charges £20 for B&B and £9 for an evening meal, and *Hillcrest Guest House* (☎ 01978-860208, 2T/3D/2F, Hill St) charging £25 for B&B and £12.50 for an evening meal. Both are conveniently central and are clean and quite adequate for a short stay.

Poplar House (☎ 01978-861772, 6T, 39–41 Regent St) is another likely option if the town is busy. They charge an economical £17.50 for B&B and a cheap £7.50 for an evening meal. They welcome dogs too.

Where to eat
Nobody visiting Llangollen should miss *Maxine's Café and Books* (☎ 01978-860334) on Castle St where you can get an excellent bacon sandwich or a full fry-up. The bookshop is awesome, stocking over 75,000 second-hand volumes. They are open seven days a week throughout the year with the sole exception of Christmas Day when Maxine has a lie-in.

Another excellent place to try for light snacks or a tasty meal is *Robbins Nest* , an intimate, welcoming restaurant in Market St opposite the big car park.

The *Bull Inn* on Castle St is a good local pub. This 18th-century coaching inn has a good choice of beers and bar meals, which include the speciality of the house, the Big Ben burger for £3.25.

If you are after a gastronomic treat head for the *Corn Mill* (☎ 01978-869555) down by the river. The chef is clearly on a nostalgia trip to his schooldays with dishes such as corned beef and black pudding hash cake with poached egg and brown sauce (£4.95) and chicken and calf's liver bubble and squeak with onion gravy (£9.95), although the full menu offers choices for all tastes.

Other places worth a try include *Simla Tandoori* on Victoria Sq for the usual Indian fare and the self explanatory *Gallery Pizza, Pasta and Steakhouse* (☎ 01978-860076) at 15 Chapel St. There are also numerous places on Bridge St, which offer value for money without exciting the craving for original cooking.

For afternoon teas and lunches, the *Cottage Tea Rooms* (☎ 01978-860076) is a busy place with helpful staff, though space is rather limited. Rucksacks outside please! Their Welsh Farmhouse tea with bara brith costs £3.60.

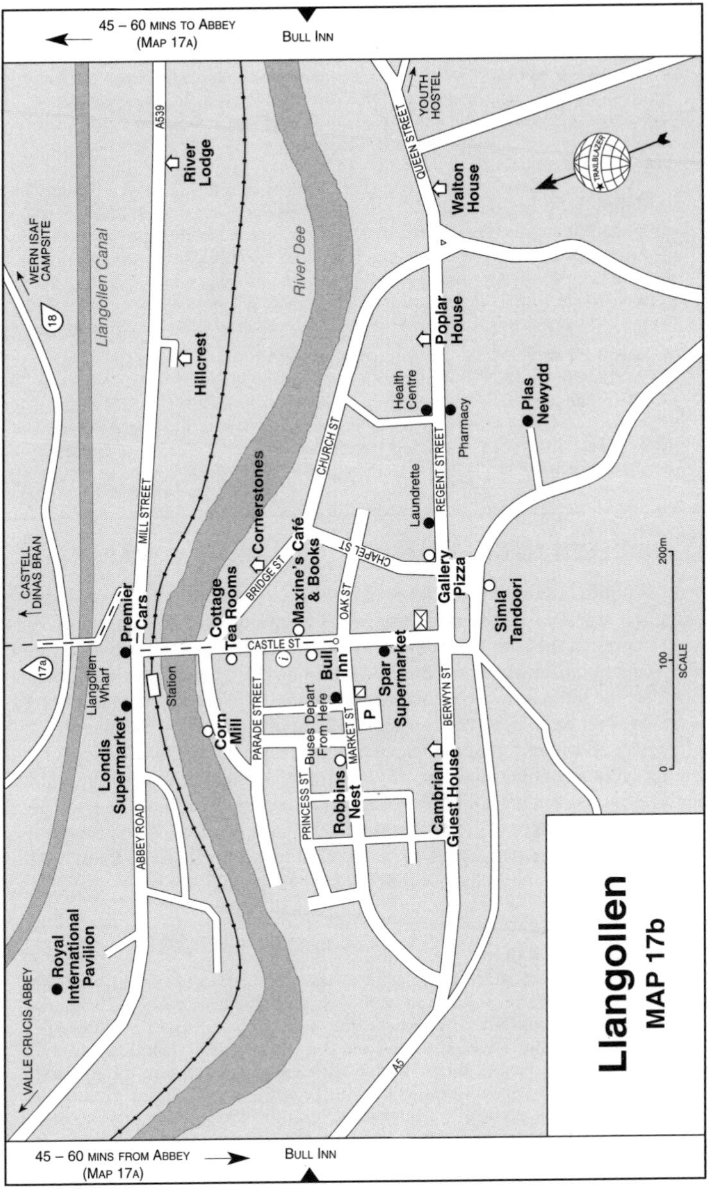

45 – 60 MINS TO ABBEY (MAP 17A)
BULL INN
45 – 60 MINS FROM ABBEY (MAP 17A)
BULL INN
Llangollen
MAP 17b
WERN ISAF CAMPSITE
CASTELL DINAS BRAN
VALLE CRUCIS ABBEY
YOUTH HOSTEL
18
17a
Llangollen Canal
River Dee
A539
A5
MILL STREET
ABBEY ROAD
QUEEN STREET
CHURCH ST
BRIDGE ST
CHAPEL ST
OAK ST
CASTLE ST
PARADE STREET
MARKET ST
PRINCESS ST
REGENT STREET
BERWYN ST
River Lodge
Hillcrest
Walton House
Poplar House
Health Centre
Pharmacy
Plas Newydd
Laundrette
Cornerstones
Maxine's Café & Books
Cottage Tea Rooms
Gallery Pizza
Simla Tandoori
Premier Cars
Llangollen Wharf
Londis Supermarket
Station
Corn Mill
Bull Inn
Buses Depart From Here
Robbins Nest
Spar Supermarket
P
Cambrian Guest House
Royal International Pavilion
TRAILBLAZER
0
100
200m
SCALE

❑ **Historic monuments around Llangollen**

● **Valle Crucis Abbey** (☎ 01978-860326, admission £2 Apr–Sept, free Oct–Mar) was founded by Cistercian monks in the 12th century. Now a ruin but with some of its original beauty surviving, it is exquisitely situated beside the River Eglwyseg, a tributary of the Dee, in a spot that would have been ideal for the solitude and peace that were an essential part of the Cistercian lifestyle.

When the white-robed monks first came to this valley to build their monastery they chose it for its remote and wild location where prayer and work could go on with minimal distractions and intrusions from the outside world. The ruins today give you a good idea, with a little imagination, of the once-glorious abbey building with its rose window and carved doorway. The fishpond remains, as does the Chapter House with its rib-vaulted roof, but perhaps the most striking impression will be left by its dramatic position below the wooded crags: a truly magical place.

● **Eliseg's Pillar** This is the surviving stump of a much higher pillar set up in memory of King Eliseg who drove out the Anglo-Saxon invaders in about AD750. It was originally surmounted by a carved stone cross from which Valle Crucis, the Valley of the Cross, takes its name. Eliseg's Pillar stands in a field to the right of the A542 road between Llangollen and Ruthin (the Horseshoe Pass). Perhaps not meriting a detour on its own, it can be taken in when you're visiting the abbey ruins.

LLANGOLLEN TO CASTLE MILL
MAPS 17a–22

This **8¹/₂-mile (14km)** section takes about **3³/₄ to 4¹/₂ hours**. The road walking along the so-called Panorama Route keeps company with the limestone crags and screes until the path leaves the road and enters **Trevor Hall Wood**, a damp, dark murky domain where you imagine there must be dragons or at least hobbits.

You can hire narrowboats at **Trevor** marina or join a day trip. It takes 1¹/₂ hours to walk back along the towpath to Llangollen, a lovely circular trail full of variety. For those pushing on, the next challenge is the crossing of the **Pontcysyllte Aqueduct** (see box, p97), one of the highlights of the entire walk. It involves no risk but it's not for anyone who suffers from vertigo. The alternative is to walk down the road to the old bridge over the River Dee. If you choose this option, you join the path again by walking through the village of **Froncysyllte** and taking a track across the canal to the towpath by the cantilever bridge.

❑ **Castell Dinas Bran**

The conical hill on which the ruins of Dinas Bran Castle stand seems an ideal stronghold but is perhaps too exposed to be of much use defensively. An interpretive board helps to obscure its historical origins in the mists of the Celtic twilight and it will appeal to fans of Dungeons and Dragons more than students of history. One thing it does have is atmosphere, its brooding presence striking a chill especially on misty evenings when nothing can be heard but the call of the ravens. Castell Dinas Bran is one of the highlights of the walk but like many ruins it's better looked at from a distance rather than examined at close quarters.

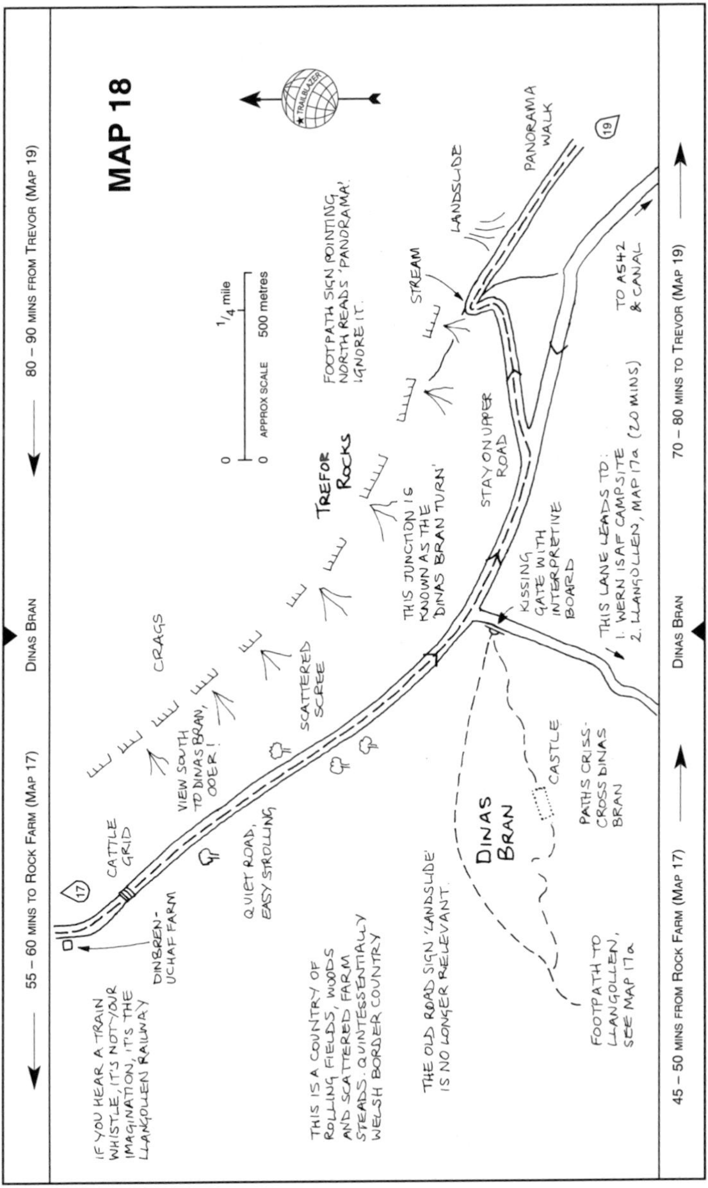
MAP 18
80 – 90 MINS FROM TREVOR (MAP 19)
DINAS BRAN
55 – 60 MINS TO ROCK FARM (MAP 17)
70 – 80 MINS TO TREVOR (MAP 19)
DINAS BRAN
45 – 50 MINS FROM ROCK FARM (MAP 17)
TRAILBLAZER
0 1/4 mile
0 APPROX SCALE 500 metres
19
17
PANORAMA WALK
LANDSLIDE
STREAM
FOOTPATH SIGN POINTING NORTH READS 'PANORAMA'. IGNORE IT.
TO A542 & CANAL
TREFOR ROCKS
STAY ON UPPER ROAD
THIS JUNCTION IS KNOWN AS THE 'DINAS BRAN TURN'
KISSING GATE WITH INTERPRETIVE BOARD
THIS LANE LEADS TO: 1. WERN ISAF CAMPSITE 2. LLANGOLLEN, MAP 17a (20 MINS)
CRAGS
SCATTERED SCREE
VIEW SOUTH TO DINAS BRAN, OOER!
CASTLE
PATHS CRISS-CROSS DINAS BRAN
DINAS BRAN
CATTLE GRID
QUIET ROAD, EASY STROLLING
DINBREN-UCHAF FARM
IF YOU HEAR A TRAIN WHISTLE, IT'S NOT YOUR IMAGINATION, IT'S THE LLANGOLLEN RAILWAY
THIS IS A COUNTRY OF ROLLING FIELDS, WOODS AND SCATTERED FARM STEADS. QUINTESSENTIALLY WELSH BORDER COUNTRY
THE OLD ROAD SIGN 'LANDSLIDE' IS NO LONGER RELEVANT.
FOOTPATH TO LLANGOLLEN, SEE MAP 17a

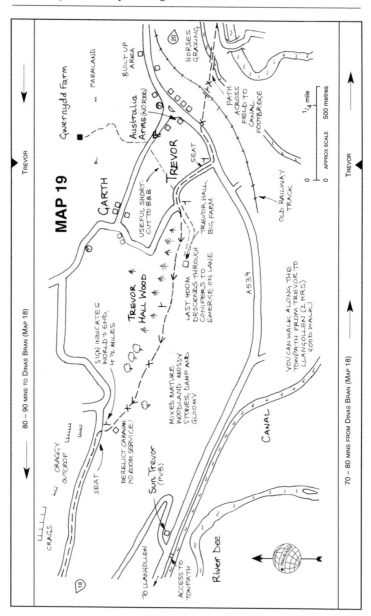

MAP 19

TREVOR

80 – 90 MINS TO DINAS BRAN (MAP 18)

70 – 80 MINS FROM DINAS BRAN (MAP 18)

Gwernydd Farm

FARMLAND

BUILT UP AREA

HORSES GRAZING

20

PATH ACROSS FIELD TO CANAL FOOTBRIDGE

1/4 mile

0   500 metres
0   APPROX SCALE

TREVOR

Australia Arms (NO FOOD)

TREVOR

SEAT

OLD RAILWAY TRACK

GARTH

USEFUL SHORT-CUT TO B&B

TREVOR HALL, BIG FARM

A539

TREVOR HALL WOOD

LAST 100M DESCENDS THROUGH CONIFERS TO EMERGE ON LANE

SIGN INDICATES WORLD'S END, 4 1/2 MILES

YOU CAN WALK ALONG THE TOWPATH FROM TREVOR TO LLANGOLLEN (2 HRS) GOOD WALK!

CRAGGY OUTCROP

SEAT

DERELICT CARAVAN NO ROOM SERVICE!

MIXED MATURE WOODLAND MOSSY STONES, DAMP AND GLOOMY

CRAGS

Sun Trevor (PUB)

CANAL

River Dee

TO LLANGOLLEN

ACCESS TO TOWPATH

18

TRAILBLAZER

TREVOR AND GARTH

There is an outstanding B&B at *Gwernydd Farm* (☎ 01978-820122, 2F), just up the hill from the Australia Arms in Trevor. It's a working farm run by Mr and Mrs Morris, lovely people, where B&B is £20 and is true value for money. Mr Morris will run you down to the Telford pub which is just that bit too far to walk, the track to the farm alone being half a mile long. *The Telford Inn* (☎ 01978-820469, 🖳 www.telfordinn. freeserve.co.uk, Map 20), has no accommodation but the bar meals are fine, catering for folk off the narrowboats which tie up at the marina in preparation for the crossing of the aqueduct. In summer they're open all day, in winter you won't be so lucky.

FRONCYSYLLTE   MAP 20

Situated astride the main A5 trunk road, the village is no place for walkers. As an overnight halt it lacks many basic amenities and your best bet would be to pass it by on the far side of the canal. On the positive side it has a rudimentary **post office** (early closing Fri), *Cliffs Café*, a transport café where you could satisfy your craving for a bacon sandwich, and *The Magna* (☎ 01692-774858) Indian restaurant.

Of the B&Bs, *Argoed Farm* (☎ 01691-772367, 2S/1T/1D/1F) is excellent at £22 for the night plus an evening meal from £10, or **camping** at £2.50, with meals and shower extra. Or you could try *Tegfan* (☎ 01691-778106, 1S/1D/1F) from £17 for B&B. They also have a **bunkhouse** sleeping 4–6 and costing £12 each.

One curiosity is a memorial fountain next to a works yard. The inscription reads: 'Erected by public subscription in memory of Private William Williams of the Royal Welsh Fusiliers, killed in action at the Battle of Frederikstad, October 25th 1900 and Private John Charles Jones, 2nd Battalion Grenadier Guards, died of enteric fever near Bloemfontein, May 10th 1900.' It's not often that you see a memorial to the Boer War.

Canal walking takes you to the so-called Irish Bridge, presumably built by Irish navvies, followed soon after by your first encounter with the earthwork which becomes evident, though not accessible, at *Plas Offa*, one of the best-known farms on the Dyke. As we went to press the farm had changed hands; it was not certain that they would continue to offer B&B and camping.

On the opposite side of the B5605 is *Cloud Hill* (☎ 01691-773359, 2T/1D), a superior quality B&B charging a reasonable £18 and an evening meal, by advance arrangement, at £10. **Camping** is £2.50.

❏ **Pontcysyllte Aqueduct** (Pronounced *Pont-see-sutley*)
Built to carry the canal over the River Dee, this is one of the wonders of the walk. Thomas Telford, among the finest engineers of the Industrial Revolution, came up with the idea of containing the water in an iron tank supported by the brick arches high above the river. Canal narrowboats are perfectly safe crossing but on the opposite side to the towpath there is nothing between them and a 126ft drop. Walkers take the towpath and there is only one rule, don't look down!

The first stone was laid on July 25, 1795, and the aqueduct took ten years to complete. It's 1007ft long with 18 piers built of local sandstone, expertly cut and dressed by Telford's masons who used a mortar consisting of lime, ox blood and water. The water is supplied from the River Dee at Berwyn, Telford having constructed the Horseshoe Falls to provide the necessary 12 million gallons needed daily. The cost of the operation was £47,000 and Telford took pride in knowing that only one life was lost during the construction.

If you decide that you want to cross the aqueduct by boat, Trevor Wharf Services (☎ 01978-821749) offers a 45-minute cruise.

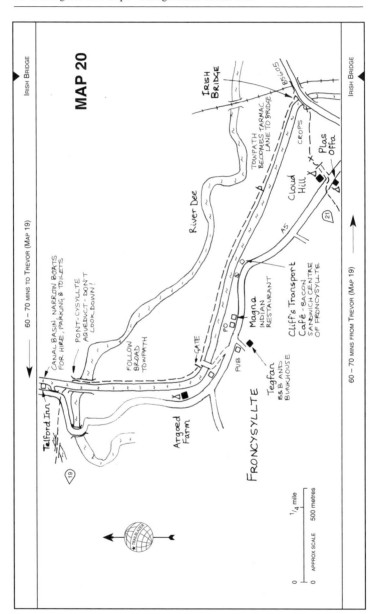

MAP 20

IRISH BRIDGE

◀ 60 – 70 MINS TO TREVOR (MAP 19)

River Dee

CANAL BASIN. NARROW BOATS
FOR HIRE, PARKING & TOILETS

PONT-CYSYLLTE
AQUEDUCT - DON'T
LOOK DOWN!

FOLLOW
BROAD
TOWPATH

TOWPATH
BECOMES TARMAC
LANE TO BRIDGE

IRISH
BRIDGE

B5605

CROPS

Cloud
Hill

Plas
Offa

A5

21

Telford Inn

19

GATE

PO

PUB

Magna
INDIAN
RESTAURANT

Cliff's Transport
Café - BACON
SANDWICH CENTRE
OF FRONCYSYLLTE

Tegfan
B&B AND
BUNKHOUSE

Arged
Farm

FRONCYSYLLTE

60 – 70 MINS FROM TREVOR (MAP 19) ▶

IRISH BRIDGE ◀

★ TRAILBLAZER

1/4 mile

0   APPROX SCALE

0   500 metres

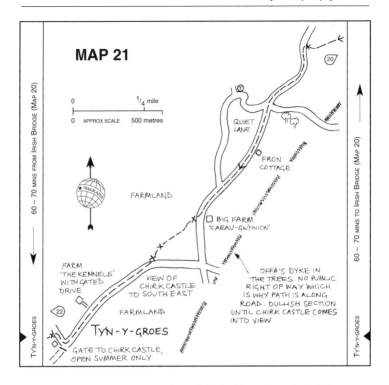

You keep to the canal towpath as far as **Irish Bridge**, where the B5605 crosses the canal, and just beyond meet the Dyke for the first time, skulking amongst a line of trees at Plas Offa Farm. You cannot join it yet, keeping pace with it along by-roads to Ty'n-y-groes where the 'garden gate' of **Chirk Castle** allows summertime access to the grounds and an alternative route to Castle Mill. A field path over farmland takes you up over a hill to descend through mixed woodland to the valley of the delightful River Ceiriog which you cross at **Castle Mill**.

❏ Chirk Castle
Chirk Castle (☎ 01691-777701, 🖥 www.nationaltrust.org.uk, Apr–Oct Wed–Sun 12–5pm, entry £6, National Trust members free) was built around 1300 by Roger Mortimer and has been lived in by the Myddleton family since 1595. Besides the interesting state rooms and the servants' hall where the tables were so arranged that the most important servants sat nearest to the fire, there is a bedroom in which King Charles I was said to have slept when visiting the castle in 1645. The gardens are delightful with their topiary hedges and views to the surrounding countryside.

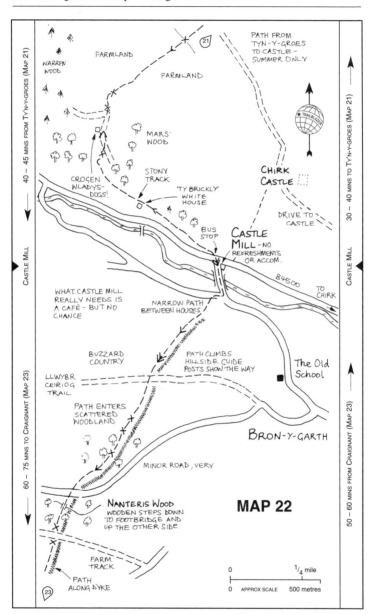

WARREN WOOD

FARMLAND

FARMLAND

PATH FROM TYN-Y-GROES TO CASTLE - SUMMER ONLY

MARS' WOOD

STONY TRACK

CROGEN WLADYS - DOGS!

'TY BRICKLY' WHITE HOUSE

★ TRAILBLAZER

CHIRK CASTLE

BUS STOP

DRIVE TO CASTLE

CASTLE MILL – NO REFRESHMENTS OR ACCOM.

B4500

TO CHIRK

WHAT CASTLE MILL REALLY NEEDS IS A CAFÉ - BUT NO CHANCE

NARROW PATH BETWEEN HOUSES

BUZZARD COUNTRY

PATH CLIMBS HILLSIDE. GUIDE POSTS SHOW THE WAY

The Old School

LLWYBR CEIRIOG TRAIL

PATH ENTERS SCATTERED WOODLAND

BRON-Y-GARTH

MINOR ROAD, VERY

NANTERIS WOOD WOODEN STEPS DOWN TO FOOTBRIDGE AND UP THE OTHER SIDE.

MAP 22

FARM TRACK

PATH ALONG DYKE

0   1/4 mile

0   APPROX SCALE   500 metres

40 – 45 MINS FROM TYN-Y-GROES (MAP 21)

CASTLE MILL

60 – 75 MINS TO CRAIGNANT (MAP 23)

30 – 40 MINS TO TYN-Y-GROES (MAP 21)

CASTLE MILL

50 – 60 MINS FROM CRAIGNANT (MAP 23)

CASTLE MILL & BRON-Y-GARTH
MAP 22

Castle Mill has no facilities but the small town of **Chirk**, 2 miles (3km) east from here along the B4500, has a train **station** on the Birmingham to Chester line (see p37). There's also a comfortable B&B some 20 minutes' walk south-east of the village at *The Old School* (☎ 01691-772546, 3T)

in Bron-y-garth, where they charge a bargain price of £17 per person, or you can **camp** for £2.50 plus 50p for the use of the shower. The only snag is the 2-mile (3km) walk to the nearest pub, although the owners will run you there for £1 and you can walk back, unsteadily.

CASTLE MILL TO RACECOURSE COMMON   MAPS 22–24

For most of the next **4¹/₂ miles (7km, 2–2¹/₂hrs)** you follow the line of **Offa's Dyke** for the first time, sometimes beside it, sometimes on the very top itself, as it climbs steeply away from Castle Mill. The path drops down to **Craignant**, a secretive little settlement in the depths of the countryside, and then climbs over the shoulder of Selattyn Hill. At the foot of **Baker's Hill** the Dyke leaves you and you are forced to follow the tarmac, a tedious plod, to the crossroads at **Racecourse Common**. Don't worry that you might arrive on race day; the course closed in Victorian times and the turf resounds to the thud of horses' hooves no more.

Where to stay and eat: Castle Mill to Racecourse Common

A few people offer B&B in **Craignant**, including Mr and Mrs Lees at *Thornhill* (☎ 01691-718990, 2D) charging a very reasonable £14 with evening meals from £6. **Campers** pay £3 per head and can take breakfast for an extra charge. *Craignant Lodge* (☎ 01691-718229, 1T/1D/1F), like Thornhill, is on the main path itself and has similar prices.

The nearest pub is *The Cross Keys* at **Selattyn** (☎ 01691-659708), just over a mile to the east along the B4579. Their place in

the *Good Beer Guide* is deserved. An hour and a half or so further on, just north of **Baker's Hill**, is the pony trekking centre *Carreg y Big* (☎ 01691-654754, 3T) where B&B costs £17.50 and an evening meal from £7.50. They allow **camping** for £2 each with use of the showers for an extra £1. Up the lane and visible from them is *The Quarry B&B* (☎ 01691-658674, 2S/1D, Apr–Oct) charging £18 for B&B and £4 for **camping** on their neat lawn using the shower in the house.

RACECOURSE COMMON TO LLANYMYNECH   MAPS 24–28

This **8¹/₂-mile (14km)** section takes about **4¹/₂ to 5¹/₄ hours**. The Old Racecourse may inspire you to set off like a thoroughbred and indeed the walking over the common and through Racecourse Wood to the **Morda Valley** is a fine start the day.

The Dyke is much in evidence with opportunities for walking on the very top of the earthwork in places until you come to the rather confusing area of **Trefonen**, **Treflach** and **Nant-Mawr**, all tidy residential areas offering little in the way of interest.

There is more than enough road walking before you get to the final hurdle, the ascent of **Llanymynech Hill**, but the stiff climb from the neat bungalows of Porth-y-waen onto the plateau-like summit is rewarded with a lovely sylvan

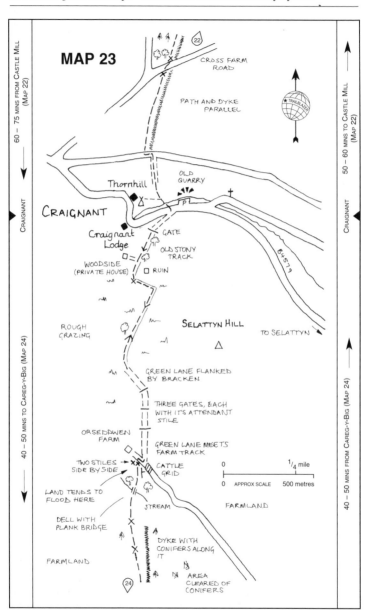

60 – 75 MINS FROM CASTLE MILL (MAP 22)

50 – 60 MINS TO CASTLE MILL (MAP 22)

CRAIGNANT

CRAIGNANT

40 – 50 MINS TO CAREG-Y-BIG (MAP 24)

40 – 50 MINS FROM CAREG-Y-BIG (MAP 24)

MAP 23

CROSS FARM ROAD

PATH AND DYKE PARALLEL

TRAILBLAZER

OLD QUARRY

Thornhill

CRAIGNANT

Craignant Lodge

GATE

OLD STONY TRACK

WOODSIDE (PRIVATE HOUSE)

RUIN

B4579

SELATTYN HILL

ROUGH GRAZING

TO SELATTYN

GREEN LANE FLANKED BY BRACKEN

THREE GATES, EACH WITH IT'S ATTENDANT STILE

ORSEDDWEN FARM

GREEN LANE MEETS FARM TRACK

TWO STILES SIDE BY SIDE

CATTLE GRID

0   ¼ mile

0   APPROX SCALE   500 metres

LAND TENDS TO FLOOD HERE

STREAM

FARMLAND

DELL WITH PLANK BRIDGE

FARMLAND

DYKE WITH CONIFERS ALONG IT

AREA CLEARED OF CONIFERS

22

24

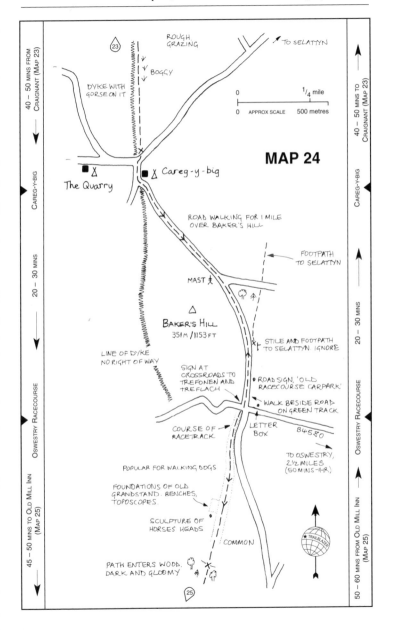

ROUGH GRAZING

TO SELATTYN

23

BOGGY

DYKE WITH GORSE ON IT

0   1/4 mile

0   APPROX SCALE   500 metres

MAP 24

The Quarry

Careg-y-big

ROAD WALKING FOR 1 MILE OVER BAKER'S HILL

FOOTPATH TO SELATTYN

MAST

BAKER'S HILL
351m / 1153 FT

LINE OF DYKE NO RIGHT OF WAY

STILE AND FOOTPATH TO SELATTYN. IGNORE

SIGN AT CROSSROADS TO TREFONEN AND TREFLACH

ROAD SIGN, 'OLD RACECOURSE CARPARK'

WALK BESIDE ROAD ON GREEN TRACK

COURSE OF RACETRACK

LETTER BOX

B4580

POPULAR FOR WALKING DOGS

TO OSWESTRY, 2½ MILES (50 MINS–1HR.)

FOUNDATIONS OF OLD GRANDSTAND. BENCHES, TOPOSCOPES.

SCULPTURE OF HORSES HEADS

COMMON

TRAILBLAZER

PATH ENTERS WOOD, DARK AND GLOOMY

25

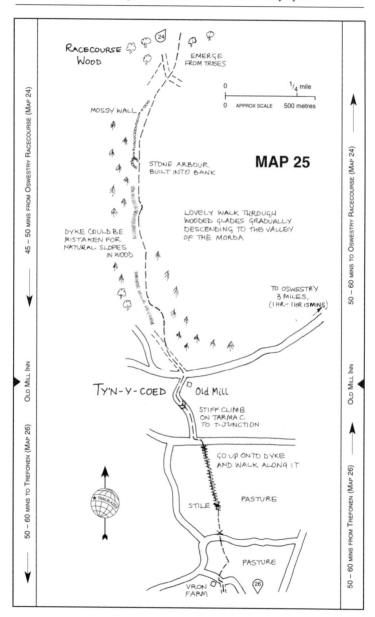

RACECOURSE WOOD
EMERGE FROM TREES

0   1/4 mile
0   APPROX SCALE   500 metres

MOSSY WALL

STONE ARBOUR BUILT INTO BANK

MAP 25

LOVELY WALK THROUGH WOODED GLADES GRADUALLY DESCENDING TO THE VALLEY OF THE MORDA

DYKE COULD BE MISTAKEN FOR NATURAL SLOPES IN WOOD

TO OSWESTRY 3 MILES, (1 HR – 1 HR 15 MINS)

TY'N-Y-COED   Old Mill

STIFF CLIMB ON TARMAC TO T-JUNCTION

GO UP ONTO DYKE AND WALK ALONG IT

STILE

PASTURE

★ TRAILBLAZER

PASTURE

VRON FARM

26

45 – 50 MINS FROM OSWESTRY RACECOURSE (MAP 24)

OLD MILL INN

50 – 60 MINS TO TREFONEN (MAP 26)

50 – 60 MINS TO OSWESTRY RACECOURSE (MAP 24)

OLD MILL INN

50 – 60 MINS FROM TREFONEN (MAP 26)

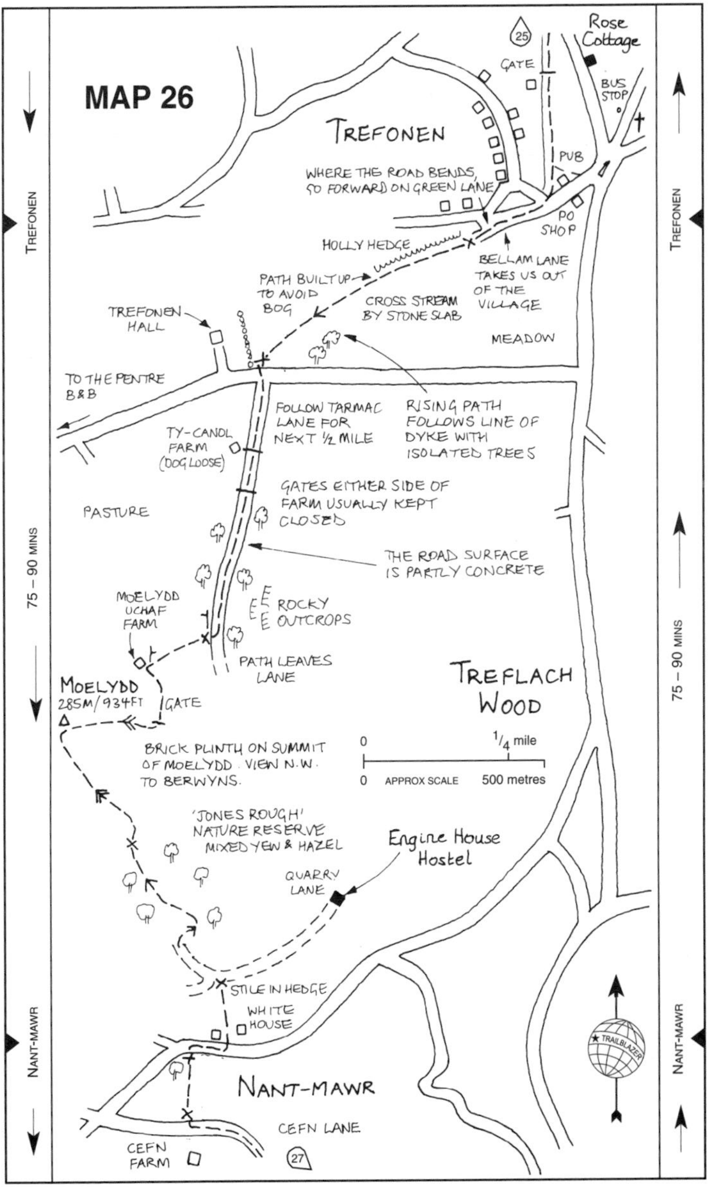
MAP 26
TREFONEN
TREFONEN
75 – 90 MINS
NANT-MAWR
Rose Cottage
25
GATE
BUS STOP
PUB
WHERE THE ROAD BENDS, GO FORWARD ON GREEN LANE
PO SHOP
HOLLY HEDGE
BELLAM LANE TAKES US OUT OF THE VILLAGE
PATH BUILT UP TO AVOID BOG
CROSS STREAM BY STONE SLAB
TREFONEN HALL
MEADOW
TO THE PENTRE B&B
FOLLOW TARMAC LANE FOR NEXT ½ MILE
RISING PATH FOLLOWS LINE OF DYKE WITH ISOLATED TREES
TY-CANOL FARM (DOG LOOSE)
GATES EITHER SIDE OF FARM USUALLY KEPT CLOSED
PASTURE
THE ROAD SURFACE IS PARTLY CONCRETE
MOELYDD UCHAF FARM
ROCKY OUTCROPS
PATH LEAVES LANE
TREFLACH WOOD
MOELYDD 285M/934FT
GATE
BRICK PLINTH ON SUMMIT OF MOELYDD. VIEW N.W. TO BERWYNS.
0 1/4 mile
0 APPROX SCALE 500 metres
'JONES ROUGH' NATURE RESERVE MIXED YEW & HAZEL
Engine House Hostel
QUARRY LANE
STILE IN HEDGE
WHITE HOUSE
NANT-MAWR
CEFN LANE
CEFN FARM
27

stroll beside the golf course through leafy glades before descending through the limestone crags and quarries. These are notable for butterflies in summer and for superb views over the **Severn Plain** to the **Breidden Hills** at any time. You are on the very border between England and Wales and indeed it is said that the Cross Keys pub is in Wales up to the bar, though the bar itself is in England. Tricky if you're applying for planning permission to alter the frontage!

Where to stay and eat: Racecourse Common to Llanymynech

Trefonen is a neat and tidy settlement with a **shop**, Martins Stores (Mon–Sat 8am–8pm, Sun 8am–1pm), where all the usual groceries are on sale and with a **post office** on the premises; two pubs, *The Efel Inn* and *The Barley Mow*, neither particularly welcoming. There is a **bus** four times a day between here and Oswestry from the bus shelter opposite the church (see map p105).

There are B&Bs in the area for those seeking accommodation, including *The Pentre* (☎ 01691-653952, 2F), a lovely old farmhouse where the charges are £35/23 for singles/doubles per person with an optional evening meal for £12. If you stay for two or more nights they will ferry you about for nothing.

In the season, Mrs Jones' charming *Rose Cottage* (☎ 01691-652050, 1T/1D, Chapel Lane) is a cheaper alternative at £15 plus £6 for an evening meal and she welcomes dogs.

The next village, **Nant-Mawr**, has few attractions, but it does have camping and accommodation. The *Engine House Hostel* (☎ 01691-659358, 🖳 www.nantmawr.com) at the Nantmawr Quarry Mountain Bike Centre has two rooms each sleeping nine and provides bed linen but not towels in the night's charge of £12.50. B&B is £15 and with an evening meal thrown in it's £23. They also allow **camping** on a patch of grass outside the bunkhouse: £4 per person including the use of the showers in the main building.

LLANYMYNECH   MAP 28

This is no beauty spot and has traffic thundering through day and night, but despite this many walkers will break their journey here. It is on the **bus** route to Oswestry and is a convenient place to call a halt, being five or six days' walk from Prestatyn, nearly 60 miles (93km). For greyhounds, it could be their fourth night on the trail but they will need to have started fit and be travelling light.

There are several pubs to choose from including the *Cross Keys* (☎ 01691-831585) where there is a full-size competition snooker table. The accommodation here is quite basic. *The Lion Hotel* (☎ 01691-830234, 2S/4T/3D/1F) charges £23 per person with meals available in the bar. **Camping** here costs £2.50 including shower.

There is also a B&B right opposite the Lion at *The Manse* (☎ 01691-831108, 2T/2D) which is situated right on the main road and charges £26 for single occupancy and £24 per head for two sharing. They have a friendly approach, making you feel very welcome.

A mile or so out of the village on the A483 is *Ty-coch* (☎ 01691-830361, 1S/1T/1D), pronounced 'Tee Coe', charging £21 a night plus £10 for an evening meal, with **camping** at £3 a head plus £1 for a shower.

There is a **post office** and **general store** (Mon–Sat 8am–6pm, Sun 8am–1pm). The **grocery shop/off-licence** at the crossroads is open every day but their café facilities have been permanently closed.

There is a **curry house**, *Bengal Spices* (☎ 01691-830170), two doors down from the post office, where standard Indian fare is available, including takeaways.

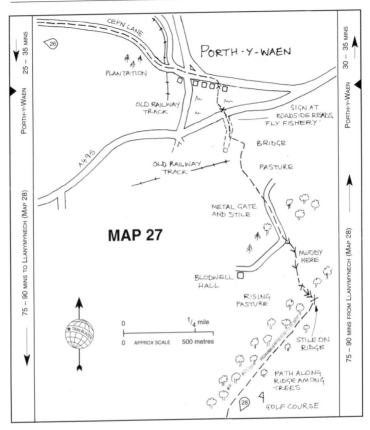

LLANYMYNECH TO BUTTINGTON

MAPS 28–32

This stretch of **10¹/₂ miles (17km, 4–4³/₄hrs)** is dead flat and straightforward, starting along the towpath of the canal. After **Four Crosses** the trail takes to the fields, passing one of the worst obstacles on the whole route, Gornel Farm, where you may have to wade through a slurry pit. Once past this quagmire you will soon find yourself keeping company with the Dyke again which in this area doubles as a flood defence, avoiding errant streams. On reaching The Nea, a private house, you join the **Tir-y-mynach Embankment** (see p111) that follows the River Severn for 4 miles (6km) to **Pool Quay**. This levée-like causeway keeps you clear of the river which has a tendency to flood in winter. The going is not particularly interesting but enlivened by views of the Breidden Hills (see p111) to the east, covered in trees and afflicted by a rash of radio masts.

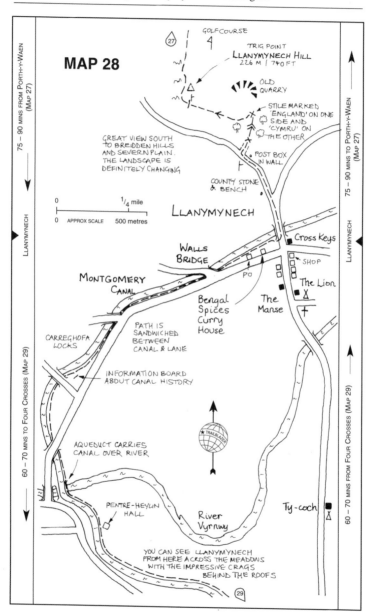

MAP 28

GOLFCOURSE

27

TRIG POINT
LLANYMYNECH HILL
226 M / 740 FT

OLD
QUARRY

STILE MARKED
'ENGLAND' ON ONE
SIDE AND
'CYMRU' ON
THE OTHER

GREAT VIEW SOUTH
TO BREIDDEN HILLS
AND SEVERN PLAIN.
THE LANDSCAPE IS
DEFINITELY CHANGING

POST BOX
IN WALL

COUNTY STONE
& BENCH

LLANYMYNECH

0   1/4 mile
0   APPROX SCALE   500 metres

Cross Keys

SHOP

WALLS
BRIDGE

PO

The Lion

MONTGOMERY
CANAL

Bengal
Spices
Curry
House

The
Manse

CARREGHOFA
LOCKS

PATH IS
SANDWICHED
BETWEEN
CANAL & LANE

INFORMATION BOARD
ABOUT CANAL HISTORY

★TRAILBLAZER

AQUEDUCT CARRIES
CANAL OVER RIVER

PENTRE-HEYLIN
HALL

River
Vyrnwy

Ty-coch

YOU CAN SEE LLANYMYNECH
FROM HERE ACROSS THE MEADOWS
WITH THE IMPRESSIVE CRAGS
BEHIND THE ROOFS

29

75 – 90 MINS FROM PORTH-Y-WAEN (MAP 27)

LLANYMYNECH

60 – 70 MINS TO FOUR CROSSES (MAP 29)

75 – 90 MINS TO PORTH-Y-WAEN (MAP 27)

LLANYMYNECH

60 – 70 MINS FROM FOUR CROSSES (MAP 29)

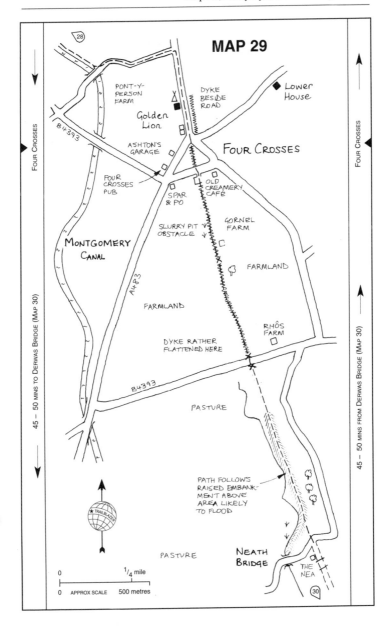

MAP 29

28

PONT-Y-PERSON FARM

Golden Lion

DYKE BESIDE ROAD

Lower House

ASHTON'S GARAGE

B4393

FOUR CROSSES PUB

FOUR CROSSES

SPAR & PO

OLD CREAMERY CAFÉ

MONTGOMERY CANAL

A483

SLURRY PIT OBSTACLE

GORNEL FARM

FARMLAND

FARMLAND

RHÔS FARM

DYKE RATHER FLATTENED HERE

B4393

PASTURE

PATH FOLLOWS RAISED EMBANKMENT ABOVE AREA LIKELY TO FLOOD

PASTURE

NEATH BRIDGE

THE NEA

30

★ TRAILBLAZER

0   1/4 mile
0   APPROX SCALE   500 metres

FOUR CROSSES

FOUR CROSSES

45 – 50 MINS TO DERWAS BRIDGE (MAP 30)

45 – 50 MINS FROM DERWAS BRIDGE (MAP 30)

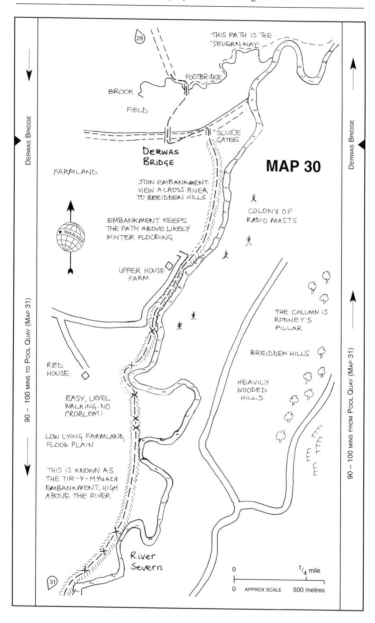

DERWAS BRIDGE

90 – 100 MINS TO POOL QUAY (MAP 31)

29

THIS PATH IS THE 'SEVERN WAY!'

FOOTBRIDGE

BROOK

FIELD

SLUICE GATES

DERWAS BRIDGE

MAP 30

FARMLAND

JOIN EMBANKMENT.
VIEW ACROSS RIVER
TO BREIDDEN HILLS

COLONY OF
RADIO MASTS

EMBANKMENT KEEPS
THE PATH ABOVE LIKELY
WINTER FLOODING

★ TRAILBLAZER

UPPER HOUSE
FARM

THE COLUMN IS
RODNEY'S
PILLAR

BREIDDEN HILLS

RED
HOUSE

HEAVILY
WOODED
HILLS

EASY, LEVEL
WALKING. NO
PROBLEM!

LOW LYING FARMLAND,
FLOOD PLAIN

THIS IS KNOWN AS
THE TIR-Y-MYNACH
EMBANKMENT, HIGH
ABOVE THE RIVER.

River
Severn

31

DERWAS BRIDGE

90 – 100 MINS FROM POOL QUAY (MAP 31)

0   1/4 mile

0   APPROX SCALE   500 metres

❏ **Breidden Hills**

Between Four Crosses and Pool Quay the path follows the River Severn as it meanders its way through the Severn Plain, an area of no outstanding beauty but characterized by the spectacular view of a compact range of hills to the east sprouting radio masts and transmitters and disfigured in part by quarrying. These are the Breidden Hills, a volcanic outcrop of dolerite rock rising to 365m (1198ft) above sea level that was used by Caractacus against the Romans in AD43. Cefn-y-castell on Middletown Hill is one of the many places where he is said to have fought his last battle. The site has only recently been cleared of the forest that was planted 300 years ago for use by the shipyards at Chatham. The monument on top of Breidden Hill commemorates Admiral Rodney who won a sea battle at Dominica in 1782.

Caractacus, also known in Welsh as Caradoc, held out against the Romans for nine years before an expedition sent by Claudius defeated him in AD51. He was taken to Rome in chains but his bearing and demeanour so impressed his judges that he was pardoned and spent the rest of his life a free man, although unable to return home to gaze once more across the Severn Plain.

The trail rejoins the towpath after Pool Quay and you can stay on it as far as **Welshpool** if you intend using the services there. If not, the main Offa's Dyke Path leaves the canal at **Buttington Wharf** and goes left to the roundabout on the A483, following the verge of the Shrewsbury road to **Buttington Bridge**. Take care as you cross the bridge.

FOUR CROSSES   **MAP 29**

The *Golden Lion* (☎ 01691-830295, 3S/2T/2D/3F) caters willingly for walkers, the path passing right outside the door. B&B costs £26 or you can **camp** for £5. Meals are available in the bar. Just off the path, *Lower House* (☎ 01691-831600, 1T/1D) on Domgay Lane charges a fairly standard £20. You can arrange a meal for an extra £10 or you can eat in the pub. The widely-acclaimed *Old Creamery Café and Takeaway* (7.30am–5pm, 5.30pm, chippie frying 12–2pm) has opened in the yard of the dairy marshalling yard, formerly the station yard. Four Crosses also has a supermarket, **Spar** (Mon–Sat 7.30am–9pm, Sun 8am–9pm) with a **post office**, and there's a second shop at **Ashton's Garage** (Mon–Fri 8am–6pm, Sat 8am–5pm and Sun 9am–12pm).

❏ **Tir-y-mynach Embankment**

You walk along the Tir-y-mynach Embankment for four miles (6km) following the course of the River Severn to Pool Quay. The walking is fairly ordinary but you can take pleasure from the swirling eddies of the Severn as it twists and turns its way to the sea. When there are occasional floods the fields are left strewn with driftwood when the waters recede. Each fence has its pile of debris – everything from twigs to whole tree trunks.

When you come to the course of the old railway line between Oswestry and Welshpool, now long abandoned, you will notice the remains of a bridge over the Severn, long since removed. The River Severn was at one time navigable as far as Pool Quay and in the early 19th century vessels of up to 30 tons were used to ship goods to Worcester and Gloucester. The weir that made the river navigable was destroyed by floods in 1881.

❏ **Strata Marcella Abbey**
Founded in 1170 by a grant from Owain Cyfeiliog, a prince of Powys, the abbey
was colonized by the Cistercian 'white monks' from Whitland near Carmarthen.
They were called white monks because they chose to use undyed cloth for their
habits. Owain himself became a monk and was buried here. At the time of the
Dissolution of the Monasteries, only three monks lived there. The site has been
plundered for stone for local building and today not one stone remains visible.
Some finds are on display at the Powysland Museum in Welshpool.

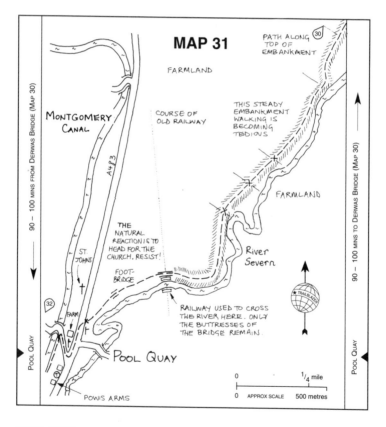

POOL QUAY **MAP 31**

The *Powis Arms* (☎ 01938-590253) is a tiny and curious pub like no other. Try it and you'll
see what we mean.

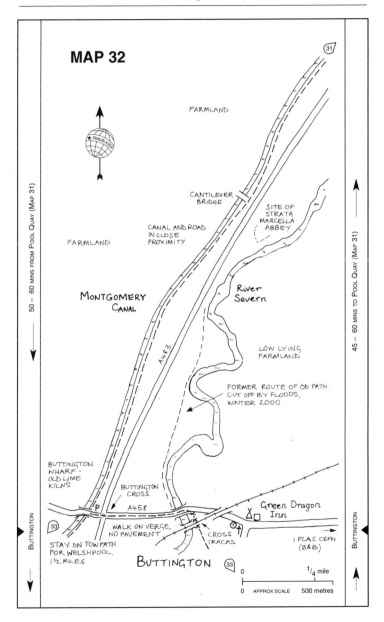

MAP 32

★ TRAILBLAZER

FARMLAND

CANTILEVER
BRIDGE

SITE OF
STRATA
MARCELLA
ABBEY

CANAL AND ROAD
IN CLOSE
PROXIMITY

FARMLAND

River
Severn

MONTGOMERY
CANAL

A483

LOW LYING
FARMLAND

FORMER ROUTE OF OLD PATH.
CUT OFF BY FLOODS,
WINTER 2000

BUTTINGTON
WHARF ·
OLD LIME
KILNS

BUTTINGTON
CROSS

P

A458

Green Dragon
Inn

33

WALK ON VERGE,
NO PAVEMENT

CROSS
TRACKS

STAY ON TOWPATH
FOR WELSHPOOL,
1½ MILES

1 PLAS CEFN
(B&B)

BUTTINGTON

33

0   ¼ mile

0   APPROX SCALE   500 metres

50 – 60 MINS FROM POOL QUAY (MAP 31)

45 – 60 MINS TO POOL QUAY (MAP 31)

BUTTINGTON

BUTTINGTON

BUTTINGTON   MAP 32

Buttington itself has few amenities, relying on one pub, *The Green Dragon Inn*
(☎ 01938-553076, food from 7.30pm),
where you can **camp** for £3 per tent, and
one B&B to earn its place on the itinerary
of Offa's Dyke walkers. Even the solitary
B&B isn't really in Buttington, being
about a mile away, making an arranged
collection necessary if you're thinking of
staying there: *1 Plas Cefn* (☎ 01938-
570225, 1S/1T/1D), is good value for
money charging an economical £16 a night
plus £6.50 if you opt for a meal. You can
camp here for £1.50. The **bus** stop is
served by the Welshpool to Shrewsbury
service (see public transport map, p38).

❏ **Buttington Wharf**
Beyond Pool Quay the Montgomery Canal leads you all the way to Buttington
Wharf, at one time an important site for limestone burning. The kilns still remain
more or less intact, if rather overgrown. A surviving accounts book tells us that in
the year 1830, 2000 tons of limestone were burnt here, most of it destined for the
fields east of the Severn. It fed the soil with the minerals needed for decent crops.
The trade in limestone along the canal was short-lived due to the coming of the rail-
ways which offered quicker, cheaper transportation.

WELSHPOOL *(Y TRALLWNG)*

Walkers on the Offa's Dyke Path may
choose to stay overnight in Welshpool due
to the limited accommodation to be found
in the vicinity of Buttington. The town is
only 1¹/₂ miles (2km) south along the towpath. However, there aren't that many
places to stay in this town either and what
there is can get booked up in peak periods.
    Very much a Welsh town, the locals
maintain that they belong first and foremost
to Montgomeryshire even if the map insists
on calling it Powys. There are frequent
reminders that this is Wales, the road signs,
bus and railway timetables, public notices
and tourist information being shown in both
languages. The town used to be known as
Pool but confusion with Poole, Dorset, led to
the council deciding to attach the 'Welsh' as
a prefix; it has been Welshpool ever since.

Transport

Rail links are to Aberystwyth and
Shrewsbury with four trains a day (see
public transport map, p38). There are plenty of **taxi** firms including Yellow Cabs (☎
01938-555533) and their rivals Amber
Cabs (☎ 01938-556611).

Services

The **tourist information centre** (☎ 01938-
552043, daily 9.30am–5.30pm) is by the
large public car park. There's a **post office**,
two **banks** with cash machines, a **laundrette** on the High St and a Boots **pharmacy** on Broad St for any necessary plas-
ters if blisters are in evidence.
    Food stocks can be replenished at a
choice of **supermarkets**, the best being
Spar (☎ 01938-552065) on Church St
which is open Monday to Sunday 7am–
11pm and Safeway on Berriew St with
similar opening times. There's an **indoor
market** on Mondays, Tuesdays and Satur-
days throughout the year.
    Alexanders of Welshpool (☎ 01938-
552329, 29 Broad St) is the only **camping
shop**, good for gas cylinders and any vital
items of clothing or equipment.
    Should you want a swim there's a
leisure centre just off the canal as you walk
into Welshpool from Buttington Bridge
called The Flash (☎ 01938-555952, Salop
Rd, £2.50). The **Medical Centre** can be
contacted on ☎ 01938-553118 and the **hospital** on ☎ 01938-553133.

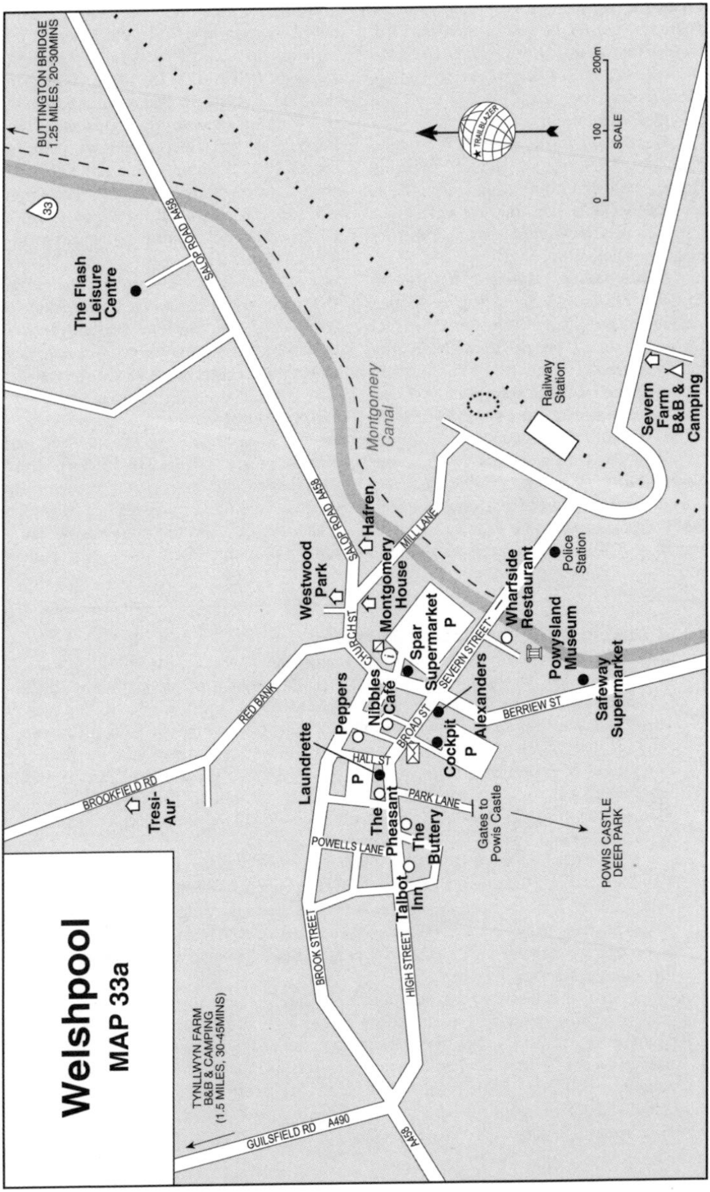

Welshpool
MAP 33a

BUTTINGTON BRIDGE
1.25 MILES, 20-30MINS

33

SHOP ROAD A483

The Flash
Leisure
Centre

Montgomery
Canal

SHOP ROAD A483

Railway
Station

Severn
Farm
B&B &
Camping

Hafren

Westwood
Park

Montgomery
House

MILL LANE

Wharfside
Restaurant

Police
Station

CHURCH ST

Spar
Supermarket

P

Powysland
Museum

Safeway
Supermarket

SEVERN STREET

RED BANK

Peppers

Nibbles
Café

BROAD ST

Alexanders

BERRIEW ST

BROOKFIELD RD

Laundrette

Cockpit

P

Tresi-
Aur

P

HALL ST

The
Pheasant

PARK LANE

Gates to
Powis Castle

POWIS CASTLE
DEER PARK

POWELLS LANE

The
Buttery

BROOK STREET

Talbot
Inn

HIGH STREET

TYNLLWYN FARM
B&B & CAMPING
(1.5 MILES, 30-45MINS)

GUILSFIELD RD A490

A483

0   100   200m

SCALE

Where to stay

There's a cluster of B&Bs on Salop Rd. *Hafren* (☎ 01938-554112, 1T/1D/1F) at No 38 is the one most likely to get booked up. Mrs Harker charges £17 to £20 per night plus £9 for an evening meal.

Westwood Park Hotel (☎ 01938-553474, 1T/1D/1F), almost opposite Hafren, charges £35-40 (room only). Meals are not available but you can walk down into the town in two minutes where there is plenty of choice.

Montgomery House (☎ 01938-552693, 1T/3F), 43 Salop Rd, is another well-appointed place nearby, priced at £25 for singles or £20 per person in the twin or family rooms.

Another neat and tidy place is *Tresi-Aur* on Brookfield Rd (☎ 01938-552430, 1S/1T/1D) at £18 a night.

Near the station is Mrs Joyce Jones' *Severn Farm*, (☎ 01938-553098, 2S/2T/2D /2F), a very well organized establishment. B&B costs £18.50, an evening meal is served at 6.30pm for £12 and **camping** is available for £3.50 per head. About a mile out of town on the Guilsfield road, set up high on the side of the hill, is *Tynllwyn Farm* (☎ 01938-553175, 1S/1T/ 1D/3F), a real find. Run by Mr and Mrs Emberton, it is a working farm with a high standard of B&B plus self-catering cottages for a longer stay. Evening meals are £11. The nearest pub is the *Raven* and Mr Emberton will run you down and leave you to get a £3 taxi ride back. **Camping** is also available at £5 per tent.

All the above will collect you from Buttington Bridge but it's no hardship to walk along the canal to the bridge over Severn St, although at the end of a hard day you might feel that this was a bridge too far.

Where to eat

At breakfast time you should seek out *Nibbles Café* (☎ 01938-556500, Bear Passage) where you might contemplate their whopping Big Breakfast Baguette which for £2.70 would quite easily feed a family of four. Possibly the best pub in

---

❏ What to see in and around Welshpool

First impressions of Welshpool are of a traditional town with traditional shops, not well known for its sophistication, but it has its curiosities. Mondays sees the **Livestock Market** in full swing, reputedly the largest in the whole of Europe. There's a beautifully restored red-brick building identified as the old **Cockpit** from the days when cock-fighting was popular. It is situated at the back of a car park. **Powysland Museum and Canal Centre** (☎ 01938-554656, admission £1) is an intriguing local museum concentrating on items relevant to the old county of Montgomeryshire. The opening times are Mon–Fri 11am–1pm, 2–5pm, closed Wed, and Sat and Sun 10am–1pm, 2–5pm.

Powis Castle (☎ 01938-551920, Apr–Oct Wed–Sun, except July and Aug Tue–Sun, 1–5pm), less than a mile south of the centre of Welshpool, is a must for those interested in the castles along the way. It is unusual, being built in a startling pink sandstone, and is reached through the deer park on foot from the town, the park gates opening at dawn and closing an hour after sunset, making an evening stroll in the summer quite achievable.

It takes a pleasant half-hour through the park, notable for its giant redwood trees, to reach the castle entrance. One passes a small plaque marking the spot where an arrow landed, shot by Sir Ralph from the castle bowling green in 1910. It does not record if it hit anyone. The castle has connections with Clive of India and contains a collection of memorabilia relevant to his career as soldier and statesman. There's also a magnificent herd of red deer in the park and peacocks provide an ornamental diversion especially in the display season.

town is *The Pheasant* (☎ 01938-553104, 43 High St) where they do meals at lunchtime and at night. A menu of standard pub meals is supplemented by the day's special which if you're lucky might be steak cooked in Guinness with puff pastry, which is excellent, or Yorkshire Bangers, a fine plateful of grilled sausages with all the trimmings. Similar fare can also be found at the *Talbot Inn* just down the street.

A meal can be enjoyed in the *Wharfside Restaurant* (☎ 01938-553271, Mon–Sun 7.30–10.30pm), the place to eat and be seen, on board a permanently-moored narrowboat. There is also a floating restaurant where for £7.95 you can cruise and enjoy a meal at the same time.

Peppers (☎ 01938-555146, Mon–Sat 8am–5pm) on Puzzle Sq is handy with a good vegetarian choice.

Finally, *The Buttery* (☎ 01938-552658) is open seven days a week for good, honest home-made meals at reasonable prices. Welshpool also has two Indian restaurants, several chippies, a pizzeria, a kebab house and a number of conventional restaurants if fast food is called for.

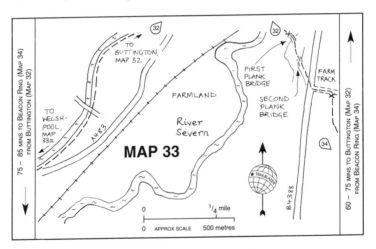

BUTTINGTON TO BROMPTON CROSSROADS   MAPS 32–40

This **12¹/₂-mile (20km, 5–6hrs)** stretch leaves the Severn and climbs for an hour to the summit of **Beacon Ring**, an Iron Age hill-fort now planted with beech trees and sprouting two unsightly transmitter masts. A largely forested ramble follows through the **Leighton** estate with its Chile pines (monkey puzzle trees) to the villages of **Kingswood** and **Forden**, then a lengthy crossing of the **Plain of Montgomery** with the Dyke in evidence throughout. The walking is low level and relatively easy as it traces the hidden hedgerows and copses of the secretive country of the **River Camlad**. The low-lying meadows through which the River Camlad flows are typical of much of this section. The views to all sides are good and the walking undemanding and rather uneventful. Near **Montgomery** the landscape of Lymore Park shows the distant town and its castle to good effect and the woods are the haunt of numerous pheasants.

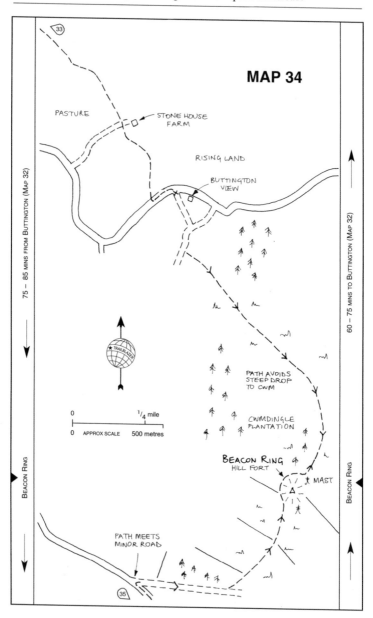

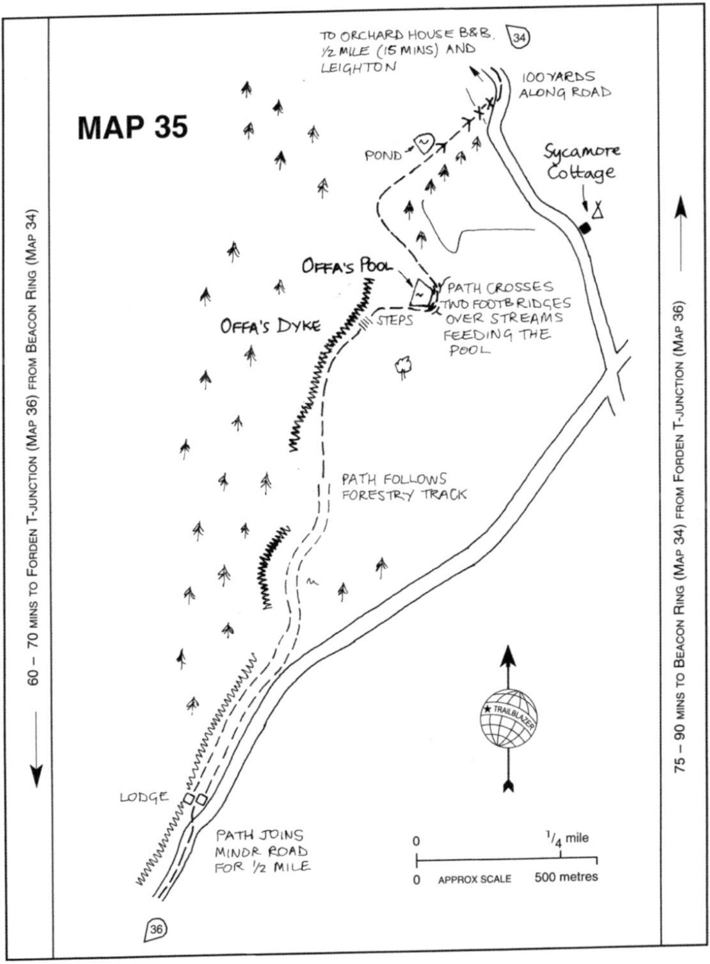

MAP 35

TO ORCHARD HOUSE B&B,
½ MILE (15 MINS) AND
LEIGHTON

34

100 YARDS
ALONG ROAD

POND

Sycamore
Cottage

OFFA'S POOL

OFFA'S DYKE

STEPS

PATH CROSSES
TWO FOOTBRIDGES
OVER STREAMS
FEEDING THE
POOL

PATH FOLLOWS
FORESTRY TRACK

LODGE

PATH JOINS
MINOR ROAD
FOR ½ MILE

36

60 – 70 MINS TO FORDEN T-JUNCTION (MAP 36) FROM BEACON RING (MAP 34)

75 – 90 MINS TO BEACON RING (MAP 34) FROM FORDEN T-JUNCTION (MAP 36)

TRAILBLAZER

0   ¼ mile
0   APPROX SCALE   500 metres

LEIGHTON   MAP 35

Leighton is not so much a village as the private estate of Leighton Hall, the houses occupied by employees from the estate and the huge farm property. There's a school and church but no shop or pub so it offers no great magnetic pull for Offa's Dyke walkers.

Sycamore Cottage (☎ 01938-553899, 4D/2F) offers rooms at £18 per head plus £8 for an evening meal. **Camping** is also available at £2.50 for a tent and you can have a shower for 50p or a bath for £1. They do snacks but not meals. Mrs Marion Pearce at *Orchard House* (☎ 01938-553 624) runs a comfortable B&B with en-suite rooms with lovely views, justifiably priced slightly higher at £20–£22 per night.

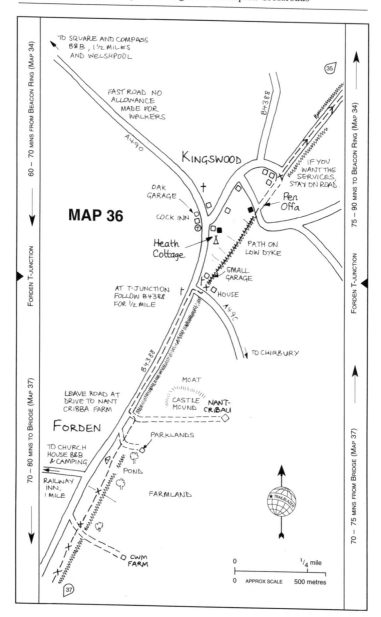

TO SQUARE AND COMPASS
B&B, 1½ MILES
AND WELSHPOOL

35

FAST ROAD. NO
ALLOWANCE
MADE FOR
WALKERS

A490

KINGSWOOD

B4388

IF YOU
WANT THE
SERVICES,
STAY ON ROAD

OAK
GARAGE

MAP 36

COCK INN

Pen
Offa

Heath
Cottage

PATH ON
LOW DYKE

SMALL
GARAGE

AT T-JUNCTION
FOLLOW B4388
FOR ½ MILE

HOUSE

A490

B4388

TO CHIRBURY

MOAT

CASTLE
MOUND

NANT-
CRIBAU

LEAVE ROAD AT
DRIVE TO NANT
CRIBBA FARM

PARKLANDS

Forden

TO CHURCH
HOUSE B&B
& CAMPING

POND

RAILWAY
INN,
1 MILE

FARMLAND

CWM
FARM

37

★ TRAILBLAZER

0   ¼ mile

0   APPROX SCALE   500 metres

60 – 70 MINS FROM BEACON RING (MAP 34)

FORDEN T-JUNCTION

70 – 80 MINS TO BRIDGE (MAP 37)

75 – 90 MINS TO BEACON RING (MAP 34)

FORDEN T-JUNCTION

70 – 75 MINS FROM BRIDGE (MAP 37)

❏ **Beacon Ring Hill-fort (*Caer Digoll*)**

Dating from the Iron Age, the fortifications housed a small village that eked out a perilous existence hunting and farming. The circular embankment and ditch would have been supplemented by a palisade made from tree trunks with an opening on the south side for a gateway. The site also contained a much older long barrow or burial mound suggesting that it would have had a sacred significance for its inhabitants.

A plantation of beech trees was established in 1953 to mark the coronation of Her Majesty Queen Elizabeth II but the commemorative stone has become defaced. To be frank, the trees spoil the site and rob it of any sense of place or space. As if the trees were not bad enough, two ugly transmitter masts with their accompanying buildings add to the lack of harmony.

In older times, beacon fires would have been lit here, hence the name, a common enough one to anyone familiar with maps of England and Wales.

To the south the skyline is dominated by the **Kerry Ridgeway** and to the west the wooded mound of **Corndon Hill** is clearly seen.

The Dyke is the border along here, although this doesn't worry the buzzards who pursue their hunting with their characteristic diligence, their cries a trademark of the deep country of the Dyke.

KINGSWOOD   MAP 36

At Kingswood you will find the hospitable *Cock Inn* (☎ 01938-580226) where the landlord welcomes customers who are walking the Dyke. Bar meals are available.

Opposite the Cock Inn is *Heath Cottage* (☎ 01938-580453, 1S/1T/2D), an appealing place for B&B or **camping**, charging £22 a night for the former and £3 including shower for the latter.

Also in the village is *Pen Offa* (☎ 01938-580513, 1T), a small, intimate B&B where for £22 you get a self-contained unit with its own entrance, ideal for a secret hideaway.

If all you need is a shop to buy a sandwich or chocolate bar, **Oak Garage** (Mon–Sat 7.30am–7pm) is a hundred metres along the main road, stocking a good selection of groceries. The Shrewsbury **bus** stops by the Cock Inn three times a day (see public transport map, p38).

Just over a mile north of Kingswood on the A490 towards the tiny airport is *The Square and Compass* (☎ 01938-580360, 2T), an unusual local where they have fitted out two self-catering flats for guests, but unfortunately not for single-night stays. The high standards are continued in the intimate and friendly bar where the beer on draught includes Worthington E. Although off the route, this place is a real find.

FORDEN   MAP 36

In Forden, a distinctly separate community from Kingswood, the *Railway Inn* (☎ 01938-580237, 3T/2D) does accommodation from £25 per person. Meals are taken in the bar. It's located about one mile west of the trail. *Church House* (☎ 01938-580353, 1T/1D/1F) would be worth trying if everywhere else is full. A small establishment, they charge a reasonable £18.50 for B&B or you can **camp** for £3 including the use of the shower. There are no evening meals but you can walk down to the pub in fifteen minutes for that good old standby, the bar meal.

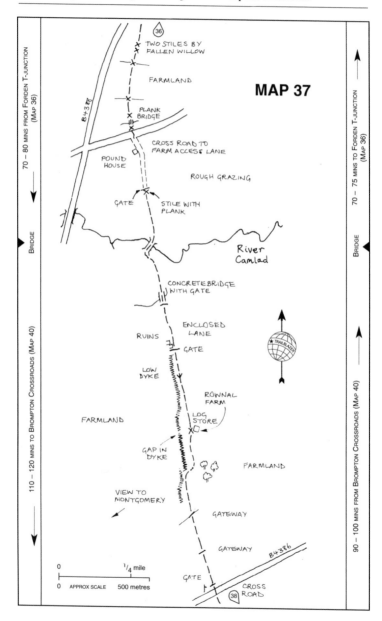

MAP 37

36

TWO STILES BY
FALLEN WILLOW

FARMLAND

B4388

PLANK
BRIDGE

CROSS ROAD TO
FARM ACCESS LANE

POUND
HOUSE

ROUGH GRAZING

GATE

STILE WITH
PLANK

River
Camlad

CONCRETE BRIDGE
WITH GATE

ENCLOSED
LANE

RUINS

GATE

LOW
DYKE

ROWNAL
FARM

LOG
STORE

FARMLAND

GAP IN
DYKE

FARMLAND

VIEW TO
MONTGOMERY

GATEWAY

GATEWAY

B4386

0   ¼ mile
0   APPROX SCALE   500 metres

GATE

38 CROSS
ROAD

TRAILBLAZER

70 – 80 MINS FROM FORDEN T-JUNCTION (MAP 36)

BRIDGE

110 – 120 MINS TO BROMPTON CROSSROADS (MAP 40)

70 – 75 MINS TO FORDEN T-JUNCTION (MAP 36)

BRIDGE

90 – 100 MINS FROM BROMPTON CROSSROADS (MAP 40)

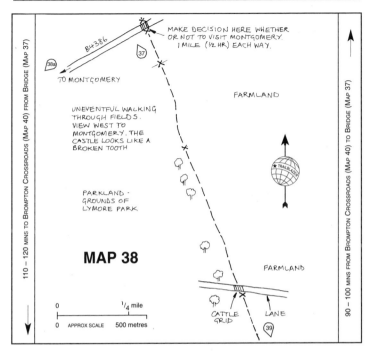

MAKE DECISION HERE WHETHER
OR NOT TO VISIT MONTGOMERY.
I MILE (½ HR) EACH WAY.

B4386

37

38a

TO MONTGOMERY

UNEVENTFUL WALKING
THROUGH FIELDS.
VIEW WEST TO
MONTGOMERY. THE
CASTLE LOOKS LIKE A
BROKEN TOOTH

PARKLAND ·
GROUNDS OF
LYMORE PARK

MAP 38

FARMLAND

★ TRAILBLAZER

FARMLAND

CATTLE
GRID

LANE

39

0   ¼ mile
0   APPROX SCALE   500 metres

110 – 120 MINS TO BROMPTON CROSSROADS (MAP 40) FROM BRIDGE (MAP 37)

90 – 100 MINS FROM BROMPTON CROSSROADS (MAP 40) TO BRIDGE (MAP 37)

MONTGOMERY *(TREFALDWYN)*
MAP 38a

The path passes to the east of the small Georgian town of Montgomery, missing it by a mile, but wayfarers may feel inclined to make a diversion to check out its attractions. It's a lovely little place and well worth the detour. It boasts a fine **Georgian Town Hall** approached by Broad St lined with elegant townhouses. The civic authorities have put up helpful notices explaining the key points of interest.

You should visit the **parish church** of St Nicholas which contains a fine open oak ceiling with arched beams and a beautiful east window, depicting the Crucifixion and Ascension in bright primary colours. In the south transept is the Herbert tomb and two effigies, one of which is of Edmund Mortimer, son-in-law to Owen Glendower, of interest to those familiar with Shakespeare's *Henry IV Part 1*.

In the churchyard is the whimsical Robbers Grave, helpfully indicated by a sign. The story goes that Robert Newton, condemned to death in 1821 for robbery, swore his innocence and maintained that the proof would be known by nothing growing on his grave for a hundred years. A rose bush marks the spot.

Montgomery was the birthplace of the poet **George Herbert** (1593–1632) known to those who studied the Oxford Book of Verse at school:

Sweet day, so cool, so calm, so bright!
The bridle of the earth and sky –
The dew shall weep thy fall tonight;
For thou must die.

Herbert's association with Montgomery included acting as MP for the town for two years although he later settled in Bemerton near Salisbury where he is better known.

Montgomery

MAP 38a

Manor House

Castle

Old Stores House

Llwyn House

Town Hall

Dragon Hotel

Arthur St

Forden Rd

Chirbury Road

38

OFFA'S DYKE PATH, 20MINS

St Nicholas Church

Montgomery Fish Bar

Checkers Hotel

Broad St

Castle Kitchen Café

Brynwylfa

TRAILBLAZER

0   100   200m
SCALE

Services

Apart from cafés, an off-licence and the **post office** where a helpful map of a nature trail is available for 30p, you would do well not to rely on Montgomery for the usual services. There are two **banks** both with cashpoints and a **public toilet** behind the town hall but that is the extent of the facilities to be found here.

Where to stay

For such a small town there is plenty of B&B accommodation. The *Checkers Hotel* (☎ 01686-668355, Broad St, 1S/2F) is a friendly local right in the middle of the town and they do B&B. Rooms are currently being refurbished.

Two others close at hand are *Brynwylfa* (☎ 01686-668555, 1T/1D/2F, 4

Bishop's Castle St) charging £22 and *Llwyn House* (☎ 01686-668576, 1S/1D/1F, Market Sq), slightly cheaper at £19. Neither of these does an evening meal but they're both clean and comfortable.

Old Stores House (☎ 01686-668617, Arthur St, 2S/1T/1D) does B&B with full Welsh breakfast for £20, or £18 with continental breakfast. Smokers and dogs are welcome, bless 'em.

The Manor House (☎ 01686-668736, Pool Rd, 1S/1T/1D) is slightly further from the centre charging £18.

Where to eat

There is a great little café in Broad St, *Castle Kitchen Café*, which is also a delicatessen and organic food shop. The menu is a treat for all foodies: courgette and chick-pea fritters with salad and yoghurt, £4.60; tapenade with toast and salad £4.90; and pissaladiere, a savoury pastry with caramelized onions, olives and anchovies £4.70. Eat your heart out Delia Smith!

You could also have a good lunch at the *Dragon Hotel* (☎ 01686-668359, Market Sq), an imposing property with fake half-timbered beams where the great and the good of the town assemble. The lunch menu offers among other delicacies gently baked pepper with goats cheese and herb couscous for £5.95 and mushroom and herb ragout in chasseur sauce (a sauce of mushrooms, shallots, tomatoes and white wine) for £6.75. Not a lot of people know it but Montgomery appears to be a haven of culinary excellence.

For those with humbler tastes, the *Montgomery Fish Bar* (☎ 01686-668911) is situated next door to the Checkers Hotel and is open in summer Monday to Saturday 6–10pm. In the winter opening times are shorter.

BROMPTON CROSSROADS MAP 40

The Blue Bell clings on to its precarious existence but offers neither food nor accommodation; visit it anyway, just to say you've been. It has remained immune to the changing fashions of the brewing industry; no one

has decided to theme it or turn it into an Irish tavern and I hope they never do. The rusting petrol pump outside is just that, a rusting petrol pump, not a furnishing accessory.

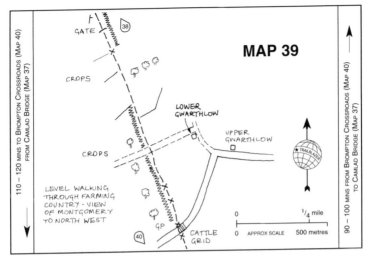

Nonetheless you will wonder if you have crossed a time barrier back into the post-war years when you walk into the bar, swallow a swift half and walk straight out again.

If you need accommodation in the area, *Little Brompton Farm* (☎ 01686-668371, 1T/1D/1F) is a good choice. One of the top ten B&Bs along the entire route, your hosts Mr and Mrs Bright take pains to make their guests comfortable. B&B costs £22; an evening meal is £12. You can **camp** too for £3 on the site reserved for caravans with the Dyke visible across a field.

A mile south of the Blue Bell and set among bluebell woods is *Mellington Hall Hotel and Caravan Park* (☎ 01588-620456, 3T/3D), a gothic pile converted into a holiday camp. It welcomes walkers either to stay in the main house for £35 or to **camp** in the grounds for £5 including showers. The grounds are over-run with rampant rhododendrons but the staff keep them tidy and well-kept for the season which brings its throngs of caravanners. The setting is superb and they have their own bar and restaurant.

BROMPTON CROSSROADS TO KNIGHTON MAPS 40–47

This **14$^{1}/_{2}$-mile (23km)** section will take about **7 to 8 hours**. Early on it crosses the east–west track of the **Kerry Ridgeway**, some 4 miles (6km) west of the captivating small town of **Bishop's Castle**, before embarking on a series of undulations known as the **Switchbacks**. The path follows the Dyke through rolling, wooded farmland, much of the time atop the Dyke itself, an opportunity to walk in the footsteps of those who worked, willingly or unwillingly, to realise the vision of King Offa.

There are many stiles to be crossed but walkers will by now be used to this obstacle which is a hallmark of the Offa's Dyke Path. The tiny chapel of St John the Baptist at **Churchtown** provides a welcome interlude and a moment of quiet reflection in a beautiful and secluded valley. Other distractions include the

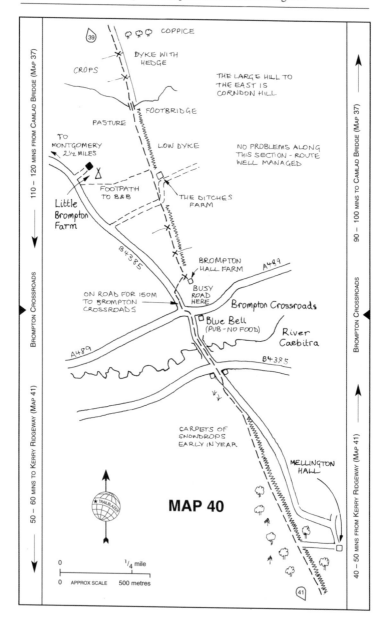

39

COPPICE

DYKE WITH HEDGE

CROPS

THE LARGE HILL TO THE EAST IS CORNDON HILL

FOOTBRIDGE

PASTURE

LOW DYKE

NO PROBLEMS ALONG THIS SECTION - ROUTE WELL MANAGED

TO MONTGOMERY 2½ MILES

FOOTPATH TO B&B

THE DITCHES FARM

Little Brompton Farm

B4385

BROMPTON HALL FARM

A489

ON ROAD FOR 150M TO BROMPTON CROSSROADS

BUSY ROAD HERE

Brompton Crossroads

Blue Bell (PUB - NO FOOD)

River Caebitra

A489

B4385

CARPETS OF SNOWDROPS EARLY IN YEAR

MELLINGTON HALL

MAP 40

★ TRAILBLAZER

0   ¼ mile

0   APPROX SCALE   500 metres

41

Left margin: 110 – 120 MINS FROM CAMLAD BRIDGE (MAP 37) • BROMPTON CROSSROADS • 50 – 60 MINS TO KERRY RIDGEWAY (MAP 41)

Right margin: 90 – 100 MINS TO CAMLAD BRIDGE (MAP 37) • BROMPTON CROSSROADS • 40 – 50 MINS FROM KERRY RIDGEWAY (MAP 41)

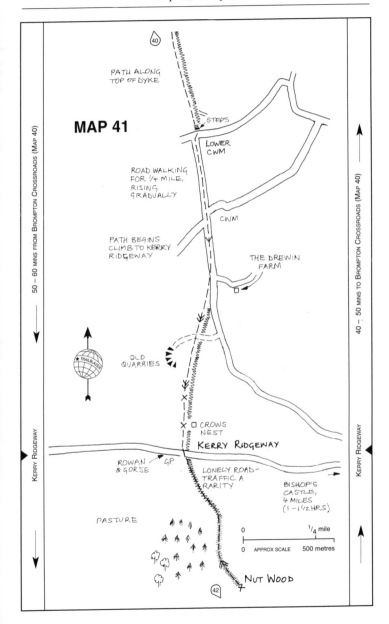

MAP 41

PATH ALONG
TOP OF DYKE

STEPS

LOWER
CWM

ROAD WALKING
FOR 1/4 MILE,
RISING
GRADUALLY

CWM

PATH BEGINS
CLIMB TO KERRY
RIDGEWAY

THE DREWIN
FARM

TRAILBLAZER

OLD
QUARRIES

CROWS
NEST

KERRY RIDGEWAY

ROWAN
& GORSE

GP

LONELY ROAD-
TRAFFIC A
RARITY

BISHOP'S
CASTLE,
4 MILES
(1 - 1 1/2 HRS)

PASTURE

0   1/4 mile

0   APPROX SCALE   500 metres

NUT WOOD

50 – 60 MINS FROM BROMPTON CROSSROADS (MAP 40)

KERRY RIDGEWAY

40 – 50 MINS TO BROMPTON CROSSROADS (MAP 40)

KERRY RIDGEWAY

40

42

❑ **Kerry Ridgeway**

The Kerry Ridgeway is an ancient trackway that, of all the drovers' roads and green lanes that criss-cross the Welsh Marches, has survived more or less intact. Nearby Bronze Age and Iron Age burial sites and stone circles are evidence that the trackway had a symbolic purpose in ancient times as well as a practical use as a line of communication.

The starting point is at Cider House Farm, once a drovers' inn on the B4355 road between Newtown and Knighton, and the finishing point is Bishop's Castle, from where a lift would have to be arranged back to your starting point. Mountain bikers and horseriders also use the route which is gently undulating and traffic-free, an ideal day's expedition through unspoilt countryside.

secluded Shropshire town of **Clun** which, being three miles (5km) off-route, may not cause most walkers to divert; for those who do it is a little gem.

The walk takes in the crossing of **Llanfair Hill**, at 430m (1408ft) the highest point on the entire Offa's Dyke Path, **Cwm-Sanaham Hill** and **Panpunton Hill**, each in its own way giving enjoyable walking and views. A bench and cairn have been placed on the latter in honour of early Offa's Dyke pioneers so you can reflect for a moment on those who made it all possible. Try not to collapse in a heap, the bench is showing its age. The character of **Knighton** viewed from here is rather spoiled by the modern housing on the outskirts. This is no Bishop's Castle, no Montgomery. But fear not, Knighton is the path's halfway mark and offers all the rest and relaxation you need to refresh you for part two of the walk.

BISHOP'S CASTLE

Four miles (6km) off route, Bishop's Castle is a good centre for those walking the trail in separate chunks rather than continuously. Parking in the town is free but taxis are not easy to obtain, there being no established taxi operator although you may be able to arrange for one to come out from Knighton. Otherwise allow at least an hour to walk up the Kerry Ridgeway to the Offa's Dyke Path. Better still, stay at one of the town's B&Bs and they'll run you up to the path and indeed collect you if necessary.

The town has shops, cafés and pubs and a good choice of accommodation. Try *The Old Brick Guest House* (☎ 01588-638471, 1T/2D/1F) charging £25 to £30 with an evening meal at £15. Alternatively,

Old Time (☎ 01588-638467, 29 High St, 2D en suite) offers cheaper and attentive accommodation at £25 per head. Single occupancy of a double room is charged at £30.

A good choice of bar meals can be had at *The Boars Head* (☎ 01588-638521), a 17th-century pub where Royalist soldiers in the Civil War left off sacking the town to slake their thirst. The food is enticing with the emphasis on meat. The High St is an interesting collection of half-timbered houses, many of them selling second-hand books and antiques, and no visit would be complete without a drink of the beer brewed on the premises of *The Three Tuns* (☎ 01588-638979), a genuine curiosity dating back to 1642.

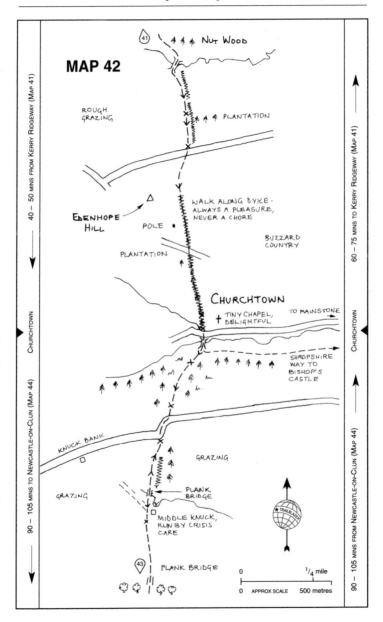

MAP 42

41

↟ ↟ ↟ NUT WOOD

ROUGH GRAZING

X ↟ ↟ PLANTATION

X

EDENHOPE HILL △

POLE •

WALK ALONG DYKE - ALWAYS A PLEASURE, NEVER A CHORE

BUZZARD COUNTRY

PLANTATION

CHURCHTOWN

✝ TINY CHAPEL, DELIGHTFUL

TO MAINSTONE

SHROPSHIRE WAY TO BISHOP'S CASTLE

KNUCK BANK

GRAZING

GRAZING

PLANK BRIDGE

MIDDLE KNUCK, RUN BY CRISIS CARE

43

PLANK BRIDGE

★ TRAILBLAZER

0   ¼ mile

0   500 metres
APPROX SCALE

40 – 50 MINS FROM KERRY RIDGEWAY (MAP 41)

CHURCHTOWN

90 – 105 MINS TO NEWCASTLE-ON-CLUN (MAP 44)

60 – 75 MINS TO KERRY RIDGEWAY (MAP 41)

CHURCHTOWN

90 – 105 MINS FROM NEWCASTLE-ON-CLUN (MAP 44)

❏ **AE Housman**

No visitor to Shropshire should overlook its connections to the lyric poet AE Housman who died in 1936. Although he knew the area hardly at all, it became for him the ideal setting for his poems of loss – lost innocence, lost love, lost ideals – that provide the basis for much of his work.

Best known for *A Shropshire Lad*, which appeared in 1896, Housman seems to catch the spirit of the place like nobody else, the 'blue remembered hills' of childhood. Housman's poems are inhabited by young men doomed to die before the flush of youth is off them, as soldiers who march away, murderers condemned to hang, girls to be forsaken and lovers betrayed. They are conceived in hope and end in death, the bourne from which no traveller returns.

NEWCASTLE-ON-CLUN   MAP 44

This tidy village clusters round the *Crown Inn* (☎ 01588-640271, 1T/1D) where B&B is £30 per person; bar meals available from about £6. Alternatively, at the crossroads stands *Newcastle Hall* (☎ 01588-640350, 1S/2T/1D/1F), a wonderful old house with a slight air of neglect where the hospitality from Mrs Reynolds is warm; she charges £23 for B&B or you can **camp** at £4 on the closely cropped lawn. She will cook you

breakfast for £5.50 but there are no showers. A mile and a half south of the village, *Springhill Farm* (☎ 01588-640337, 1T/1D/1F) is a working farm. B&B costs £23.50 or you can **camp** on their lawn for £2 using the shower in the house. An evening meal costs £11. It's a good half-hour walk to the pub, the return uphill, so you're better off staying put.

CLUN   MAP 44a

You could choose to ignore Newcastle-on-Clun and settle for the rather wider choice of accommodation offered in Clun, 3 miles (5km, 1¼–1½hrs) east of the main path, which AE Housman described as one of the 'quietest places under the sun'. The quickest route to the village is from Lower Spoad down the busy B4368. The walk will take just over an hour and is enlivened in the

latter stages by the view of the romantic-looking castle ruin on its mound close to the road.

The village has cafés, pubs, shops and a **bus** service to Bishop's Castle, a 25-minute ride away (see public transport map, p38).

A variety of accommodation is readily available, including *Clun Mill Youth Hostel* (☎ 01588-640582, 24 beds), one of

❏ **Environmentally Sensitive Areas**

In the Clun area you may come across interpretive panels explaining the intentions behind the ESA Scheme. Introduced by MAFF, now DEFRA, the designation claims to 'conserve and enhance characteristic landscapes, wildlife habitats and historic features'. Farmers participating in this voluntary scheme are encouraged to manage their land in ways that benefit the environment. They can help to do this by allowing the natural regeneration of woodland and using only native species when replanting. Hedge restoration plays an important part involving not only laying, but coppicing, which is the cutting down to ground level to encourage new growth.

The Clun ESA is an area of smooth rounded hills and wooded valleys. Fields are mostly small and bordered by hedgerows. The valley land is under grass while the wooded riverbanks are home to a variety of wildlife including otters.

MAP 43

(42)

GP

SHROPSHIRE
WAY

SHED WITH
CORRUGATED
IRON ROOF

△
HERGAN
408m/1340FT

FINE WALKING
ALONG DYKE
LONG ADOPTED
AS GREEN ROAD

STEPS INFILLED WITH
LIMESTONE

GATE TO
ENCLOSED LANE

'LOWER MOUNT'
COTTAGE

STREAM

FOOTBRIDGE

BRIDGE
FARM

LINE OF ORNAMENTAL
CONIFERS - RATHER SUBURBAN

STILE

GOOD WAYMARKING
ALONG HERE

△ GRAIG HILL
369m/1210FT

DYKE OVERGROWN

DYKE LINED BY OLD LARCHES
MUCH BLOWN BY THE WIND

(44)

0   1/4 mile

0   APPROX SCALE   500 metres

90 – 105 MINS TO NEWCASTLE-ON-CLUN (MAP 44) FROM CHURCHTOWN (MAP 42)

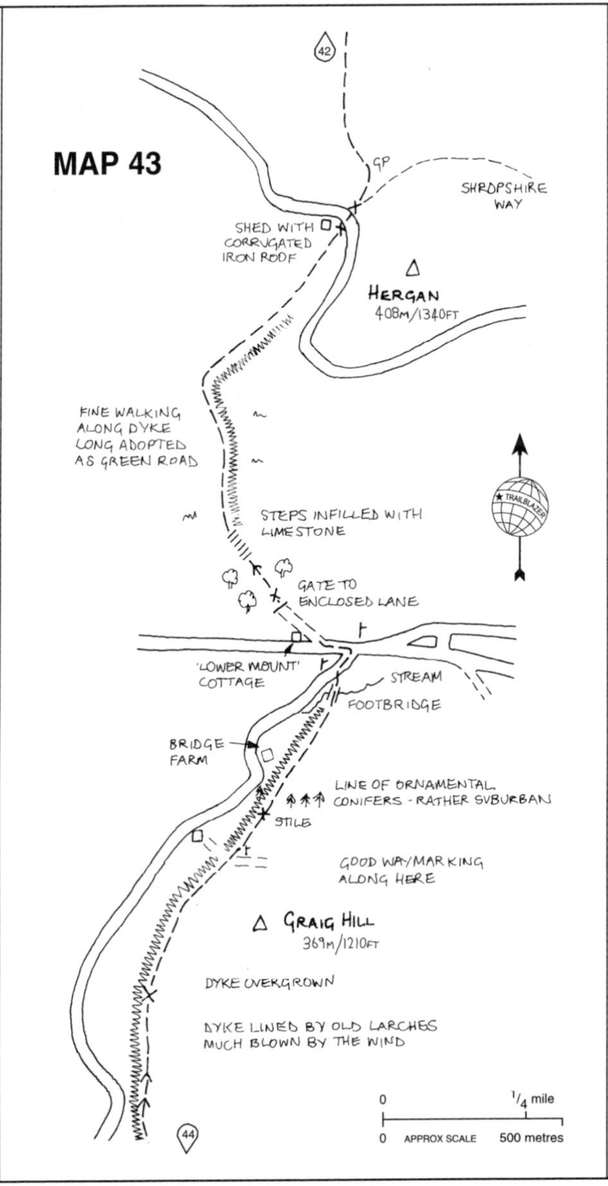

90 – 105 MINS FROM NEWCASTLE-ON-CLUN (MAP 44) TO CHURCHTOWN (MAP 42)

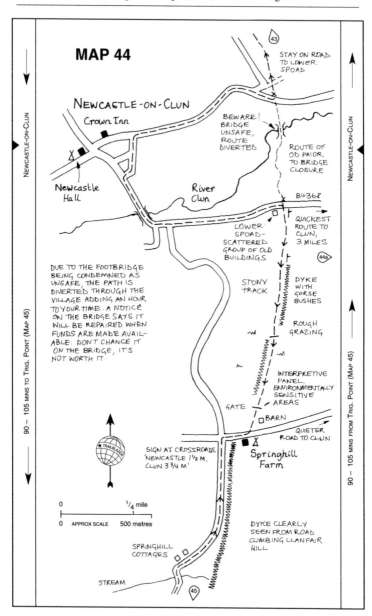

MAP 44

NEWCASTLE-ON-CLUN

Crown Inn

Newcastle Hall

River Clun

B4368

STAY ON ROAD TO LOWER SPOAD

BEWARE! BRIDGE UNSAFE, ROUTE DIVERTED

ROUTE OF OLD PRIOR TO BRIDGE CLOSURE

QUICKEST ROUTE TO CLUN, 3 MILES

LOWER SPOAD - SCATTERED GROUP OF OLD BUILDINGS

STONY TRACK

DYKE WITH GORSE BUSHES

ROUGH GRAZING

INTERPRETIVE PANEL, ENVIRONMENTALLY SENSITIVE AREAS

DUE TO THE FOOTBRIDGE BEING CONDEMNED AS UNSAFE, THE PATH IS DIVERTED THROUGH THE VILLAGE ADDING AN HOUR TO YOUR TIME. A NOTICE ON THE BRIDGE SAYS IT WILL BE REPAIRED WHEN FUNDS ARE MADE AVAILABLE. DON'T CHANCE IT ON THE BRIDGE, IT'S NOT WORTH IT.

GATE

BARN

QUIETER ROAD TO CLUN

Springhill Farm

SIGN AT CROSSROADS, 'NEWCASTLE 1½ M, CLUN 3¾ M'

TRAILBLAZER

0 ¼ mile

0 APPROX SCALE 500 metres

SPRINGHILL COTTAGES

STREAM

DYKE CLEARLY SEEN FROM ROAD CLIMBING LLANFAIR HILL

43

44a

45

NEWCASTLE-ON-CLUN

NEWCASTLE-ON-CLUN

90 – 105 MINS TO TRIG. POINT (MAP 45)

90 – 105 MINS FROM TRIG. POINT (MAP 45)

the very few along the entire length of the Path. It's open April–August and is self catering only. For B&B, try **Clun Farm House** (☎ 01588-640432, 2S/1T/2D/1F), quiet and comfortable at £25, evening meals at £15–£18; or **Crown House** (☎ 01588-

640780, 1T/1D) where the rooms (£23 per head) are in a self-contained cottage. The best pub, **The Sun Inn** (☎ 01588-640559, 1S/1T/4D/1F), has accommodation for £30-35 per person in the converted stables and a good selection of meals in the cosy bar.

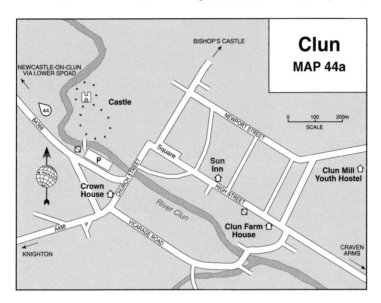

KNIGHTON (*TREF Y CLAWDD*) MAP 47

The Welsh name for Knighton means the town on the Dyke. This is literally true, being a town that actually bestrides the Dyke, as opposed to those like Llangollen and Welshpool that just miss it. It is also regarded as the halfway point on the Offa's Dyke Path, so for those who need one, this could be the excuse for a minor celebration.

It is unlikely that its attractions would be sufficient to draw you if your feet had not brought you here but it has its charms and is worth wandering round if you have any energy left at the end of the day, say between a pint and a meal.

Transport

Trains run to Shrewsbury and Swansea four times a day in the week with one only

on Sunday (see public transport map, p38-9). There is one local **taxi** firm, Knighton Taxis (☎ 01547-528165).

Services

The **tourist information centre** is home to the **Offa's Dyke Association** (☎ 01547-528753) open 9am–5.30pm, daily from Easter to October (Mon-Fri, Oct-Easter), on West St. There's an interpretive centre with interactive monitors.

Knighton has two **banks** (Barclays and HSBC) both on Broad St and both with cashpoints, and a **post office** near the clock-tower in the centre of town. There's a **supermarket**, Tuffins (☎ 01547-528645) on Bridge St, which is open seven days a week.

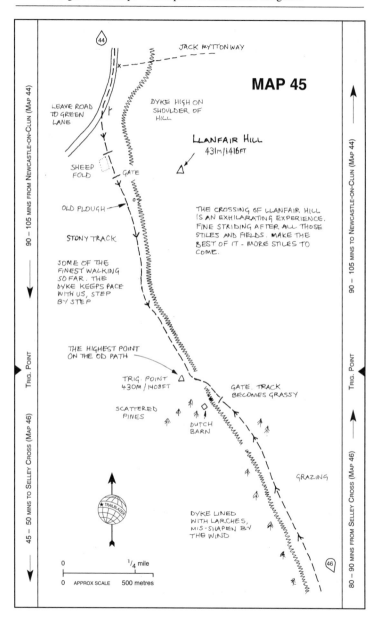

44

JACK MYTTON WAY

MAP 45

LEAVE ROAD
TO GREEN
LANE

DYKE HIGH ON
SHOULDER OF
HILL

LLANFAIR HILL
431m/1416FT

SHEEP
FOLD

GATE

OLD PLOUGH

STONY TRACK

THE CROSSING OF LLANFAIR HILL
IS AN EXHILARATING EXPERIENCE.
FINE STRIDING AFTER ALL THOSE
STILES AND FIELDS. MAKE THE
BEST OF IT - MORE STILES TO
COME.

SOME OF THE
FINEST WALKING
SO FAR. THE
DYKE KEEPS PACE
WITH US, STEP
BY STEP

THE HIGHEST POINT
ON THE OD PATH

TRIG. POINT
430M / 1408FT

GATE. TRACK
BECOMES GRASSY

SCATTERED
PINES

DUTCH
BARN

GRAZING

DYKE LINED
WITH LARCHES,
MIS-SHAPEN BY
THE WIND

46

★ TRAILBLAZER

0   ¹/₄ mile

0   APPROX SCALE   500 metres

90 – 105 MINS FROM NEWCASTLE-ON-CLUN (MAP 44)

TRIG. POINT

45 – 50 MINS TO SELLEY CROSS (MAP 46)

90 – 105 MINS TO NEWCASTLE-ON-CLUN (MAP 44)

TRIG. POINT

80 – 90 MINS FROM SELLEY CROSS (MAP 46)

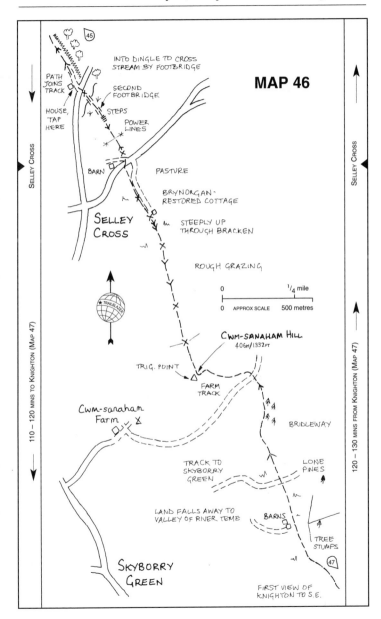

MAP 46

INTO DINGLE TO CROSS
STREAM BY FOOTBRIDGE

45

PATH
JOINS
TRACK

SECOND
FOOTBRIDGE

HOUSE,
TAP
HERE

STEPS

POWER
LINES

BARN

PASTURE

SELLEY
CROSS

BRYNORGAN -
RESTORED COTTAGE

STEEPLY UP
THROUGH BRACKEN

ROUGH GRAZING

0   ¼ mile

0   APPROX SCALE   500 metres

★ TRAILBLAZER

CWM-SANAHAM HILL
406m/1332FT

TRIG. POINT

FARM
TRACK

Cwm-sanaham
Farm

BRIDLEWAY

TRACK TO
SKYBORRY
GREEN

LONE
PINES

LAND FALLS AWAY TO
VALLEY OF RIVER TEME

BARNS

SKYBORRY
GREEN

TREE
STUMPS

47

FIRST VIEW OF
KNIGHTON TO S.E.

SELLEY CROSS

SELLEY CROSS

110 – 120 MINS TO KNIGHTON (MAP 47)

120 – 130 MINS FROM KNIGHTON (MAP 47)

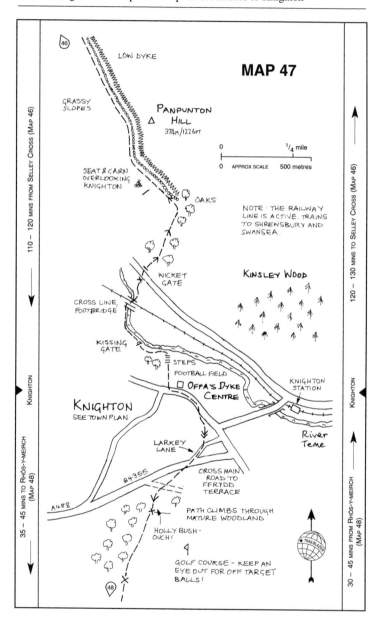

MAP 47

46

LOW DYKE

GRASSY SLOPES

PANPUNTON HILL
△ 374M/1226FT

0 ... ¹/₄ mile

0 ... APPROX SCALE ... 500 metres

SEAT & CAIRN OVERLOOKING KNIGHTON

OAKS

NOTE: THE RAILWAY LINE IS ACTIVE. TRAINS TO SHREWSBURY AND SWANSEA.

KINSLEY WOOD

WICKET GATE

CROSS LINE, FOOTBRIDGE

KISSING GATE

STEPS

FOOTBALL FIELD

KNIGHTON STATION

□ OFFA'S DYKE CENTRE

KNIGHTON
SEE TOWN PLAN

LARKEY LANE

River Teme

B4355

CROSS MAIN ROAD TO FFRYDD TERRACE

A488

PATH CLIMBS THROUGH MATURE WOODLAND

HOLLY BUSH - OUCH!

GOLF COURSE - KEEP AN EYE OUT FOR OFF TARGET BALLS!

48

★ TRAILBLAZER

110 – 120 MINS FROM SELLEY CROSS (MAP 46)

KNIGHTON

35 – 45 MINS TO RHÓS-Y-MEIRCH (MAP 48)

120 – 130 MINS TO SELLEY CROSS (MAP 46)

KNIGHTON

30 – 45 MINS FROM RHÓS-Y-MEIRCH (MAP 48)

If you're into **antiques**, there are a number of interesting shops in The Narrows, the lane that climbs up a cobbled street from the clocktower. Have a quick look at the **Tower House Gallery** (☎ 01547-529530) on the High St for paintings by local artists. The opening times are Tuesday to Saturday 10am–5.30pm, although you may find them open on busy Sundays in summer. **Market day** is Thursday and **early closing** Wednesday.

Where to stay

Camping is scarce around Knighton. There's extremely cheap camping for 70p per person plus £1 for a shower at *Cwm Sanaham Farm* (☎ 01547-528431) north of the town, below the hill with the same name. They also do B&B from £15 per person. Nearer the centre of town, **camping** is available on the owner's lawn for £3 each at *15 Mill Green* (☎ 01547-520075, 2S/1T) plus £1 for the use of a shower or bath, or B&B for a reasonable £16.

There is a good choice of B&B accommodation in Knighton, finely tuned by long exposure to Offa's Dyke walkers. *Offa's Dyke House* (☎ 01547-529816, 4 High St, 2S/2T/3D) is an excellent place. They charge £20 for B&B.

The *George and Dragon* (☎ 01547-528532, Broad St, 3T/2D) has converted the stables at the back and furnished them with tools and bric-a-brac. Charges are £25 per person per night plus a supplement for single occupancy.

There are two reliable B&Bs along West St, both charging £20 for a night: *9 West St* (☎ 01547-529021, 1T/1D) run by Bob and Anne Maslen-Jones and Mrs Roberton's *Wesley House* (☎ 01547-520296, West St, 1S/1T/1D).

The *Red Lion* pub (☎ 01547-528231, 1D/4F), on the corner of Church St and West St, is a homespun place and with luck there will be Old Speckled Hen on draught in the bar. B&B is from £20 per person.

The *Fleece House* (☎ 01547-520168, Market St, 6T) caters for walkers and thoughtfully provides a colourful bench to sit on when removing your boots before going indoors. B&B costs from £25 and if you are content with a light breakfast they will deduct £2 from the bill. The restaurant menu looks interesting.

For something that's a cut above the rest, try *The Great House* (☎ 01547-529123, 🖥 www.oldmansionhouse.freese rve.co.uk, Bridge St, 1S/2T) a listed Jacobean townhouse with panelled rooms.

❏ **Glyndwr's Way**

It is not uncommon for wayfarers doing the Offa's Dyke Path to be so captivated by the area that they think of returning to renew their acquaintance with mid-Wales. Such enthusiasts could well turn to Glyndwr's Way which can either be linked to the Offa's Dyke Path or tackled on its own. It meets the Offa's Dyke Path in two places, east of Welshpool and at Knighton and visits many sites associated with the 15th-century hero Owain Glyndwr.

The 132-mile (212km) route describes a rough circle starting and finishing in Knighton. Walking clockwise, the trail goes west through the Radnorshire hills to Machynlleth then crosses the Cambrian Mountains to touch Lake Vyrnwy before wandering east to Welshpool to join the Offa's Dyke Path south to Knighton through the rolling Shropshire hills. Less well known than the Offa's Dyke Path, Glyndwr's Way is nonetheless a splendid route through a variety of marvellous country that would otherwise be overlooked. If you have time, go for it without hesitation. If not, plan to return another day.

For further information contact the Glyndwr's Way Officer (☎ 01654-703376, 🖥 www.glyndwrsway.co.uk), Powys County Council, Heol Maengwyn, Machynlleth, Powys, SY20 8EE.

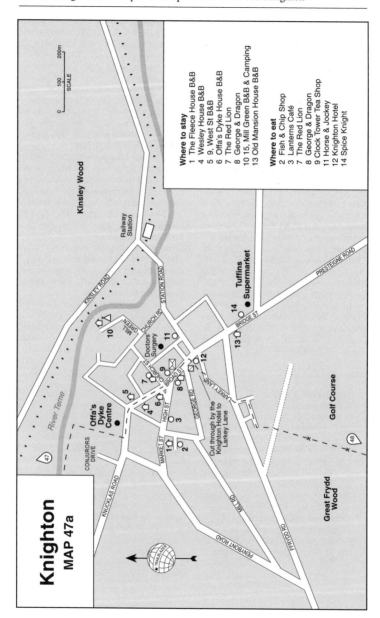

Knighton
MAP 47a

Where to stay
1 The Fleece House B&B
4 Wesley House B&B
5 West St B&B
6 Offa's Dyke House B&B
7 The Red Lion
8 George & Dragon
10, 15, Mill Green B&B & Camping
13 Old Mansion House B&B

Where to eat
2 Fish & Chip Shop
3 Lanterns Café
7 The Red Lion
8 George & Dragon
9 Clock Tower Tea Shop
11 Horse & Jockey
12 Knighton Hotel
14 Spice Knight

All the rooms are en suite and the charge is £23.50 plus £12.75 for an evening meal.

Where to eat
Knighton cannot be described as the gastronomic capital of the Borders but if it's fast food you're after there's the obligatory *chip shop* on Castle Rd (Mon–Sat 12–2pm, 5–10.30pm) and an Indian Restaurant, *Spice Knight Balti House* (☎ 01547-528510) on Bridge St.

The *George and Dragon* (see p137) and *Red Lion* (see p137) do standard pub grub and you have a choice of the *Horse and Jockey* (☎ 01547-520062) or the steak bar at the *Knighton Hotel* (☎ 01547-520530) for more formal meals.

The Clock Tower Tea Shop (☎ 01547-528354) is a good place for a coffee and they also do lunchtime meals of a rather conventional sort, such as cheese and onion flan with jacket potato and coleslaw for £3.90, or lasagne with jacket potato for the same price.

Lanterns Café (☎ 01547-528922, Mon 9.30am–2.30pm, Tues–Sat 9.30am–4pm) in The Narrows offers all-day breakfasts and coffee.

KNIGHTON TO KINGTON   MAPS 47–53

This 13^1/$_2$-mile (22km) section fits conveniently into a day's walking of **6 to 6**^{1}/$_2$ **hours**. Knighton is left behind with a stiff climb up to the golf links, then the route becomes agricultural with more of the all-too-familiar stiles to add to your tally. At least you see plenty of the Dyke on this stretch, in places high and formidable with a well-defined ditch.

Two hills are crossed, **Hawthorn Hill** and **Furrow Hill**, fine open airy walking that will raise your spirits and put a spring in your step. **Dolley Green** is merely a point on the map but for anyone intending to stay in **Presteigne**, a wise choice, your B&B host will almost certainly collect you from here and deliver you back to resume the walk the next day.

More switchbacks follow and more agricultural perambulations with plenty of walking on top of the Dyke. Over **Rushock Hill** you encounter extraordinary scenery, bracken and gorse, heathland and wooded country, that is full of variety followed by a summit ridge with nothing but the wind and soaring buzzards for company.

The long descent to **Kington** ensnares you in a tiresome succession of fields where the waymarking needs improving until the sight of a manicured green tells you that you are on course – another golf course, to be exact, the highest in England. Luckily the final mile into Kington is probably the best waymarked section along the entire path, so honours are even. You approach the town by the back door, over a fast by-pass and a footbridge leading to neat bungalows and into The Square where two pubs vie for your custom.

❏ **Important note – walking times**
Unless otherwise specified, **all times in this book refer only to the time spent walking**. You will need to add 20-30% to allow for rests, photography, checking the map, drinking water etc. When planning the day's hike count on 5-7 hours actual walking.

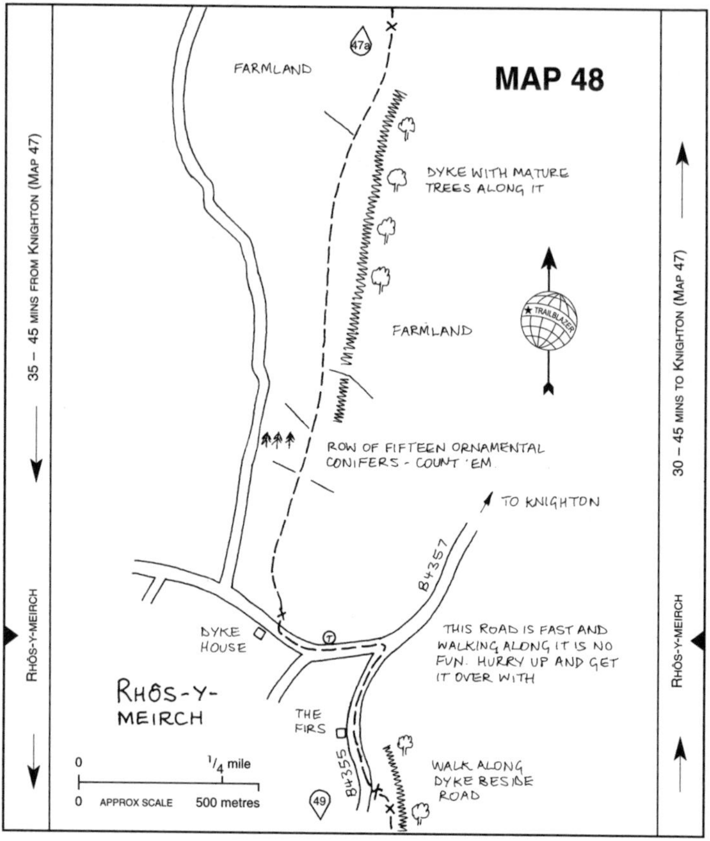

MAP 48

47a ×

FARMLAND

DYKE WITH MATURE TREES ALONG IT

★ TRAILBLAZER

FARMLAND

35 – 45 MINS FROM KNIGHTON (MAP 47)

30 – 45 MINS TO KNIGHTON (MAP 47)

ROW OF FIFTEEN ORNAMENTAL CONIFERS - COUNT 'EM.

TO KNIGHTON

B4357

RHOS-Y-MEIRCH

RHOS-Y-MEIRCH

DYKE HOUSE

17

THIS ROAD IS FAST AND WALKING ALONG IT IS NO FUN. HURRY UP AND GET IT OVER WITH

RHÔS-Y-MEIRCH

THE FIRS

B4355

WALK ALONG DYKE BESIDE ROAD

49

0 — ¼ mile
0 APPROX SCALE 500 metres

DOLLEY GREEN **MAP 50**

Dolley Green itself has no services but there are two campsites and a B&B very close by. *Gumma Farm* (☎ 01547-560243, 1S/1T/1D) is reached by walking east from Dolley Green to the bridge over the River Lugg then taking the next right along the Discoed road where you will find the farm on the left. B&B costs from £23 per person. Tents cost £2 and you can book an evening meal for £13.50. The alternative will mean a walk of 1½ miles (2km) into Presteigne along a fast road, so do take a torch for the return. The other, more commercial, site is *Rock Bridge Park Caravan Site* (☎ 01547-560300). It is well signposted and situated beside the B4356 about a mile east of Dolley Green heading towards Presteigne. Single tents are welcome at a rather steep charge of £5 per person including the use of a decent shower block. There is no shop on site but there are shops open in Presteigne until 10pm.

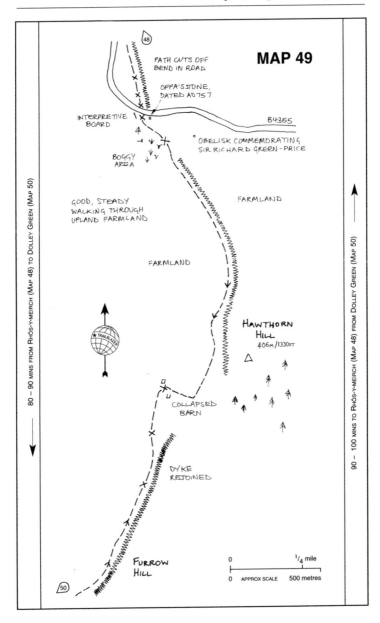

MAP 49

48

PATH CUTS OFF
BEND IN ROAD

OFFA'S STONE,
DATED AD 757

INTERPRETIVE
BOARD

B4365

OBELISK COMMEMORATING
SIR RICHARD GREEN-PRICE

BOGGY
AREA

GOOD, STEADY
WALKING THROUGH
UPLAND FARMLAND

FARMLAND

FARMLAND

HAWTHORN
HILL
406m/1330ft

★ TRAILBLAZER

COLLAPSED
BARN

DYKE
REJOINED

FURROW
HILL

50

0   ¼ mile

0   APPROX SCALE   500 metres

80 – 90 MINS FROM RHÔS-Y-MEIRCH (MAP 48) TO DOLLEY GREEN (MAP 50)

90 – 100 MINS TO RHÔS-Y-MEIRCH (MAP 48) FROM DOLLEY GREEN (MAP 50)

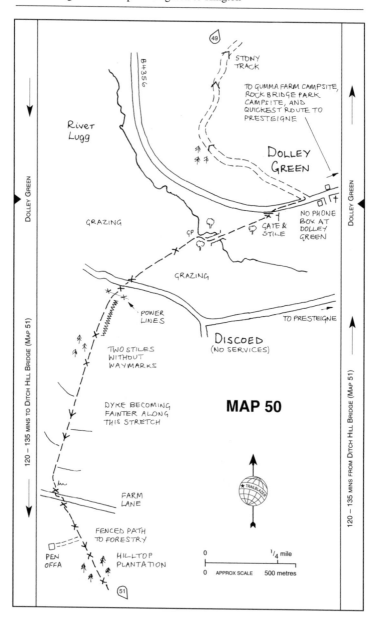

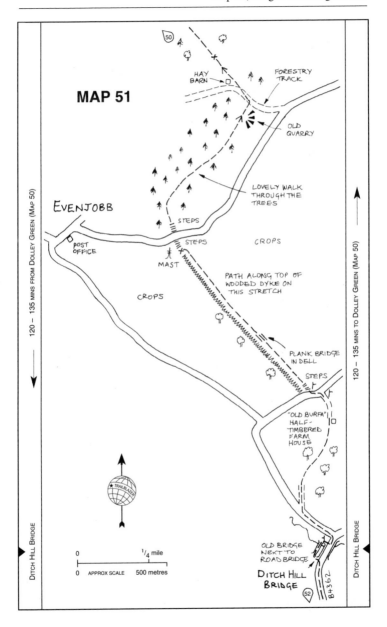

MAP 51

EVENJOBB

POST OFFICE

HAY BARN

FORESTRY TRACK

OLD QUARRY

LOVELY WALK THROUGH THE TREES

STEPS

STEPS

MAST

CROPS

CROPS

PATH ALONG TOP OF WOODED DYKE ON THIS STRETCH

PLANK BRIDGE IN DELL

STEPS

"OLD BURFA" HALF-TIMBERED FARM HOUSE

120 – 135 MINS FROM DOLLEY GREEN (MAP 50)

120 – 135 MINS TO DOLLEY GREEN (MAP 50)

DITCH HILL BRIDGE

DITCH HILL BRIDGE

0   ¼ mile

APPROX SCALE

0   500 metres

TRAILBLAZER

OLD BRIDGE NEXT TO ROAD BRIDGE

DITCH HILL BRIDGE

B4362

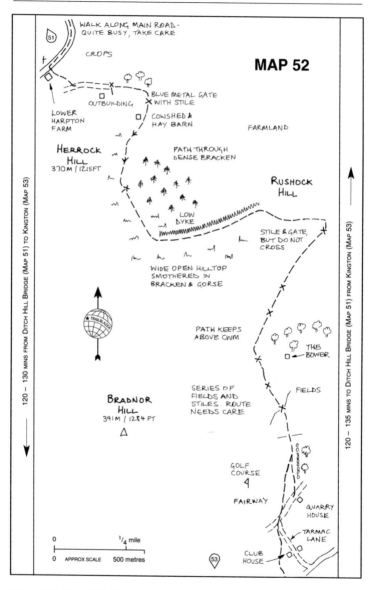

MAP 52

WALK ALONG MAIN ROAD - QUITE BUSY, TAKE CARE

(51)

CROPS

BLUE METAL GATE WITH STILE

OUTBUILDING

LOWER HARPTON FARM

COWSHED & HAY BARN

FARMLAND

HERROCK HILL 370M / 1215FT

PATH THROUGH DENSE BRACKEN

RUSHOCK HILL

LOW DYKE

STILE & GATE, BUT DO NOT CROSS

WIDE OPEN HILLTOP SMOTHERED IN BRACKEN & GORSE

TRAILBLAZER

PATH KEEPS ABOVE CWM

THE BOWER

BRADNOR HILL 391M / 1284 PT

SERIES OF FIELDS AND STILES ROUTE NEEDS CARE

FIELDS

GOLF COURSE

FAIRWAY

QUARRY HOUSE

TARMAC LANE

CLUB HOUSE

(53)

0 ¼ mile
0 APPROX SCALE 500 metres

120 – 130 MINS FROM DITCH HILL BRIDGE (MAP 51) TO KINGTON (MAP 53)

120 – 135 MINS TO DITCH HILL BRIDGE (MAP 51) FROM KINGTON (MAP 53)

(Opposite) Top: Chirk Castle (see p99). **Bottom:** Canoeing in the River Dee, Llangollen (see p90).

PRESTEIGNE *(LLANANDRAS)*

Only 2¼ miles (4km) off the Offa's Dyke Path from Dolley Green, Presteigne is a useful little town with accommodation and services of a quality which singles it out as a pleasant place to break your journey. Most B&B hosts will be happy to collect you from Dolley Green. The best B&B, *Carmel Court* (☎ 01544- 267986, 1S/3T/5D /1F), is a former Carmelite nunnery charging from £22.50 for B&B with a breakfast unequalled from sea to shining sea. The house is homely with a guests' lounge and helpful, attentive hosts. The chapel next door was built by nuns with their bare hands whilst living in sheds in the grounds. A photo album in the breakfast room tells the story, so no complaining of hardship on your day's walk ahead! For an evening meal there is an unusual restaurant in the High St, *The Hat Shop* (☎ 01544-260017, Mon–Sat 12–2pm, 6.30–9pm), offering an imaginative choice of food with an emphasis on healthy eating including a range of kebabs at £6.50 with salad, hoummus and pitta bread. With wine and coffee to finish, a meal here will cost about £12. How's that for good value?

You can find **supermarkets**, **cash-points** and a **post office** in town and at least one good tourist attraction, the **Judge's Lodging**, (☎ 01544-260650, 🖳 www.judges lodging.org.uk) a former winner of Britain's Local Museum of the Year Award. The restored judges' apartments with servants' quarters below give a fascinating insight into the upstairs-downstairs world of the Victorian era. From March to October it's open daily 10am–6pm, and in November and December from Wednesday to Sunday 10am–4pm; admission £4.50. It also houses the **tourist information centre**.

The **taxi** firm AT Garrod (☎ 01544-267220) is used to transporting walkers and their luggage to all points of the compass, even over long distances, eg you could park in Presteigne and get them to take you to Chepstow from where you could walk north to your car again. They are flexible and the only thing to worry about is the cost.

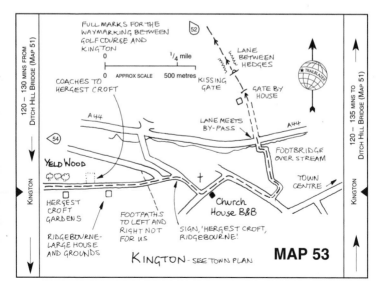

(**Opposite**) **Top**: Old Burfa Farm (see p143). **Bottom**: In the woods near Knighton (see p143).

KINGTON   MAP 53a

Although on the western side of Offa's Dyke, Kington has always been an English town and belongs to Herefordshire. Its charms are rather faded and offer more to the motorized tourist than to the walker.

The church is worth a visit, a fine building started in the 12th century and later added to, especially in the reign of Queen Victoria. In a side chapel is the effigy of Sir Thomas Vaughan and his wife, Ellen the Terrible, named, rumour has it, for her cooking.

Services

The services in Kington are not extensive. The **tourist information centre** on Mill St (☎ 01544-230778) has plenty of leaflets but isn't always open when you need it. The opening times from Easter to September Mon–Fri 10am–5pm and it's closed for lunch 1–2pm.

There are **buses** to Hereford, Ludlow, Presteigne, Bishop's Castle and Knighton (see public transport map, p38-9). **Taxis** are available from out of town; try Country Cabs (☎ 01544-267976) who are familiar with the needs of walkers.

The town possesses three **cashpoints**, one at Barclays on the High St, one at the Spar **supermarket** (Mon–Sat 7am–11pm, Sun 8am–11pm) and one at the BP garage on Headbrook. Otherwise you can cash a cheque at HSBC Bank or at the **post office** (early closing Wed) provided you have a cheque book with you.

There is a **health centre** (☎ 01544-230302) at The Meads, off Victoria Rd, and a **laundrette** (Mon–Sun 7.30am–9pm) near the post office on Bridge St.

Market day is Tuesday and **early closing** Wednesday and, believe me, when they say early closing they mean it.

Where to stay

Fleece Meadow Caravan and Camping Park (☎ 01544- 231235, Mill St) is an efficient riverside site where they charge £3 per person. You can also **camp** at the B&B at *Bell Cottage* on Church Rd (☎ 01544-230596) for £4 a head including a bath and you can get breakfast, too. They also do

B&B for £22 per person. *Cambridge Cottage* (☎ 01544 -231300, 19 Church St, 1S/1F) also has space for **tents** at £2.50 a head or you could sleep in a bed for £19.

Church House (☎ 01544-230534, Church Rd, 1T/1D) is right on the route and only a short walk from the pub. It will cost you £25 for the night.

Another small yet comfortable B&B, this one in a modern bungalow, is *2 Bradnor View Close* (☎ 01544-231208, 1S/1T) charging a remarkable £15, possibly the cheapest B&B on the entire walk.

The Royal Oak (☎ 01544-230484, Church St, 1S/2T/1D/1F) is a genuine old-style inn with a welcoming host and hostess with simple, straightforward, clean accommodation and good, homely meals. The charge for a night's B&B is £20 per person and it may be possible to camp here (£3 per person; £2 for a shower).

The Swan Hotel (☎ 01544-230510, 🖳 www.swanhotelkington.co.uk, Church St, 1S/1T/2D/2F) nearly opposite is a couple of rungs higher up the ladder. They charge £32.50 for B&B and the bar has quite a classy menu.

Where to eat

Eating out in Kington is not likely to be an experience to remember but there are several pubs that do the usual pub grub. Try *The Queens Head* (☎ 01544-231106, Bridge St) which promises home-cooked meals.

There are several Chinese restaurants: *Li Wain* (☎ 01544-231089, Church St), closed on Monday and Tuesday and also the *Taste of Orient* (☎ 01544-231291, High St) which is closed on Tuesday.

You won't find much in the way of fast food but there is a reliable chippy, *Kington Fish and Chip Shop* (☎ 01544-230906, 17 High St) open at lunchtime and in the evening, again except Monday and Tuesday when the town is dead. There are one or two coffee shops in the town but as with other shops their hours of opening are erratic, depending on if there are people about. If not, they tend to close up and go home.

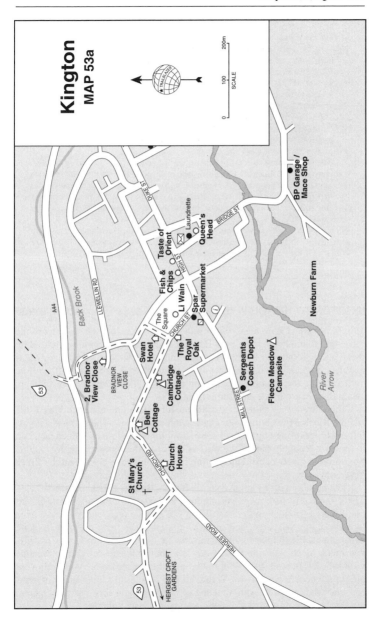

Kington
MAP 53a

SCALE
0   100   200m

BP Garage /
Mace Shop

DUKE ST

Back Brook

A44

LLEWELLIN RD

Newburn Farm

Laundrette

BRIDGE ST

Taste of
Orient

Queen's
Head

HIGH ST

Fish &
Chips

Li Wain

Spar
Supermarket

The Square

CHURCH ST

River Arrow

2, Bradnor
View Close

BRADNOR
VIEW CLOSE

Swan
Hotel

The
Royal
Oak

Sergeants
Coach Depot

Fleece Meadow
Campsite

Cambridge
Cottage

MILL STREET

Bell
Cottage

St Mary's
Church

Church
House

CHURCH RD

HERGEST ROAD

HERGEST CROFT
GARDENS

53

❏ **The Marches**

This term is used to describe the border country between England and Wales which has been contested and fought over for centuries. It has now become peacefully established as a kind of middle ground, partly Welsh, partly English, characterized by its rounded hills, wooded river valleys and secluded fields and lanes.

It is an area populated by a race who have been described as the Anglo-Welsh, the place names straying either side of the border as if uncertain to which side they belong. Genuine border towns such as Oswestry, Montgomery, Knighton, Kington, Presteigne and Hay-on-Wye are all ports of call on the walker's progression along the Dyke and the unique identity of these towns will not be lost on the discerning observer.

The term 'March' derives from an Anglo-Saxon word *mearc* meaning simply a boundary. It was William the Conqueror who resolved to sort out the lawless Welsh once and for all by granting Marcher lordships to his followers. These were virtually independent fiefdoms with the authority to act as they saw fit, owing only their final allegiance to the king. They could impose the force of law on the country, raise taxes and build castles, many of which remain in places like Chepstow, Monmouth, White and Chirk, all milestones along the Offa's Dyke Path. The Marcher lords were a significant factor in the control of England and names such as Roger Mortimer, William Fitzosbern and Gilbert de Clare remind us of turbulent times.

KINGTON TO HAY-ON-WYE   MAPS 53–60

This **14^1/2-mile (23km, 6^1/2–7^1/2hrs)** walk includes possibly the best part of the entire trail, namely the route over **Hergest Ridge**, an open common grazed by sheep and wild ponies. Farmers cut the bracken on Hergest Ridge and bale it like they do grass elsewhere, for use as bedding for their animals. It can't be used as fodder, being poisonous. By cutting it they allow grass to grow through, making better use of the land for grazing.

There are lovely views of the **Shropshire Hills** and ahead to **Hay Bluff** and the **Black Mountains**, your challenge for tomorrow. The going is delightfully easy on springy turf, cropped by sheep for centuries and indeed raced on in the past. Roughly half of the walk is on roads, the route having to wind its way through a network of lanes before it meets the noisy A438 and the **River Wye**.

The highlight of the latter stages is **Bettws Dingle**, a dark and shaded glen where the broad path takes you through a plantation of conifers and mixed tree cover, silent and mysterious. When you emerge on to the A438 you have to walk along the verge, and must keep well away from the tarmac along which the traffic thunders with no thought for the humble wayfarer. Crossing, you make touch with the languorous Wye but sadly no delightful riverside walk follows. Instead, a series of fields has to be crossed before you attain your goal of the book town **Hay-on-Wye**. This will have been a longish day of highs and lows and it will be with a feeling of relief that you seek out your accommodation, too tired at first to browse among the dusty volumes.

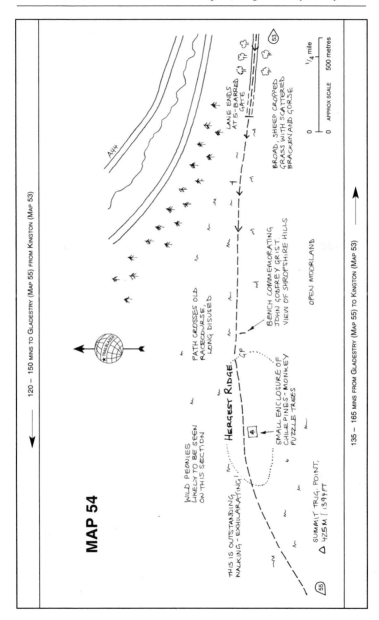

MAP 54

A44

THIS IS OUTSTANDING
WALKING – EXHILARATING!

WILD PEONIES
LIKELY TO BE SEEN
ON THIS SECTION

HERGEST RIDGE

PATH CROSSES OLD
RACECOURSE,
LONG DISUSED

BENCH COMMEMORATING
JOHN GODFREY GRIST,
VIEW OF SHROPSHIRE HILLS

OPEN MOORLAND

SMALL ENCLOSURE OF
CHILE PINES – MONKEY
PUZZLE TREES

△ SUMMIT TRIG. POINT,
425 M / 1394 FT

LANE ENDS
AT 5-BARRED
GATE

BROAD, SHEEP CROPPED
GRASS WITH SCATTERED
BRACKEN AND GORSE

53

0 ¼ mile
0 500 metres
APPROX SCALE

55

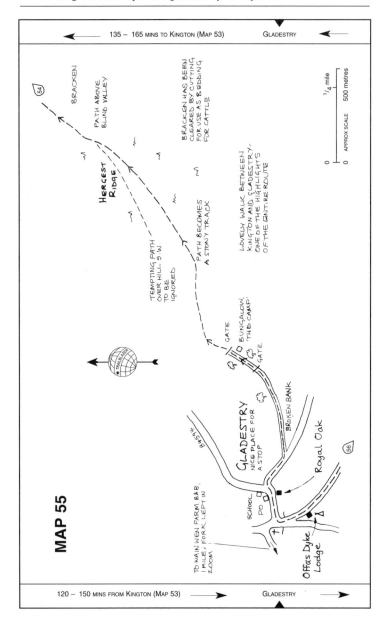

MAP 55

54

BRACKEN

PATH ABOVE
BLIND VALLEY

BRACKEN HAS BEEN
CLEARED BY CUTTING
FOR USE AS BEDDING
FOR CATTLE

HERGEST RIDGE

LOVELY WALK BETWEEN
KINGTON AND GLADESTRY-
ONE OF THE HIGHLIGHTS
OF THE ENTIRE ROUTE

PATH BECOMES
A STONY TRACK

TEMPTING PATH
OVER HILL, S.W.
TO BE
IGNORED

¹/₄ mile

500 metres

0   APPROX SCALE

0

★ TRAILBLAZER

GATE

BUNGALOW
'THE CAMP'

GATE

BROKEN BANK

GLADESTRY
NICE PLACE FOR
A STOP

Royal Oak

56

B4594

SCHOOL

PO

TO WAIN WEN FARM B&B,
1 MILE, FORK LEFT IN
2.00KM

Offas Dyke
Lodge

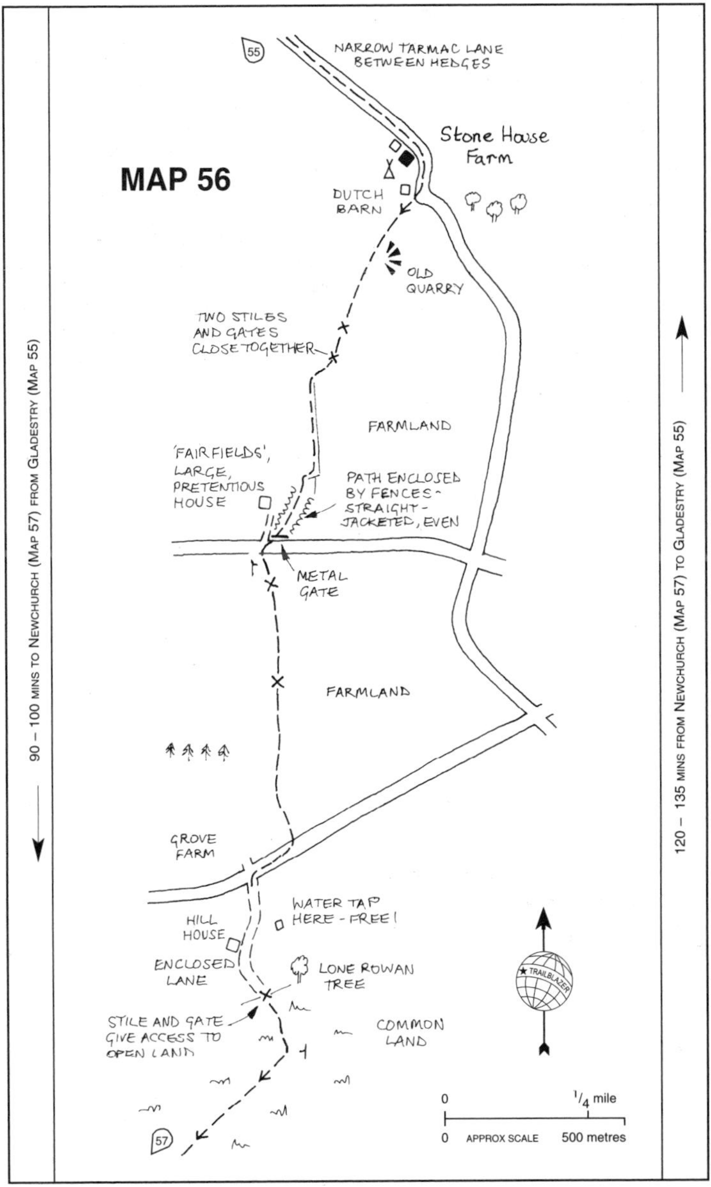

MAP 56

NARROW TARMAC LANE BETWEEN HEDGES

55

Stone House Farm

DUTCH BARN

OLD QUARRY

TWO STILES AND GATES CLOSE TOGETHER

FARMLAND

'FAIRFIELDS', LARGE, PRETENTIOUS HOUSE

PATH ENCLOSED BY FENCES - STRAIGHT - JACKETED, EVEN

METAL GATE

FARMLAND

GROVE FARM

HILL HOUSE

ENCLOSED LANE

WATER TAP HERE - FREE!

LONE ROWAN TREE

STILE AND GATE GIVE ACCESS TO OPEN LAND

COMMON LAND

57

90 – 100 MINS TO NEWCHURCH (MAP 57) FROM GLADESTRY (MAP 55)

120 – 135 MINS FROM NEWCHURCH (MAP 57) TO GLADESTRY (MAP 55)

TRAILBLAZER

0   1/4 mile

0   APPROX SCALE   500 metres

GLADESTRY   MAP 55

Gladestry would be a good place to stop. It's a pity it falls part way between two towns both with extensive facilities, otherwise its popularity would be assured. One of Gladestry's main claims to fame, perhaps its only one, is the *Royal Oak* (☎ 01544-370669, 2S/1T/1D), an excellent hostelry strongly biased in favour of walkers. Meals are taken in the bar. A room here will cost £20 each or you can **camp** for £2 including a bath.

Opposite the pub is the **post office**. The village shop has sadly succumbed to commercial pressures in common with many rural businesses and has closed.

For B&B, the *Offa's Dyke Lodge* (☎ 01544-370341, 2T/2D) is an establishment

with a swimming pool earning it four richly deserved stars from the tourist board: B&B is from £25, **camping** £2.50 and an evening meal £15.

Half a mile from the village but on the path is *Stone House Farm* (☎ 01544-370651, 1S/1T/1D) charging £16 for B&B, with evening meals by arrangement; camping costs £2 a head. However, Stone House was closed early 2004 for refurbishment so you'll need to check that it has opened again.

A little further out is *Wain Wen Farm* (☎ 01544-370226, 2S/1T/1D) another bargain at £20 for B&B plus evening meals by arrangement.

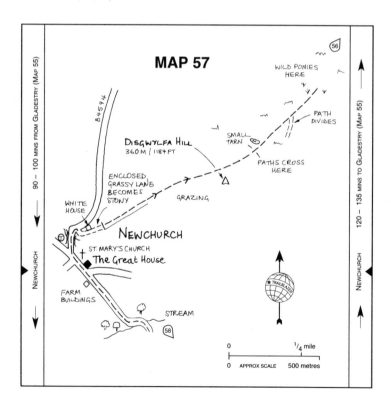

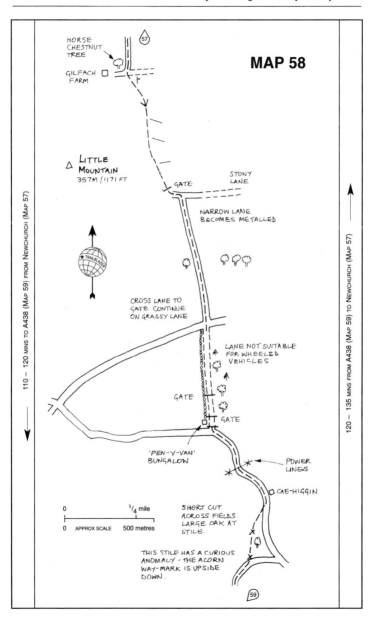

HORSE CHESTNUT TREE

57

GILFACH FARM

MAP 58

F

△ LITTLE MOUNTAIN
357M / 1171 FT

GATE

STONY LANE

NARROW LANE BECOMES METALLED

★ TRAILBLAZER

CROSS LANE TO GATE. CONTINUE ON GRASSY LANE

LANE NOT SUITABLE FOR WHEELED VEHICLES

GATE

GATE

'PEN-Y-VAN' BUNGALOW

POWER LINES

CAE-HIGGIN

0   ¼ mile
0   APPROX SCALE   500 metres

SHORT CUT ACROSS FIELDS. LARGE OAK AT STILE.

THIS STILE HAS A CURIOUS ANOMALY - THE ACORN WAY-MARK IS UPSIDE DOWN.

59

110 – 120 MINS TO A438 (MAP 59) FROM NEWCHURCH (MAP 57)

120 – 135 MINS FROM A438 (MAP 59) TO NEWCHURCH (MAP 57)

NEWCHURCH   MAP 57

There are no facilities here at all except a telephone kiosk and one B&B, *The Great House* (☎ 01544-370257, 2F, sleeps 6), a wonderful old building where £20 will accommodate you for the night and £10 will feed you. **St Mary's Church** occupies an ancient sacred site, probably of pre-Christian origin. Graves are grouped on the south side, the north side by local custom being the Devil's side. In the churchyard to the right of the steps leading up from the road lies the grave of the Vaughan family. The Rev David Vaughan was curate of the parish for 17 years and then vicar for 33 years until his death, aged 83 years in 1903. Under the granite cross lies his daughter,

Emmeline, who died aged 14 years. Her sad figure haunts a passage in *Kilvert's Diary* of 14 March 1873: 'As I stooped over the green grave by the churchyard gate, placing the primrose bunches in a cross upon the turf, large flakes of snow still fell thickly upon us but melted as they fell, and the great yew tree bent weeping upon the grave.' The yew tree fell in a great storm in January 1991, narrowly missing the church. It had stood for 1100 years. Within the church these lines by RS Thomas are inscribed: 'In cities that have outgrown their promise, people are becoming pilgrims again if not to this place then to the re-creation of it in their own spirits.'

HAY-ON-WYE (*Y-GELLI*)   MAP 60a

Don't miss the opportunity of an overnight stay in one of the most interesting towns on your route. In recent times Hay-on-Wye has acquired a considerable reputation on account of the numerous secondhand book-shops on its narrow streets. Bibliophiles and the curious can browse for hours, fasci-nated by the cornucopia of titles on sale from cheap paperbacks to antiquarian rari-ties costing astronomical sums. Hay-on-Wye was effectively rescued from obscuri-ty by Richard Booth, the self-styled 'King of Hay' who resolved to turn a previously rundown town into the second-hand book capital of the Western world. Today it has a bookshop for every 30 of the population.

Richard Booth resides in the **castle** which houses yet another bookshop including a courtyard open to the sky where the walls are lined with books at the single price of 50p. One of the biggest bookshops is housed in the old **Hay Cinema**, (☎ 01497-820071), open every day (Mon–Sat 9am–7.30pm, Sun 11.30am–5.30pm) except Christmas Day and Easter Sunday.

Every year in late May, Hay hosts the **Hay Festival of Literature** when the great and the good from the world of books visit to speak on their chosen subject or promote their latest publication. It's now an interna-tional event: recent speakers have included past US presidents.

It makes sense to avoid the town during the festival since you won't get a room or, if you are lucky enough to track one down, you'll be charged twice the price because of demand.

Another busy period is during the **Royal Welsh Show** held at nearby Builth Wells in late July, since this also makes great demands on the accommodation available in the town.

Transport

There is no rail link, the nearest station being about 20 miles (32km) away at Hereford, but there are five **buses** a day to and from Hereford and six to Brecon (see public transport map, p39). You won't have any luck if you want a bus to Kington, which is a pity for those doing the trail in daily stages and thus trying to get back to their starting point. It will mean a taxi cost-ing around £15.

Taxi operators include Border Taxis (☎ 01497-821266).

Services

Hay is well supplied with all the services you're likely to need. A starting point for your enquiries is the excellent **tourist infor-mation centre** (☎ 01497-820144, 10am–5pm daily, closed 1–2pm for lunch in the winter) adjoining the Craft Centre on Oxford Rd.

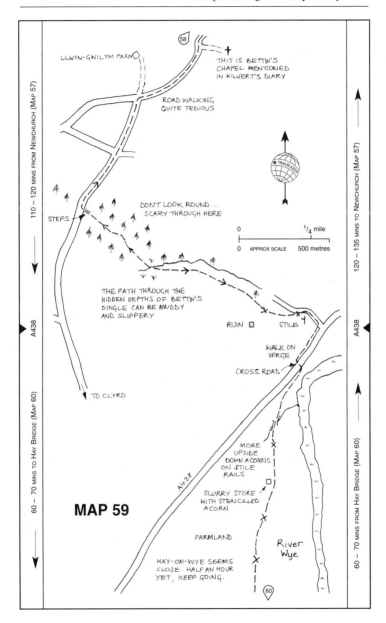

58

LLWYN-GWILYM FARM

THIS IS BETTW'S CHAPEL MENTIONED IN KILVERT'S DIARY

ROAD WALKING QUITE TEDIOUS

★ TRAILBLAZER

DON'T LOOK ROUND... SCARY THROUGH HERE

STEPS

0   1/4 mile
0   APPROX SCALE   500 metres

THE PATH THROUGH THE HIDDEN DEPTHS OF BETTW'S DINGLE CAN BE MUDDY AND SLIPPERY

RUIN

STILE

WALK ON VERGE

CROSS ROAD

TO CLYRO

MORE UPSIDE DOWN ACORNS ON STILE RAILS

A438

SLURRY STORE WITH STENCILLED ACORN

MAP 59

FARMLAND

HAY-ON-WYE SEEMS CLOSE. HALF AN HOUR YET, KEEP GOING.

River Wye

60

110 – 120 MINS FROM NEWCHURCH (MAP 57)

A438

60 – 70 MINS TO HAY BRIDGE (MAP 60)

120 – 135 MINS TO NEWCHURCH (MAP 57)

A438

60 – 70 MINS FROM HAY BRIDGE (MAP 60)

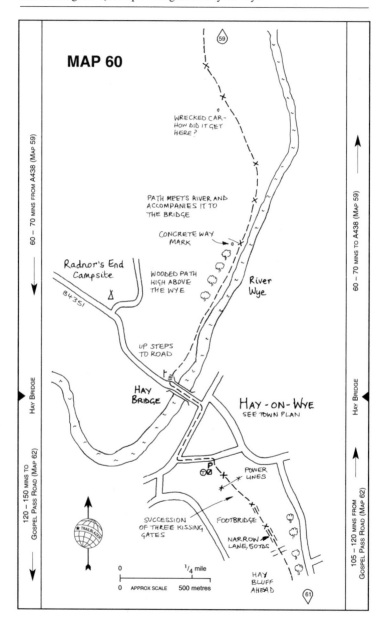

MAP 60

59

WRECKED CAR –
HOW DID IT GET
HERE?

PATH MEETS RIVER AND
ACCOMPANIES IT TO
THE BRIDGE

CONCRETE WAY
MARK

Radnor's End
Campsite

B4351

WOODED PATH
HIGH ABOVE
THE WYE

River
Wye

UP STEPS
TO ROAD

HAY
BRIDGE

HAY-ON-WYE
SEE TOWN PLAN

P

POWER
LINES

SUCCESSION
OF THREE KISSING
GATES

FOOTBRIDGE

NARROW
LANE, 50 YDS

HAY
BLUFF
AHEAD

61

TRAILBLAZER

0   1/4 mile

0   500 metres
APPROX SCALE

60 – 70 MINS FROM A438 (MAP 59)

HAY BRIDGE

120 – 150 MINS TO
GOSPEL PASS ROAD (MAP 62)

60 – 70 MINS TO A438 (MAP 59)

HAY BRIDGE

105 – 120 MINS FROM
GOSPEL PASS ROAD (MAP 62)

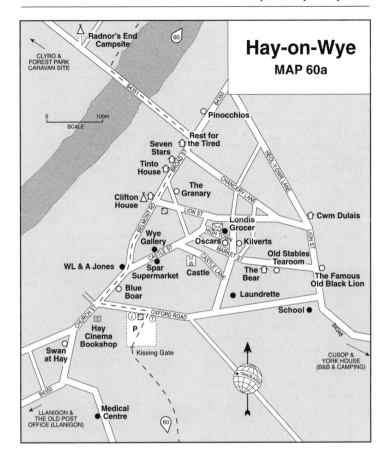

Hay-on-Wye
MAP 60a

Three **banks** in the town have **cashpoints** (Barclays, NatWest and HSBC) and the **post office** can be found on the narrow street called High Town.

The major **supermarket** chains are notable by their absence but you will find Londis (Mon–Sat 8am–8pm, Sun 9.30am–6pm) on High Town and there's a Spar (daily 8am–6.30pm) located on Castle St.

WL & A Jones on Church St nearly opposite the Blue Boar pub have a small stock of **camping accessories** including Camping Gaz and Coleman fuel. In the season they are open all week. You will find a **laundrette** (daily 8am–9pm) just off Oxford Rd across from the big public car park. **Market day** is Thursday and **early closing** Tuesday.

Hay is rich in **galleries** which art-lovers will not want to miss if time allows. The Wye Gallery (Mon–Sat 10am–5pm, Sun 11am–4pm) on Castle St has original limited-edition prints of high quality.

Where to stay

Radnor's End Camping (☎ 01497-820780), a five-minute uphill walk from the town, can fit in 15 tents and charges £3.50 per person. The showers are a coin-in-the-slot system so have some change handy. Across the river at Clyro on Painscastle Rd is *Forest Park Caravan Site* (☎ 01497-820156) which will take tents at £6 per tent. *Clifton House* (☎ 01497-821618, 1 Belmont Rd, 1D/1F) is a B&B that also takes tents, charging £25 per person for a bed or £4 if you are under canvas.

Rest for the Tired (☎ 01497-820550, 6 Broad St, 1T/2D) is a nicely furnished B&B above a second-hand bookshop. You'll know it by the buckled bicycle wheel sign, a relic from the days when it was a cherished café for cyclists. The tariff is £22.50 a head for two sharing but beware the single occupancy supplement of £5.

Broad St has a selection of B&Bs worth trying including the *Seven Stars* (☎ 01497-820806, 3T/8D/2F) which has an indoor heated pool and sauna. The charge is from £30 for two or more sharing, £22.50 for single occupancy and £28 for en suite. Also on Broad St is the smaller but no less comfortable *Tinto House* (☎ 01497-820590, 1T/2D/1F) charging from £27.50. They have a nice garden at the back overlooking the River Wye.

Two more B&Bs deserving a mention are *The Bear* (☎ 01497-821302, 💻 www.thebear-hay-on-wye.co.uk, 2 Bear St, 1T/2D), from £24 or £29 for an en suite room, a truly charming establishment furnished in tasteful style, and *Cwm Dulais House* (☎ 01497-820179, 1T/2D, Heol-y-Dwr Ln) where there is space to sit in the garden and enjoy the spectacle of the caged birds, including parakeets and canaries.

If you prefer hotels to the more homely world of the B&B, *Kilverts* (☎ 01497-821042, 2S/3T/5D/1F) is right in the middle of town and ideally placed to catch the buzz. The cost of a room is £35–£40 and in the season it is always busy. It's the best pub in town and the bar meals are a treat.

Ten minutes' walk from the centre of town, *York House* (☎ 01497-820705,

1T/2D/1F) offers B&B for £26 and an evening meal for £16, or you can **camp** on the level lawn for £4 a head; quite expensive by Offa's Dyke Path standards. Showers are taken at the top of the house in a small bathroom set aside for campers.

If all the B&Bs in town are full you could try the *Old Post Office* at Llanigon (☎ 01497-820008, 1T/2D), an interesting and unusual old cottage with low beams and rickety floors, furnished with taste and enterprise by Linda Webb. Rooms cost £20 (£28 en suite) a head and remember not to ask for bacon or sausage at breakfast: the house is vegetarian.

Where to eat

There are **tea shops** and coffee houses aplenty in the town of which those that deserve a mention include *Oscars* (☎ 01497 -821193) opposite the post office, open daily except Tuesday 10.30am–5pm for baguettes, filled jacket potatoes, quiches and various sandwiches. They are also licensed.

Old Stables Tea Room (☎ 01497-820563) on Bear St does nice light lunches and afternoon teas but was only open on Thursdays at the time of writing.

The Granary (☎ 01497-820790) is great for morning coffee and lunch and is open daily from 10am to 5.30pm, sometimes later at busy weekends.

For fast food, try *Pinocchios* (Mon–Fri 12–3pm, 6–10pm, Sat 11am–3pm, 5–11pm, Sun 12–3pm, 5– 10pm) on Broad St with the usual selection of Tex-Mex style food.

The *Blue Boar* (☎ 01497-820884) is a welcoming hostelry at the junction of Oxford Rd and Church St where the beers are Flowers and Brains and the usual bar meals are provided.

Kilverts (☎ 01497-821042) in The Bull Ring in the centre of town is a good bet where a pizza and pasta menu ensures that your evening meal shouldn't cost more than £10 including a pint of Hancocks HB. There are daily specials on the blackboard if you want to push the boat out, such as braised hock of lamb in rich root vegetable and redcurrant sauce for £12 or grilled skate wing with capers and black pepper for £11.

Smart as it may look, the *Swan at Hay* (☎ 01497-821188) also does excellent bar meals.

The Famous Old Black Lion (☎ 01497-820841) on Lion St is a cut above the average, serving mainly gourmet meals and earning an accolade from a national newspaper which places it among the top 100 food inns in the country.

❏ Francis Kilvert (1840–1879)

Francis Kilvert was curate of the parish of Clyro near Hay for seven years from 1865–1872 during which time he kept a diary. Never intended for publication, the wife whom he married five weeks before his sudden death from peritonitis destroyed large parts of it, but the remainder was published in 1938 and achieved immediate notice. Kilvert's simple, honest description of life in the villages around Hay-on-Wye and his love of the countryside and in particular his eye for pretty young girls have endeared him to a reading public ever since.

He records with close attention to detail the landscape which he loved and through which he constantly walked. Many of the places he describes are much the same today as they were in the Victorian era.

Kilvert left Clyro to become vicar of Chippenham in Wiltshire but returned to what was then Radnorshire to become vicar of Bredwardine for the last year of his life. He is buried there and on his tombstone are the words 'He being dead, yet speaketh'. He was 38 years old when he died.

He would not have welcomed Offa's Dyke walkers judging by this entry from his diary of April 5, 1870:

'What was our horror to see two tourists with staves and shoulder belts all complete postured among the ruins in an attitude of admiration, one of them discoursing learnedly to his gaping companion and pointing out objects of interest with his stick. If there is one thing more hateful than another it is being told what to admire and having objects pointed out to one with a stick. Of all noxious animals too the most noxious is a tourist. And of all tourists the most vulgar, illbred, offensive and loathsome is the British tourist.'

HAY-ON-WYE TO PANDY   MAPS 60–69

This **17¹/₂ miles (28km, 8¹/₂–10hrs)** is one of the most demanding days on the entire walk and needs some thought before it is tackled. For the average walker, traversing the long spine of the **Hatterrall Ridge** will call for some preparation, both mentally and practically. Food, drink (essential en route) and clothing must be adequate for the terrain which is wild, open moorland around 600 metres (2000ft) in altitude with hardly any shelter and few options for escaping to the valleys to the east or west.

The going underfoot is good, aided in many places by heavy mill flagstones laid end to end as part of the erosion control programme by Brecon Beacons National Park Authority. These won't please everybody since they introduce a man-made element to what are natural surroundings but it is an alternative to the erosion steadily getting worse as the traffic in walkers increases.

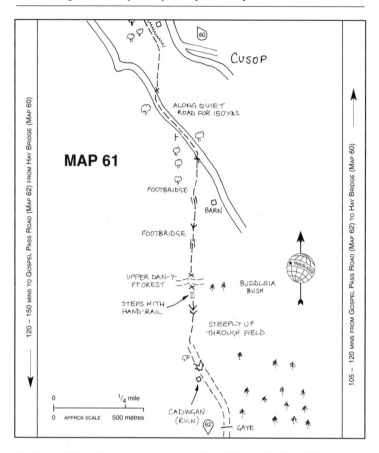

MAP 61

CUSOP

60

ALONG QUIET
ROAD FOR 150YDS

FOOTBRIDGE

BARN

FOOTBRIDGE

UPPER DAN-Y-
FFOREST

STEPS WITH
HAND-RAIL

STEEPLY UP
THROUGH FIELD

BUDDLEIA
BUSH

★ TRAILBLAZER

GP

CADWGAN
(RUIN)   62   GATE

0   1/4 mile
0   APPROX SCALE   500 metres

120 – 150 MINS TO GOSPEL PASS ROAD (MAP 62) FROM HAY BRIDGE (MAP 60)

105 – 120 MINS FROM GOSPEL PASS ROAD (MAP 62) TO HAY BRIDGE (MAP 60)

❏ Stone waymarkers on the Hatterrall Ridge
Between the Gospel Pass road and Hatterrall Hill the Brecon Beacons National Park
Authority has erected a series of waymarkers like gravestones with the acorn and
directional details hand carved, as part of a European-funded project for the National
Trail. The design was based on traditional Parish/boundary markers in the Black
Mountains; the Old Red Sandstone came from a quarry near Abergavenny. Local
carvers were employed to carve the stones. They have done a good job although it is
to be feared that erosion will obliterate the text eventually; even now they are not particularly easy to read. Meanwhile they make a welcome addition to the multiplicity
of waymarkings used on the Offa's Dyke Path and chime well with the surroundings.

(Opposite) Top: St Mary's Chapel, Capel-y-ffin (see p167). **Bottom**: Hay Castle (see p154).

Coming off **Hatterrall Hill** the main road at Pandy is clearly seen with houses clustered along it and you are buoyed up by the prospect of the end of your walk in sight. Grit your teeth since it will be another hour before you find yourself in front of a pint at the Lancaster Arms, contemplating the specials menu chalked above the bar and resting your tired limbs. The last two miles (3km) along lanes and through fields lead finally across the railway line and over the river to reach civilization a few yards from the pub's back door.

Where to stay and eat: Hay-on-Wye to Pandy

For most walkers, the section between Hay-on-Wye and Pandy will be undertaken as a challenge for a single day and it is probably best treated as such rather than split into two with an overnight stop. However, if the idea is too daunting or the weather particularly bad the crossing could be broken by an overnight stop in the Vale of Ewyas to the west at **Capel-y-ffyn** or **Llanthony**, or to the east in **Longtown**. The descent off the ridge to either is no problem, but the climb back would be a stiff test of the legs first thing the following morning. Another way to Capel-y-ffyn and Llanthony is to follow the valley road over Gospel Pass (see Maps 62 and 64–66) rather than ascending Hay Bluff and walking along the Hatterrall Ridge. It's just under four miles (6km) along this quiet lane to Capel-y-ffin Youth Hostel, but a rather soul-destroying eight miles (13km) if you wanted to tread tarmac all the way to Llanthony Abbey.

❏ **White Castle**

Between Kington and Llantilio-Crossenny your walk is enriched by the impressive ruins of White Castle. Once known as Llantilio Castle, the white plaster rendering on the outer walls, still visible in places, earned it the name it is known by today.

The castle has many distinctive features, not least the almost complete moat, still filled with water and in the summer a happy hunting ground for dragonflies. This is crossed by a wooden bridge to enter the outer ward through the 13th-century gate. The inner gateway has twin towers that can be climbed via a staircase to a gallery from which marvellous views can be enjoyed, including to the north the prominent scarp of The Skirrid (see p168) with all the land in between that you have traversed on your way. The inner buildings are well preserved and include the remains of a chapel, a hall and the kitchens and there is a deep well covered by a grill from which the garrison would have drawn their water.

White Castle was one of the 'Three Castles' forming a powerful defensive presence in mid-Wales, the other two being Skenfrith and Grosmont, neither as well preserved as White. A walk links them, the 'Three Castles Walk', and signposting can be seen as you emerge on to the lane by the entrance. Even if you don't take the time for a visit you will at least take photographs of these massive towers dominating the surrounding countryside, a reminder of a more troublesome past.

(**Opposite**) **Top**: The knight, the angel and the miller: carvings above Geoffrey's Window, The Priory, Monmouth (see p109). Geoffrey was a 12th century Benedictine monk and chronicler best known as the author of the *History of the Kings of Britain*. **Bottom**: White Castle (see above).

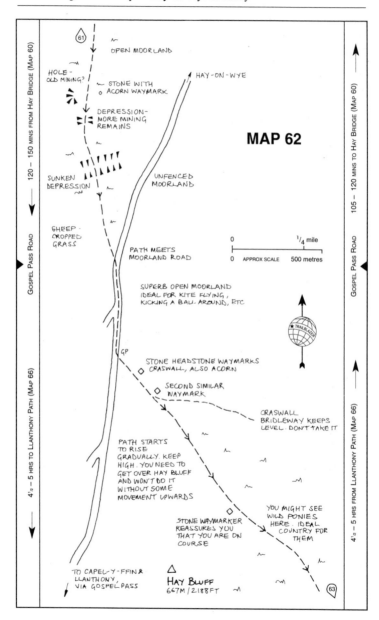

MAP 62

61

OPEN MOORLAND

HOLE - OLD MINING?

STONE WITH o ACORN WAYMARK

HAY-ON-WYE

DEPRESSION - MORE MINING REMAINS

SUNKEN DEPRESSION

UNFENCED MOORLAND

SHEEP - CROPPED GRASS

PATH MEETS MOORLAND ROAD

0   1/4 mile
0   APPROX SCALE   500 metres

SUPERB OPEN MOORLAND IDEAL FOR KITE FLYING, KICKING A BALL AROUND, ETC

★ TRAILBLAZER

GP

STONE HEADSTONE WAYMARKS CRASWALL, ALSO ACORN

SECOND SIMILAR WAYMARK

CRASWALL BRIDLEWAY KEEPS LEVEL. DON'T TAKE IT

PATH STARTS TO RISE GRADUALLY. KEEP HIGH. YOU NEED TO GET OVER HAY BLUFF AND WON'T DO IT WITHOUT SOME MOVEMENT UPWARDS

YOU MIGHT SEE WILD PONIES HERE. IDEAL COUNTRY FOR THEM

STONE WAYMARKER REASSURES YOU THAT YOU ARE ON COURSE

TO CAPEL-Y-FFIN & LLANTHONY, VIA GOSPEL PASS

HAY BLUFF 667M / 2188FT

63

GOSPEL PASS ROAD — 120 – 150 MINS FROM HAY BRIDGE (MAP 60)

4½ – 5 HRS TO LLANTHONY PATH (MAP 66)

GOSPEL PASS ROAD — 105 – 120 MINS TO HAY BRIDGE (MAP 60)

4½ – 5 HRS FROM LLANTHONY PATH (MAP 66)

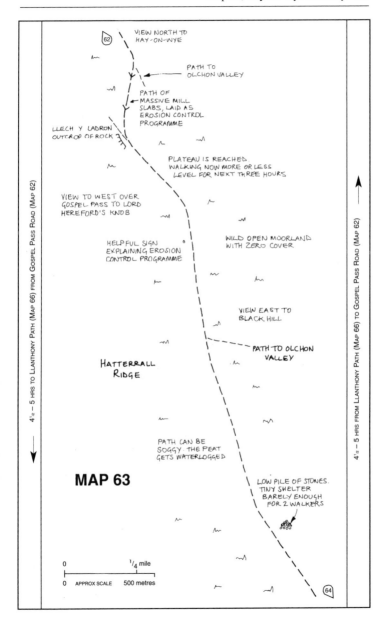

62

VIEW NORTH TO
HAY-ON-WYE

PATH TO
OLCHON VALLEY

PATH OF
MASSIVE MILL
SLABS, LAID AS
EROSION CONTROL
PROGRAMME

LLECH Y LADRON
OUTCROP OF ROCK

PLATEAU IS REACHED.
WALKING NOW MORE OR LESS
LEVEL FOR NEXT THREE HOURS

VIEW TO WEST OVER
GOSPEL PASS TO LORD
HEREFORD'S KNOB

WILD OPEN MOORLAND
WITH ZERO COVER

HELPFUL SIGN
EXPLAINING EROSION
CONTROL PROGRAMME

VIEW EAST TO
BLACK HILL

PATH TO OLCHON
VALLEY

HATTERRALL
RIDGE

PATH CAN BE
SOGGY. THE PEAT
GETS WATERLOGGED

MAP 63

LOW PILE OF STONES.
TINY SHELTER
BARELY ENOUGH
FOR 2 WALKERS

0   ¹/₄ mile

0   APPROX SCALE   500 metres

64

4½ – 5 HRS TO LLANTHONY PATH (MAP 66) FROM GOSPEL PASS ROAD (MAP 62)

4½ – 5 HRS FROM LLANTHONY PATH (MAP 66) TO GOSPEL PASS ROAD (MAP 62)

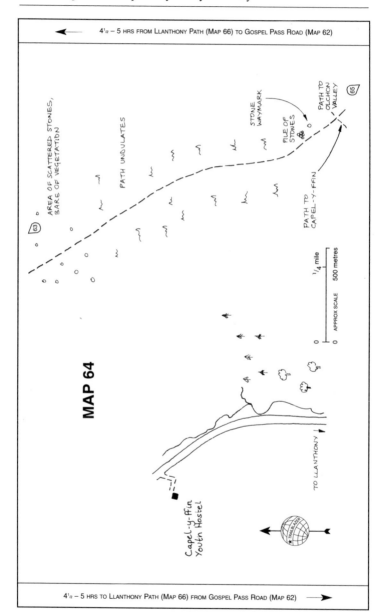

MAP 64

AREA OF SCATTERED STONES, BARE OF VEGETATION

PATH UNDULATES

STONE WAYMARK

PILE OF STONES

PATH TO OLCHON VALLEY

PATH TO CAPEL-Y-FFIN

¼ mile
500 metres
APPROX SCALE

Capel-y-ffin Youth Hostel

TO LLANTHONY

TRAILBLAZER

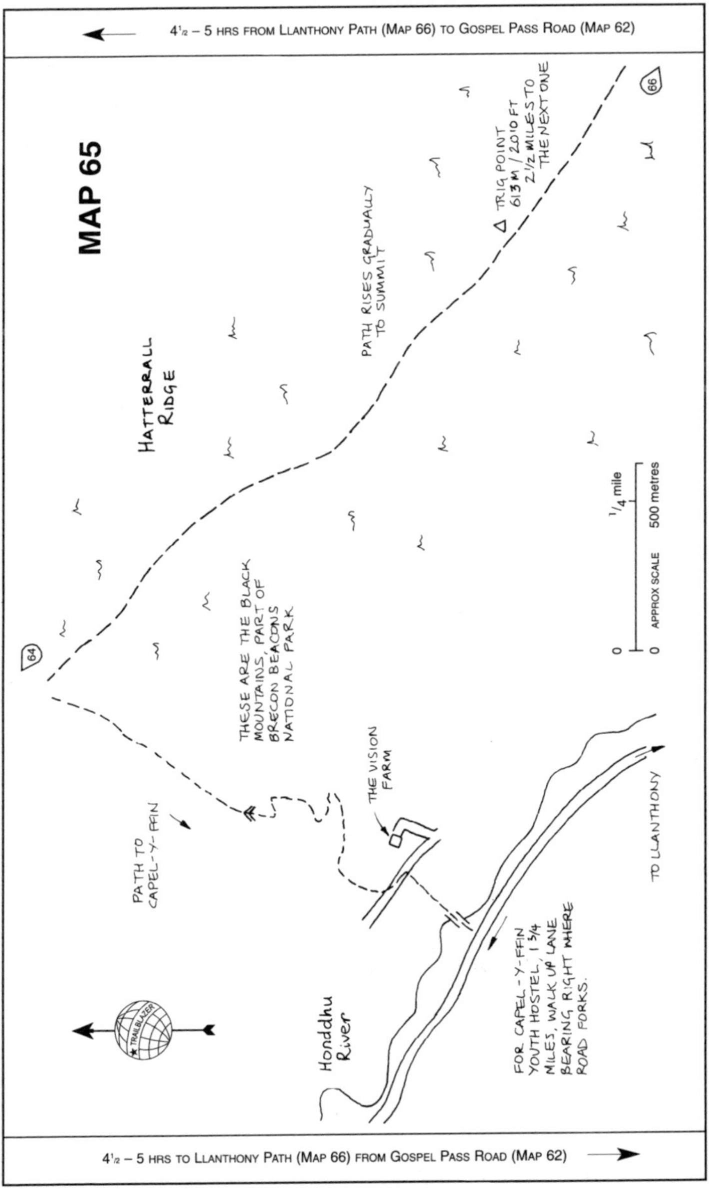
4½ – 5 HRS FROM LLANTHONY PATH (MAP 66) TO GOSPEL PASS ROAD (MAP 62)
MAP 65
HATTERRALL RIDGE
PATH RISES GRADUALLY TO SUMMIT
TRIG POINT 613M / 2010 FT 2½ MILES TO THE NEXT ONE
66
64
THESE ARE THE BLACK MOUNTAINS, PART OF BRECON BEACONS NATIONAL PARK
THE VISION FARM
PATH TO CAPEL-Y-FFIN
Honddhu River
FOR CAPEL-Y-FFIN YOUTH HOSTEL, 1¾ MILES, WALK UP LANE BEARING RIGHT WHERE ROAD FORKS.
TO LLANTHONY
0 ¼ mile
0 APPROX SCALE 500 metres
TRAILBLAZER
4½ – 5 HRS TO LLANTHONY PATH (MAP 66) FROM GOSPEL PASS ROAD (MAP 62)

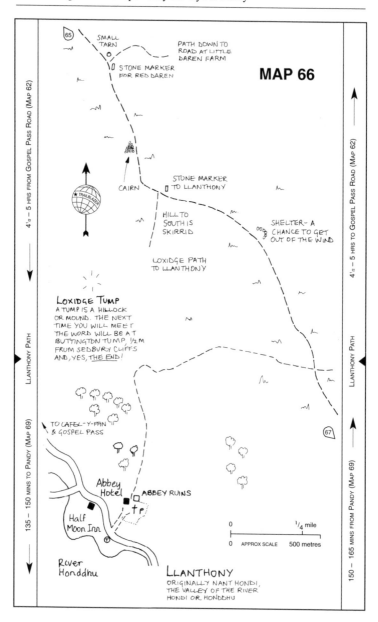

MAP 66

65

SMALL TARN

PATH DOWN TO ROAD AT LITTLE DAREN FARM

STONE MARKER FOR RED DAREN

CAIRN

STONE MARKER TO LLANTHONY

SHELTER– A CHANCE TO GET OUT OF THE WIND

HILL TO SOUTH IS SKIRRID

LOXIDGE PATH TO LLANTHONY

★ TRAILBLAZER

LOXIDGE TUMP
A TUMP IS A HILLOCK OR MOUND. THE NEXT TIME YOU WILL MEET THE WORD WILL BE AT BUTTINGTON TUMP, ½ M FROM SEDBURY CLIFFS AND, YES, THE END!

67

TO CAPEL-Y-FFIN & GOSPEL PASS

Abbey Hotel

ABBEY RUINS

Half Moon Inn

River Honddhu

LLANTHONY
ORIGINALLY NANT HONDI, THE VALLEY OF THE RIVER HONDI OR HONDDHU

0 ———— ¼ mile
0 ———— 500 metres
APPROX SCALE

4½ – 5 HRS FROM GOSPEL PASS ROAD (MAP 62)

LLANTHONY PATH

135 – 150 MINS TO PANDY (MAP 69)

4½ – 5 HRS TO GOSPEL PASS ROAD (MAP 62)

LLANTHONY PATH

150 – 165 MINS FROM PANDY (MAP 69)

CAPEL-Y-FFIN   MAP 64

The first possible place to stay that you come to is in the Vale of Ewyas at *Capel-y-ffin Youth Hostel* (☎ 01873-890650, 38 beds) where the charge is £9 with evening meals from £5. Don't leave it to chance though; this hostel often gets booked up by groups and has complex opening times so it's essential to phone ahead to reserve a space.

To reach it from the ridge leave the Offa's Dyke Path at the signpost pointing west to Capel and east to Olchon (see Maps 64 and 65). The path descends the open hillside steeply heading towards the farm buildings of Vision Farm where the path turns right to meet the road. Right again leads to the little cluster of buildings at St Mary's Chapel, built in 1762 on an earlier site, the ancient yews in the churchyard shielding the tiny chapel from the elements. A further mile along the road north brings you to a track on the left climbing up to the isolated youth hostel. It's two and a half miles (4km) off the route and the climb back on to the ridge in the morning will be steep.

❑ The Vale of Ewyas

Here, you feel, is the Glencoe of the Welsh Border, a place marked indelibly by conflict. **John Hillaby**, *Journey through Britain*

The Vale of Ewyas in which Llanthony sits has attracted its share of dreamers. In 1807, Walter Savage Landor bought an estate that cost him the then colossal sum of £20,000, hoping to create for himself an escape from the world but instead finding nothing but dispute, resentment and trouble with his neighbours. Washing his hands of it, he loathed the Black Mountains for the rest of his life.

At Capel-y-ffin, what is now the youth hostel was acquired by one Father Ignatius who established a British order of Benedictine monks. He laboured ceaselessly as Francis Kilvert (see box, p159), a regular visitor, testified but when he died in 1907, there was no one of sufficient energy to carry on his work.

Eric Gill, artist, sculptor and typographer of genius, took over the estate in 1924 with his extended family, believing that the surroundings would help create a new life of harmony and creativity.

Some of his best work was indeed done here but eventually his vision came to nothing. The only reminder of his time here are some headstones in the tiny chapel of St Mary's, their bold sharp lettering speaking for the skill of the carver. These visionaries all departed, strangers who had convinced themselves that the landscape could compensate anyone for anything. But they were each defeated by the harsh and unforgiving surroundings. Dreams are not enough.

LLANTHONY   MAP 66

Three miles (5km) or so further along the ridge are several paths west to the atmospheric and long-abandoned Llanthony Abbey. A side trip from the ridge to the abbey would take about two hours.

Amongst the ruins is the excellent *Abbey Hotel* (☎ 01873-890487, 2T/3D) which offers accommodation and refreshment. Note that it's open daily from April to October but at weekends only for the rest of the year. B&B costs £30-33 per person, more at weekends.

Nearby is the remarkable *Half Moon Inn* (☎ 01873-890611, 1S/2T/4D/2F) in a stunning location and on a par with the best walkers' pubs in the land. Accommodation costs from £22.50; meals are available at the bar.

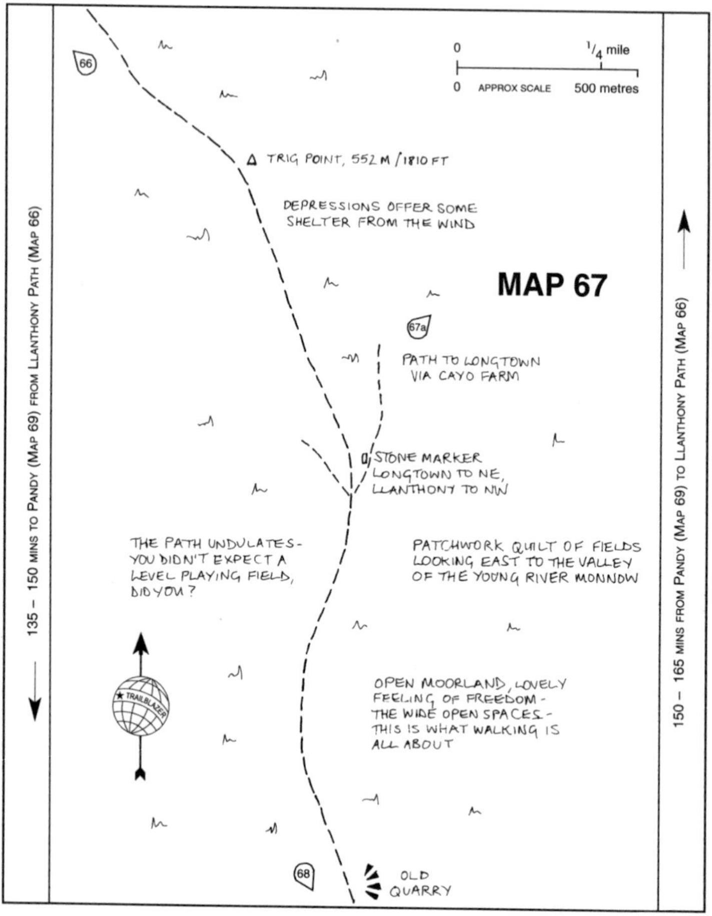

66

0 — — — — 1/4 mile
0   APPROX SCALE   500 metres

△ TRIG POINT, 552 M / 1810 FT

DEPRESSIONS OFFER SOME
SHELTER FROM THE WIND

MAP 67

67a

PATH TO LONGTOWN
VIA CAYO FARM

STONE MARKER
LONGTOWN TO NE,
LLANTHONY TO NW

THE PATH UNDULATES –
YOU DIDN'T EXPECT A
LEVEL PLAYING FIELD,
DID YOU?

PATCHWORK QUILT OF FIELDS
LOOKING EAST TO THE VALLEY
OF THE YOUNG RIVER MONNOW

★ TRAILBLAZER

OPEN MOORLAND, LOVELY
FEELING OF FREEDOM –
THE WIDE OPEN SPACES –
THIS IS WHAT WALKING IS
ALL ABOUT

68   OLD
      QUARRY

135 – 150 MINS TO PANDY (MAP 69) FROM LLANTHONY PATH (MAP 66)

150 – 165 MINS FROM PANDY (MAP 69) TO LLANTHONY PATH (MAP 66)

❑ The Skirrid (*Ysgyrid Fawr*)

Dominating the view southwards as you approach Pandy, the long whale-backed hill of the Skirrid, also known as St Michael's Mount or the Holy Mountain, has long been a place of superstition and pilgrimage. Rising to 486m (1595ft), the summit is encircled by an Iron Age hill-fort, a low rampart visible on the north side. The highest point is marked by an OS triangulation column. Nearby, two square stones and a shallow depression mark the site of St Michael's Chapel, once used by persecuted Catholics for secret worship. The northern slope was created by an ice-age landslip, although local superstition suggests it occurred at the very moment of the crucifixion.

LONGTOWN   Map 67a

Longtown is almost two miles (3km) off-route to the east of Hatterrall Ridge and has accommodation, most notably *Tan House Farm* (☎ 01873-860221, 1F) with B&B for £25, or you can **camp** for £4 including a shower. The pub, *The Crown Inn* (☎ 01873-860217), is just down the road.

Olchon Cottage Farm (☎ 01873-860233, 2F), Turnant Rd, also offers a good standard of accommodation with B&B from £22.50 per person.

To reach Longtown, take the path east from the stone marker (Map 67) then descend for half a mile on a clear green track with a wall on the right. Keep to the upper path above trees then swing right through fields to Cayo Farm.

Follow the concrete farm lane to reach a bridge over the Olchon Brook and follow the lane till you reach Longtown.

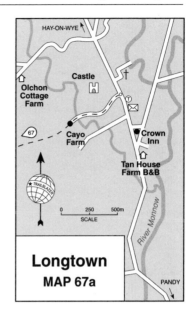

PANDY   MAP 69

Reaching the busy A465 at the fabled Lancaster Arms you are in Pandy. Hardly a village, it has nonetheless attracted along its main road a number of B&Bs, a smart hotel and at least three pubs.

Since walkers began to use the Offa's Dyke Path in some numbers Pandy has grown up as a regular stopping-off point for them, poised midway between Hay-on-Wye and Monmouth, a distance of 34 miles (55km), too far for the average walker in one day. A quarter of a mile before you reach the main road is an old country house, *Brynhonddhu* (☎ 01873-890535, 1T/2D) charging £20 for a room without a bath, or £27.50 for en suite.

Right on the main road itself and hence a little subject to traffic noise is *The Lancaster Arms Inn* (☎ 01873-890699, 2T), a welcoming pub with few refinements and limited accommodation at £25 per person or £22 per head for doubles. The rather good pub grub in the bar redeems an other-

wise fairly bog-standard hostelry. You may be intrigued enough to try chicken tikka Cassandra, a remarkable variation on the most popular dish in the UK.

A bit further along the road and 400 yards from the path is *The Old Pandy Inn* (☎ 01873-890208), which includes the bunkhouse (*The Black Mountain Lodge*) sleeping up to eight people from £14.50 per person including breakfast and bedding.

The *Park Hotel* (☎ 01873-890271, 6S/2T/4D/2F) is a large establishment charging from £25 per person. Meals are taken in the bar and start at around £8.

Campers can pitch at *Oldcastle Court Farm* (☎ 01873-890285, 1S/1T/1D) for £3.50 a head including shower, with B&B available at a reasonable £20, but it's 1¹/₂ miles to the pub.

Buses run between Abergavenny and Hereford (see public transport map, p39).

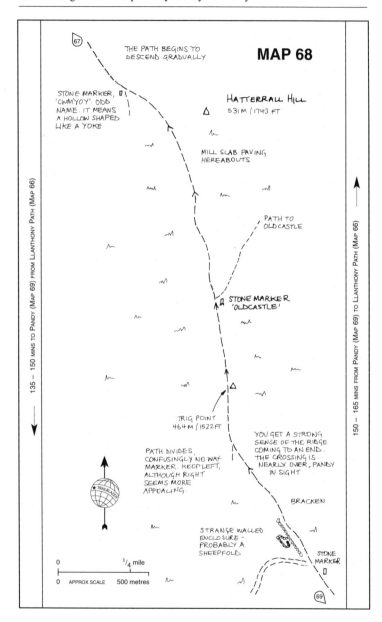

67

THE PATH BEGINS TO
DESCEND GRADUALLY

MAP 68

STONE MARKER,
'CWMYOY'. ODD
NAME. IT MEANS
A HOLLOW SHAPED
LIKE A YOKE

HATTERRALL HILL
531M / 1743 FT
△

MILL SLAB PAVING
HEREABOUTS

PATH TO
OLDCASTLE

STONE MARKER
'OLDCASTLE'
△

TRIG POINT
464M / 1522FT
△

YOU GET A STRONG
SENSE OF THE RIDGE
COMING TO AN END.
THE CROSSING IS
NEARLY OVER, PANDY
IN SIGHT

PATH DIVIDES,
CONFUSINGLY NO WAY-
MARKER. KEEP LEFT,
ALTHOUGH RIGHT
SEEMS MORE
APPEALING.

★ TRAILBLAZER

BRACKEN

STRANGE WALLED
ENCLOSURE –
PROBABLY A
SHEEPFOLD

STONE
MARKER

0   ¹/₄ mile

0   APPROX SCALE   500 metres

69

135 – 150 MINS TO PANDY (MAP 69) FROM LLANTHONY PATH (MAP 66)

150 – 165 MINS FROM PANDY (MAP 69) TO LLANTHONY PATH (MAP 66)

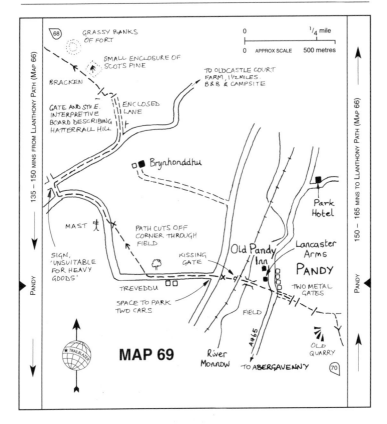

MAP 69

PANDY TO LLANTILIO-CROSSENNY

MAPS 69–73

There are some highlights on this **7¹/₂-mile (12km, 3¹/₂–4¹/₂hrs)** walk through mainly agricultural land, including the charming village of **Llangattock-Lingoed**, its few houses clustered near the church of St Cadoc and the cheerful pub. The trail takes you up to the very walls of **White Castle** (*Castell Gwyn*), see box p161, one of the best preserved of the Marcher castles and well worth visiting if you have the time. There are no facilities here unfortunately and the kiosk is seldom manned: no ice-cream van, no telephone, nothing to detain you unless you intend wandering among the ruins which are, it must be said, one of the seven wonders of the Offa's Dyke Path.

Llantilio-Crossenny first shows you its church peeping from amongst the trees as you approach, field by field, until at last you meet a lane that takes you into the village.

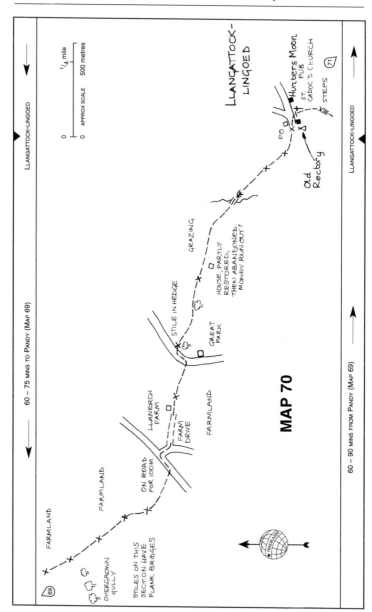

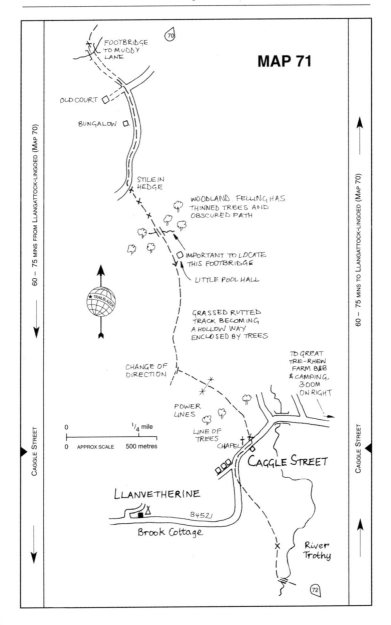

FOOTBRIDGE TO MUDDY LANE

70

MAP 71

OLD COURT

BUNGALOW

STILE IN HEDGE

WOODLAND FELLING HAS THINNED TREES AND OBSCURED PATH

IMPORTANT TO LOCATE THIS FOOTBRIDGE

LITTLE POOL HALL

★ TRAILBLAZER

GRASSED RUTTED TRACK BECOMING A HOLLOW WAY ENCLOSED BY TREES

CHANGE OF DIRECTION

TO GREAT TRE-RHEW FARM B&B & CAMPING, 300M ON RIGHT

POWER LINES

LINE OF TREES

CHAPEL

CAGGLE STREET

0   ¼ mile
0   APPROX SCALE   500 metres

LLANVETHERINE

B4521

Brook Cottage

River Trothy

72

CAGGLE STREET

CAGGLE STREET

LLANGATTOCK-LINGOED

The small hamlet of Llangattock-Lingoed is an unassuming place hiding itself from the world. At its heart stands the church of St Cadog around which the houses have clustered since its earliest known dedication in the 6th century. A quiet, neat settlement, the walker may pass through without seeing a soul, which is the way it should be.

Hunter's Moon Inn (☎ 01873-821499, 4D) would be even better if it could be relied on to be open at lunchtime. The rooms, all en suite, cost £22.50 to £30 per person.

MAP 70

The Old Rectory (☎ 01873-821326, 1S/1T/2D/1F) is a comfortable B&B charging from £25, and £11 for a three-course evening meal. They have space for five tents: you can **camp** for £2.50 including shower.

There is also a **post office** here, open Mon, Wed, Thur and Fri 9am–12pm, 2–4.30pm, Tues 9am–1pm and Sat 9am–12pm.

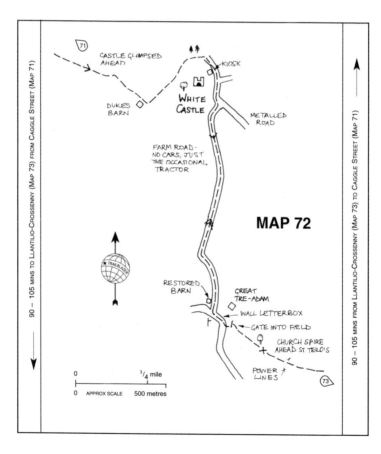

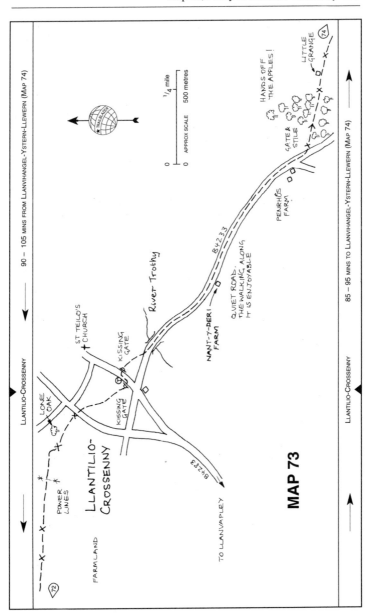

90 – 105 MINS FROM LLANVIHANGEL-YSTERN-LLEWERN (MAP 74)

LLANTILIO-CROSSENNY

85 – 95 MINS TO LLANVIHANGEL-YSTERN-LLEWERN (MAP 74)

LLANTILIO-CROSSENNY

TRAILBLAZER

¼ mile

0   500 metres

0   APPROX SCALE

74

LITTLE GRANGE

HANDS OFF THE APPLES!

GATE & STILE

PENRHÔS FARM

B4233

River Trothy

ST TEILO'S CHURCH

KISSING GATE

NANT-Y-DERI FARM

QUIET ROAD. THE WALKING ALONG IT IS ENJOYABLE

MAP 73

KISSING GATE

LONE OAK

POWER LINES

LLANTILIO-CROSSENNY

FARMLAND

72

B4233

TO LLANVAPLEY

CAGGLE STREET/LLANVETHERINE

If you have no intention of walking from Pandy to Monmouth in one go you might decide to break the journey at Caggle Street or Llanvetherine, or walk to Llantilio-Crossenny and stay at Llanvetherine.

You will find a choice of establishments offering B&B including *Great Trerhew Farm* (☎ 01873-821268, 1S/1T/2D /1F) at £20 or a mere £1 if you prefer to **camp**. Book an evening meal from £12.50 per person.

MAP 71

Brook Cottage (☎ 01873-821315, 1S/1D) is another option, only 100 yards from the pub, with B&B at £18 and **camping** at £3 each including £1 for a shower.

For a **taxi** to ferry you on to Monmouth, back to Pandy or into Abergavenny, Lewis of Abergavenny (☎ 01873 -854140) or Jay-Bee Taxis of Monmouth (☎ 07974-496102) are reliable.

LLANTILIO-CROSSENNY TO MONMOUTH   MAPS 73–77

This **9-mile (14km, 4–4^1/$_2$hrs)** stretch follows the valley of the **River Trothy**, an area of sequestered calm where you will see hardly anyone and can enjoy the peace. It is undulating country, the ground descending gradually from the Black Mountains.

The tiny church of St Michael at **Llanfihangel-Ystern-Llewern** is another of the many beautiful small churches that you pass on the Offa's Dyke Path and it is a shame that it has to be kept locked.

The other attraction in the village is **Offa's Vineyard**, a surprising discovery but one of those curiosities that make the path so fascinating. Abbey Bridge and Abbey Cottage are the only reminders of the Cistercian monastery of **Grace Dieu** founded in 1226 by John of Monmouth but destroyed by Henry VIII. Not a trace remains and you have to rely on your imagination to picture the site bustling with activity.   (*Continued on p181*)

❑ **Offa's Vineyard**
A stencilled sign on a gate just as you join the drive to Sunnybank Farm in the tiny hamlet of Llanfihangel-Ystern-Llewern invites you to taste the wines of Offa's Vineyard. This is not a joke. There really is a vineyard, actively involved in producing wines labelled under the name of Offa's Vineyard. Peter Johnson grows grapes, the red under polythene tunnels, the white in the open air on the west facing slopes overlooking the River Trothy. Although never likely to challenge the great growths, the wines are very drinkable and the vineyard a real 'find'. Why not slip a bottle of the sparkling into your rucksack to open when you reach Sedbury Cliffs?

In these days of supermarket domination it is a delight to discover a local producer relying solely on his own skills and instincts to produce a product of quality and interest. Cheers, Peter!

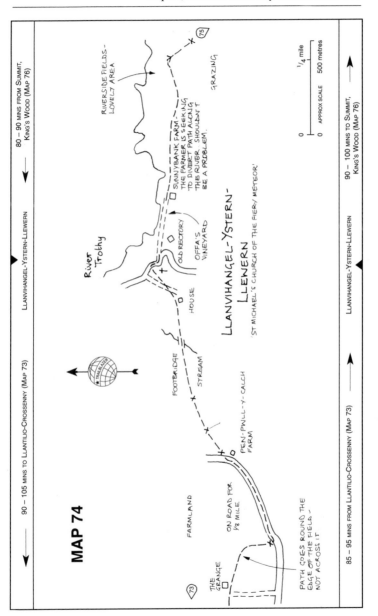

MAP 74

THE GRANGE

FARMLAND

ON ROAD FOR ½ MILE

PATH GOES ROUND THE EDGE OF THE FIELD – NOT ACROSS IT

PEN-PWLL-Y-CALCH FARM

STREAM

FOOTBRIDGE

HOUSE

River Trothy

OLD RECTORY

OFFA'S VINEYARD

SUNNYBANK FARM: THE FARMER IS SEEKING TO DIVERT PATH ALONG THE RIVER. SHOULDN'T BE A PROBLEM.

RIVERSIDE FIELDS – LOVELY AREA

GRAZING

LLANVIHANGEL-YSTERN-LLEWERN
ST MICHAEL'S CHURCH OF THE FIERY METEOR'

¼ mile

0   APPROX SCALE   500 metres

— 90 – 105 MINS TO LLANTILIO-CROSSENNY (MAP 73) —   LLANVIHANGEL-YSTERN-LLEWERN   — 80 – 90 MINS FROM SUMMIT, KING'S WOOD (MAP 76) —

— 85 – 95 MINS FROM LLANTILIO-CROSSENNY (MAP 73) →   LLANVIHANGEL-YSTERN-LLEWERN   — 90 – 100 MINS TO SUMMIT, KING'S WOOD (MAP 76) —

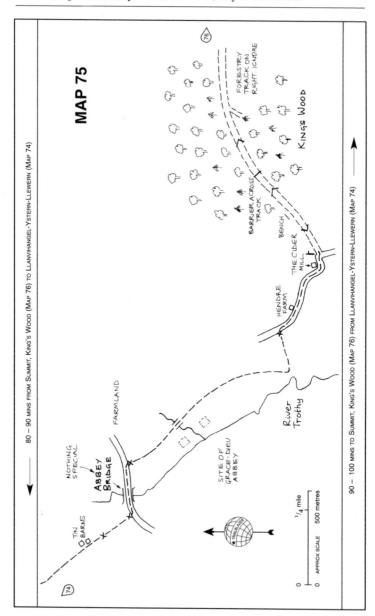

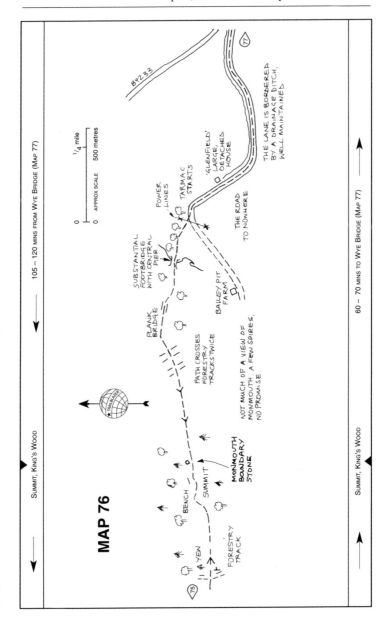

Summit, King's Wood

105 – 120 mins from Wye Bridge (Map 77)

MAP 76

BK233

0   APPROX SCALE   500 metres
0   ¼ mile

THE LANE IS BORDERED BY A DRAINAGE DITCH, WELL MAINTAINED

'GLENFIELD' LARGE, DETACHED HOUSE

THE ROAD TO NOWHERE

TARMAC STARTS

POWER LINES

SUBSTANTIAL FOOTBRIDGE WITH CENTRAL PIER

BAILEY PIT FARM

PLANK BRIDGE

PATH CROSSES FORESTRY TRACKS TWICE

NOT MUCH OF A VIEW OF MONMOUTH A FEW SPIRES. NO PROMISE.

TRAILBLAZER

BENCH

SUMMIT

MONMOUTH BOUNDARY STONE

YEW

FORESTRY TRACK

75

77

Summit, King's Wood

60 – 70 mins to Wye Bridge (Map 77)

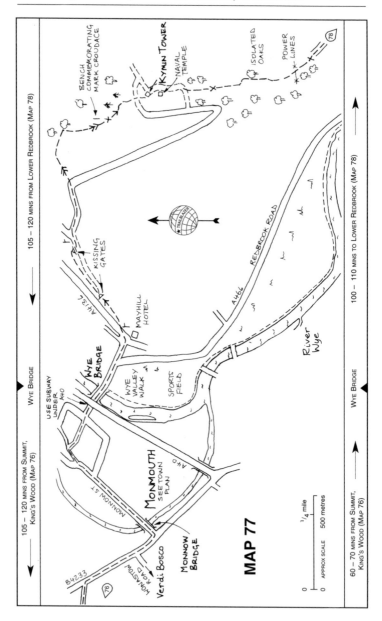

MAP 77

The patchwork of meadow and field divided up by broad hedgerows of black-thorn, hawthorn, elder, dogwood and maple merge with scattered woodland to create an area which grows on you as you move through it. At times it seems that it has been deserted since its inhabitants are seldom seen apart from an occasional tractor or children getting off the school bus, but well-kept fields and neat farms bear witness to the agricultural importance of the area.

Your approach to the town of **Monmouth** is over the mound of **Kings Wood**, a mixture of broadleafed trees and conifers where forestry operations are likely to be heard if not seen. There is no sudden vista of the town from the north and you pass along the edge of a succession of potato fields to reach Watery Lane which gradually leads into a neat and mushrooming housing development. Once you stand on Monnow Bridge, however, you know you have arrived. Tomorrow the Wye Valley awaits.

MONMOUTH *(TREFYNWY)* MAP 77a

Monmouth is a delightful town set in the heart of the Wye Valley. It's the birthplace of Henry V (see box p183) and has links to Nelson, but is perhaps best known for the 13th-century Monnow Bridge which compares with that in Cahors, France, in having a fortified tower. Those who have chosen to walk south to north may very well make this their first night's stopover although to walk more than 17 miles (28km) on your first day may be a severe test of character.

Services

Most of the services you will need are to be found on the main street which runs uphill from Monnow Bridge to Agincourt Square. This is where the town's heart beats and where, in the Shire Hall, the **tourist information centre** (☎ 01600-713899, 10am–5.30pm, closed for lunch 1–2pm in the winter) is to be found.

Buses to Chepstow run at two-hourly intervals throughout the day, a journey of under an hour, and there are six buses a day to Gloucester (see public transport map, p39). There is no railway station, the nearest being at Chepstow. **Taxi** firms are JMC Taxis (☎ 01600-890998) and Amber Cars (☎ 01600-712200).

Stock up on any groceries either at Waitrose **supermarket** (Mon–Tues 8.30am–7pm, Wed–Thu 8.30am–6pm, Fri 8.30am–9pm, Sat 8.30am–7pm and Sun 10am–4pm) or at Londis on Cinderhill St (Mon–Sun 6am–10.30pm). There are cash points at four **banks** and Thomas Cook are open for **foreign exchange** transactions from 9am to 5.30pm Mon–Sat, closed Sun. For those making an early start, Morgam **newsagents** opens at 5.30am if the papers have arrived and can be handy for laying in a few essentials for the day. You can also get cash-back but they don't take cheques.

If you need a **doctor**, Dixton Surgery (☎ 01600-712152) is a little way down Dixton Rd, or there's Monmouth Hospital (☎ 01600-713522).

The Savoy Theatre (☎ 01600-772467) is a charming small **cinema** on Church St; a nice place to while away an evening. You should also try to find the time to visit the **Regimental Museum** (☎ 01600-772175, The Castle, summer 2–5pm daily, winter Sat–Sun 2–4pm, admission free) which is a gem. It has a fascinating description of the Battle of Agincourt and the English bow-men, many of whom came from Monmouthshire.

Where to stay

Monnow Bridge Caravan and Camping Site (☎ 01600-714004, Drybridge St) is a small **campsite** that is happy to take tents and will always squeeze you in somewhere if arriving late. It's only a two-minute walk from town and charges £4 for a one-person tent or £6 for a two-person tent. The shower takes 20p pieces in a coin box. A little further out is *Monmouth Caravan Park* (☎ 01600-714745, Rockfield Rd) which will

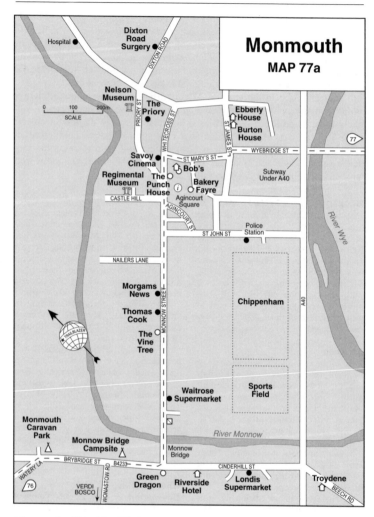

take tents for £5 a night. This is a formal site with a lounge bar and pool table mainly for static caravanners but it's convenient, being right on the route of the path.

Budget-priced B&Bs are thinly spread but there are a number of places where you will be comfortable and welcome including

Ebberley House (☎ 01600-713602, St James Sq, 1T/1D/1F) charging £20, with the double room being en suite. Mrs Dawes will do you a packed lunch for £4.50 but does not do meals.

If you have no luck there you could try *Burton House* (☎ 01600-714958, 19 St

James Sq, 1T/1D/1F) next door, slightly cheaper at £19 and with packed lunches for £4.50.

In the centre of town in the pedestrianized Church St is *Bob's* (☎ 01600-712600, 7 Church St, 2T/6D) where the rather small but quite comfortable rooms are en suite which is reflected in the higher price of £22.50 each (£30 single). The restaurant is probably the best in town.

The Riverside Hotel (☎ 01600-715577, Cinderhill St, 9T/6D/2F) welcomes walkers and offers comfortable, if rather pricey, accommodation from £25 to £35 for B&B. There are evening meals from £7.

Finally, two small local houses offer a warm welcome to wayfarers during the summer months and would be an excellent choice for those walking alone or as a couple. *Verdi Bosco* (☎ 01600-714441, 65 Wonastow Rd, 1D) and *Troydene* (☎ 01600-712260, 16 Beech Rd, 1S/1T) both charge £19 a head and £3.50 for a packed lunch.

Where to eat

The town offers a wide choice of pubs of which two deserve mention, being unreconstructed in the standard brewery-chain way. *The Green Dragon* (☎ 01600-712561, St Thomas Sq) is distinctive in its yellow and green exterior and earns its place in the *Good Beer Guide*. A jazz group plays on several nights of the week, making it the coolest hang-out in town. They serve a full breakfast (though only from 11am to 12 noon) for £3.95 and will do packed lunches for £3.50, handy for those who have camped just down the road. Hancocks HB is the beer on draught.

The Punch House (☎ 01600-713855, Agincourt Sq) is the other pub of note with bags of character, serving Brains beer, the slogan for which is 'It's Brains you want'; a rather unfortunate catchphrase.

Reasonably-priced gourmet food is found at *Bob's* (see above) where you might choose onion and garlic tart as a starter followed by tortellini mimosa or possibly tuna fagioli with balsamic vinegar and come away having paid £9 for your meal.

Halfway down Monnow St is *The Vine Tree* (☎ 01600-713935), a good place if you are looking for pub grub.

For a quick sandwich to take away, *Bakery Fayre* (Tue–Sat 9am–5.30pm) makes stunning 'designer' baguettes, such as a demi sausage baguette with mustard at £1.50, plus hot tea or coffee.

❏ **Henry V**
In Shakespeare's *Henry V*, reference is made to Henry's connections with the Wye Valley in a conversation after the Battle of Agincourt with the Welsh Captain Fluellen. In it Fluellen reminds him of the Battle of Crecy when

' . . . *the Welshmen did good service in a garden where leeks did grow, wearing leeks in their Monmouth caps; which your majesty know, to this hour is an honourable badge of the service; and I do believe your majesty takes no scorn to wear the leek upon Saint Tavy's day.'*
King Henry: *I wear it for a memorable honour;*
For I am Welsh, you know, good countryman.
Fluellen: *All the water in Wye cannot wash your majesty's Welsh blood out of your body, I can tell you that; God bless it and preserve it, as long as it pleases his grace, and his majesty too!'*

It seems, however, that having left Wales as an infant Henry's attachment to his place of birth was not sufficiently strong to make him wish to return, for he never did.

❑ **The Longbow**
The museum at Monmouth has a reconstruction of a longbow, the decisive weapon at the battles of Crecy (1346) and Agincourt (1415), when bowmen made up half the mass of the infantry in the English army. The longbow was made of yew but as this depleted the churchyards, bowyers were ordered to make four bows of wych hazel, elm or ash to every one of yew.

Longbows were five feet long (1.5m) and the shaft was a cloth yard, ie 27¹/₂inches (70cm). They had an accurate range of 300 yards (275m) and six to ten arrows could be fired each minute. In 1182 a Welsh archer in Abergavenny fired an arrow through a 4-inch-thick (10cm) door. In wet weather bowstrings were kept dry under the conical hats of hard boiled leather, their Monmouth caps preferred by the archers to metal helmets.

MONMOUTH TO CHEPSTOW   MAPS 77–86

This **16¹/₂-mile (27km, 8¹/₄–9hrs)** section is long and arduous, all the harder for being almost the last leg. Many walkers divide it into two stages, stopping at **Brockweir** or **Tintern**.

The route follows the beautiful **Wye Valley**, characterized by densely wooded slopes above the gently flowing river. It is a tourist area and in the season is crowded with visitors, the roads are busy all day, and there is no shortage of services along the way. The solitude that you may have relished through the hidden country of the Borders is unlikely to be found here.

The **Wye Valley Walk**, which hugs the river, can be taken as an easier alternative to the Offa's Dyke Path which runs parallel and inland of the river, remaining cloaked in woodland throughout. When you finally come across a sign saying 'Sedbury Cliffs 3 miles' you feel a quickening of the pulse and a surge of energy that will sustain you over these last tiring miles. The path stealthily avoids the town of **Chepstow** and it is possible to miss it altogether although there is no mistaking the presence of urban sprawl which has to be navigated.

REDBROOK   MAP 78
Redbrook was once known for its pubs but the only one that now remains is *The Boat Inn* (☎ 01600-712615) reached by crossing a footbridge over the Wye from the recreation park alongside the main Monmouth–Chepstow road. It's a lovely welcoming pub with a selection of ales and the meals are enterprising and original – try pan heggarty with bacon, a Scottish dish made with layers of potatoes, onions, garlic and cheese, great value at £5.90.

Tresco (☎ 01600-712325, 2S/2D/1F) is a well-known B&B in the area offering warm and economical hospitality for £17.50 a night or you can **camp** for £3. A party of up to six can be accommodated in a mobile home for £10 a head, breakfast extra.

The other B&B in Lower Redbrook is *Barque House* (☎ 01600-772936, 1T/2D), further along the main road, charging £18 a head. They do evening meals if booked in advance. They have a breakfast room with a wood-burning stove to hang out in, which is useful if you've time on your hands. If you fancy a cup of tea or coffee only,

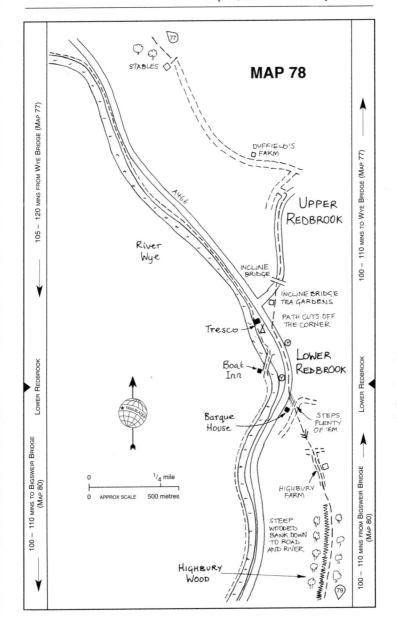

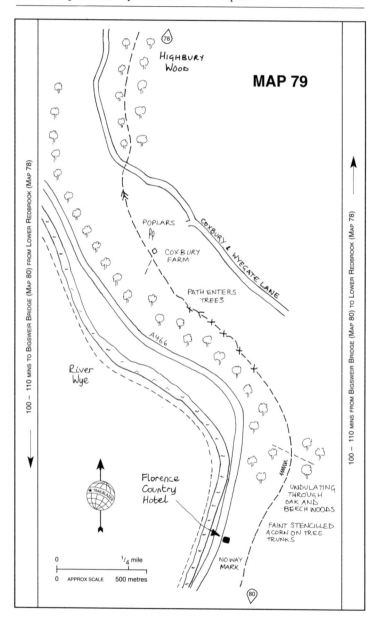

MAP 79

HIGHBURY WOOD

78

COXBURY & WYEGATE LANE

POPLARS

COXBURY FARM

PATH ENTERS TREES

A466

River Wye

Florence Country Hotel

UNDULATING THROUGH OAK AND BEECH WOODS

FAINT STENCILLED ACORN ON TREE TRUNKS

NO WAY MARK

80

TRAILBLAZER

0   1/4 mile

0   APPROX SCALE   500 metres

100 – 110 MINS TO BIGSWEIR BRIDGE (MAP 80) FROM LOWER REDBROOK (MAP 78)

100 – 110 MINS FROM BIGSWEIR BRIDGE (MAP 80) TO LOWER REDBROOK (MAP 78)

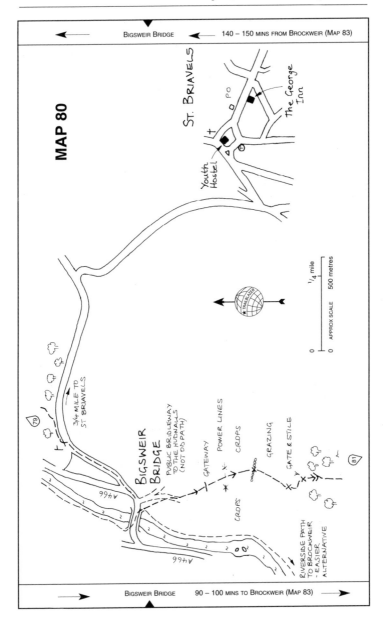

Incline Bridge Tea Gardens (☎ 01600-713863, open in summer) is a good place to sit on the decking and ease your feet for a while. The incline bridge was part of the Monmouth to Coleford Tramway opened in 1812 and used for transport with horse-drawn wagons until 1916. Half a mile short of Bigsweir Bridge on the A466 is *The*

Florence Country Hotel (☎ 01594-530830, 1S/1T/6D/1F) a charming establishment on the banks of the Wye. It's a little dearer than the average B&B but comes with many extras. It will cost £36 a night with dinner from £13.50. They have a soft spot for walkers.

ST BRIAVELS   MAP 80

This unusual hilltop village is 1½ miles (2km) off route and notable for its *youth hostel* (☎ 01594-530272, 70 beds). It is situated in the castle which was once used as a hunting lodge by King John. Beds are £11 and evening meals are available for £5. You can usually count on the place being open at weekends but mid-week and off-season a telephone booking would be necessary, rather than turning up on spec.

The George Inn (☎ 01594-530228, 1T/3D) is known for its home-made local food and traditional ales. They do accommodation too, from £35 to £55 per person. It's an interesting place to stay, off the beaten track. Hidden away on St Briavels Common is the enterprising *Oak Cottage* (☎ 01594-530440, 2S/2D, Map 81), a secluded house offering B&B at the outstandingly cheap price of £17.50 a head, or **camping** at £5 per person plus £1.50 for a shower or bath. Meals, veggie only, are available at £7.50 and if this won't do, the pub is 2 miles (3km) away.

❏ Tintern Abbey

Tintern Abbey (☎ 01291-689251, Apr–Sept 9.30am–6pm, Oct 9am–5pm, Nov–Mar 9.30am–4pm, admission £3) was founded in 1131 by Cistercian monks, the most successful of the various monastic orders of the period. The name comes from their first establishment at Citeaux in France, Cistercium in Latin, established in 1098. Known as the White monks from their custom of wearing habits made from undyed cloth, they followed a regime of strict abstinence, forsaking personal possessions and any unnecessary ornamentation. They sought out remote places far away from the concourse of men and it was this that brought them to beautiful river valleys such as Tintern, Strata Marcella and Grace Dieu, all on your route. At their height there were over 500 foundations spread right across northern Europe, 85 in Britain alone.

At the time of the Dissolution of the Monasteries by Henry VIII the monastery at Tintern had declined and was reduced to only a few monks, and after they were expelled it fell into ruin and destitution. However, the area was known for iron working and the ruins were soon appropriated as dwellings by the iron workers.

Wordsworth came here twice as a tourist and the scene of romantic desolation soon had him reaching for his pen, composing the long poem *Lines Written a Few Miles Above Tintern Abbey* in 1798. Tintern isn't mentioned but the poet was obviously impressed by the scenery:

How oft, in spirit, have I turned to thee
O sylvan Wye! Thou wanderer through the woods
How often has my spirit turned to thee!

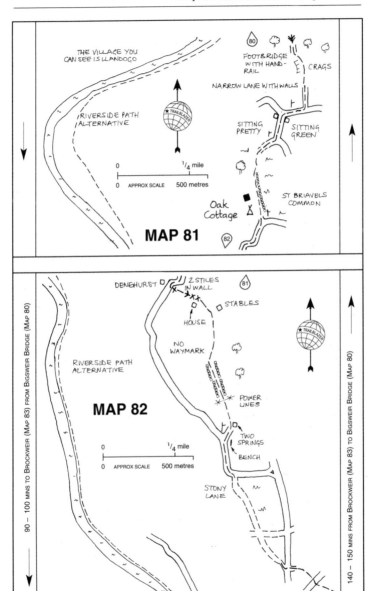

THE VILLAGE YOU CAN SEE IS LLANDOGO

(80)

FOOTBRIDGE WITH HAND-RAIL

CRAGS

NARROW LANE WITH WALLS

RIVERSIDE PATH ALTERNATIVE

★ TRAILBLAZER

SITTING PRETTY

SITTING GREEN

0   ¼ mile

0   APPROX SCALE   500 metres

Oak Cottage

ST BRIAVELS COMMON

MAP 81

(82)

DENEHURST

2 STILES IN WALL

(81)

STABLES

HOUSE

NO WAYMARK

RIVERSIDE PATH ALTERNATIVE

★ TRAILBLAZER

MAP 82

POWER LINES

0   ¼ mile

0   APPROX SCALE   500 metres

TWO SPRINGS

BENCH

STONY LANE

(83)

90 – 100 MINS TO BROCKWEIR (MAP 83) FROM BIGSWEIR BRIDGE (MAP 80)

140 – 150 MINS FROM BROCKWEIR (MAP 83) TO BIGSWEIR BRIDGE (MAP 80)

BROCKWEIR   MAP 83

Brockweir is used by canoeists since it has a quay where they can get their boats out of the river. For walkers its main attraction is the *Brockweir Country Inn* (☎ 01291-689548), a hostelry whose idiosyncrasies grow on you. The beers are well chosen with an eye for flavour and taste and the bar meals, though rather limited, offer a rea-

sonable choice. B&B accommodation can be found up the hill at *Honeyfields Farm* (☎ 01291-689859, 4T) which Michael Murphy runs with care and attention to detail. B&B costs £20 per head in the house or £25 per person in one of the two self-contained en-suite rooms to the side of the house.

TINTERN   MAP 83

Tintern Abbey (see box p188) is another wonder of the walk and well worth a look, but walkers short of time or energy may have to give it a miss because it's just over a mile off route. A clear signposted path leads down through the thickly wooded hillside to reach the riverside path which takes you to the old tramway bridge across the Wye. Once over the plank-boarded (but safe) bridge the abbey ruins are left along the road a quarter of a mile away. There are several hotels of a superior kind here as well as cafés, pubs, a post office and shops all used by the busy tourist trade, for this is a favourite venue for coach trips.

The Abbey Mill Tea Rooms (☎ 01291-689228) is open every day between 10am and 5.30pm, although on visitor-less winter days they may go home early. Try the tasty and sustaining Welsh tea, a plate of two Welsh cakes, a slice of bara brith and a pot

of tea. A square meal can be had at *The Rose and Crown* (☎ 01291-689254), notable for its sizzling steaks served with all the trimmings on a skillet: a juicy rump costs from £6.95. They also offer B&B for £40 per room (en suite) but the rooms were being refurbished early in 2004.

There are a number of B&Bs in Tintern from which to choose, including *Bellevue* (☎ 01291-689826, Monmouth Rd, 2D) above an 'antiquarian' book shop costing from £22.50.

Holmleigh (☎ 01291-689521, 1S/1T/2D) is clean and comfortable at £18 a night, while for a more 'pubby' ambience try *Wye Valley Hotel* (☎ 01291-689441, 2S/2T/2D/1F), a friendly family-run hotel but rather dearer at £35 per person per night.

The **bus** between Chepstow and Monmouth runs every two hours (see public transport map, p39).

CHEPSTOW (*CAS-GWENT*) MAP 86a

Journey's end is in sight. Prestatyn seems a world away and by now you will be feeling a certain pride in your achievement and may have acquired a feeling of belonging to the fellowship of travellers. You can say, with James Elroy Flecker:

We are Pilgrims, Master; we shall go
Always a little further: it may be
Beyond that last blue mountain barred
*   with snow*
Across that angry or that glimmering sea.

Chepstow offers everything the overnighter could need, from accommodation to good rail and road links; just think, from London

it only takes two and a half hours by train. There's a good selection of places to eat and things to do and see, including an impressive castle to add to your list.

Like Monmouth, it has a main street that climbs from the river to the top of the town where the Town Gate manfully resists the traffic pollution as it has done for four hundred years. There is a good by-pass to keep the through traffic away from the shopping area of the town yet cars are still the worst drawback. Is it time the main street became a pedestrian-only zone? Perhaps Chepstow will see a surge of interest as the birthplace of the creator of the Harry Potter books, JK Rowling.

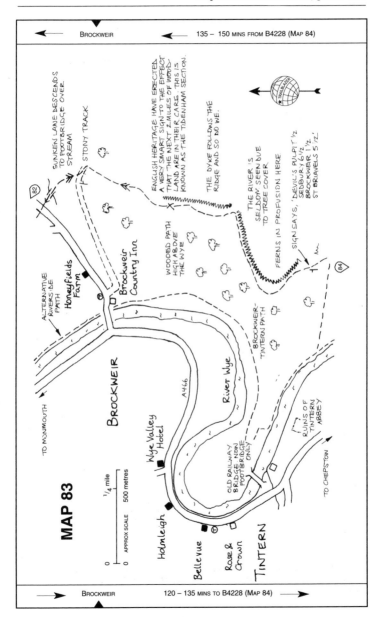

SUNKEN LANE DESCENDS TO FOOTBRIDGE OVER STREAM

STONY TRACK

ENGLISH HERITAGE HAVE ERECTED A VERY SMART SIGN TO THE EFFECT THAT THE NEXT 2 MILES OF WOODLAND ARE IN THEIR CARE. THIS IS KNOWN AS THE TIDENHAM SECTION.

THE DYKE FOLLOWS THE RIDGE AND SO DO WE.

THE RIVER IS SELDOM SEEN DUE TO TREE COVER

FERNS IN PROFUSION HERE

SIGN SAYS, 'DEVIL'S PULPIT 1/2 SEDBURY 6 1/2 BROCKWEIR 1 1/2 ST BRIAVELS 5 1/2'

82

84

WOODED PATH HIGH ABOVE THE WYE

ALTERNATIVE RIVERSIDE PATH

Honeyfields Farm

Brockweir Country Inn

Brockweir–Tintern Path

TO MONMOUTH

BROCKWEIR

A466

River Wye

RUINS OF TINTERN ABBEY

TO CHEPSTOW

MAP 83

1/4 mile

500 metres

0   APPROX SCALE

0

Wye Valley Hotel

Holmleigh

Bellevue

Rose & Crown

OLD RAILWAY BRIDGE NOW FOOTBRIDGE ONLY

TINTERN

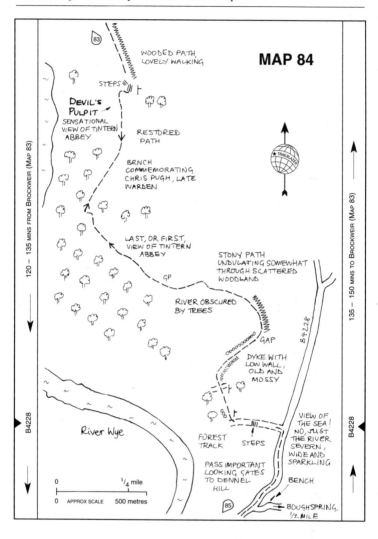

MAP 84

83

WOODED PATH,
LOVELY WALKING

STEPS

DEVIL'S
PULPIT
SENSATIONAL
VIEW OF TINTERN
ABBEY

RESTORED
PATH

BENCH
COMMEMORATING
CHRIS PUGH, LATE
WARDEN

LAST, OR FIRST,
VIEW OF TINTERN
ABBEY

STONY PATH
UNDULATING SOMEWHAT
THROUGH SCATTERED
WOODLAND

GP

RIVER OBSCURED
BY TREES

GAP

B4228

DYKE WITH
LOW WALL,
OLD AND
MOSSY

River Wye

FOREST
TRACK

STEPS

VIEW OF
THE SEA!
NO, JUST
THE RIVER
SEVERN,
WIDE AND
SPARKLING

PASS IMPORTANT
LOOKING GATES
TO DENNEL
HILL

BENCH

85

BOUGHSPRING,
½ MILE

0   ¼ mile
0   APPROX SCALE   500 metres

120 – 135 MINS FROM BROCKWEIR (MAP 83)

B4228

135 – 150 MINS TO BROCKWEIR (MAP 83)

B4228

(Opposite) Monnow Bridge in Monmouth (see p181) is the only intact example of a 13th century fortified bridge. (Photo © Bryn Thomas). **Overleaf: Top:** Redbrook and the Wye Valley (see p184). **Bottom:** Rennie's Bridge, Chepstow (see p195).

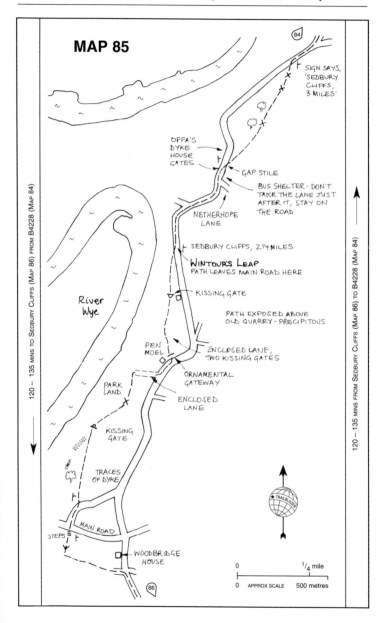

MAP 85

SIGN SAYS, 'SEDBURY CLIFFS, 3 MILES'

OFFA'S DYKE HOUSE GATES

GAP STILE

BUS SHELTER - DON'T TAKE THE LANE JUST AFTER IT, STAY ON THE ROAD

NETHERHOPE LANE

SEDBURY CLIFFS, 2¼ MILES

WINTOUR'S LEAP
PATH LEAVES MAIN ROAD HERE

KISSING GATE

PATH EXPOSED ABOVE OLD QUARRY - PRECIPITOUS

River Wye

PEN MOEL

ENCLOSED LANE, TWO KISSING GATES

ORNAMENTAL GATEWAY

PARK LAND

ENCLOSED LANE

KISSING GATE

TRACES OF DYKE

MAIN ROAD

STEPS

WOODBRIDGE HOUSE

120 – 135 MINS TO SEDBURY CLIFFS (MAP 86) FROM B4228 (MAP 84)

120 – 135 MINS FROM SEDBURY CLIFFS (MAP 86) TO B4228 (MAP 84)

TRAILBLAZER

0   ¼ mile
0   APPROX SCALE   500 metres

84

86

Transport

The **rail** links are to Cardiff and Birmingham New Street with eight trains a day. **Buses** to Bristol run every hour (see public transport map, p39). A reliable **taxi** firm is Town Gate Cars (☎ 01291-627733).

Services

The **tourist information centre** (☎ 01291-623772) is located just by the castle car park and is open seven days a week from 10am to 5.30pm but closes for lunch 1-2pm. For anyone in need of extra cash, the town is liberally supplied with **cashpoints** from all the main high street banks while **foreign exchange** transactions can also be conducted at the **post office** in Albion Square. Medical needs are available through all of the five **health centres**. Town Gate Practice (☎ 01291-636444) is the most central.

Early closing day is Wednesday but the main shops remain open including the huge **Tesco** next to the station which is open 24 hours during the week, closing at 10pm on Saturday night but opening again on Sunday from 10am to 4pm.

Where to stay

Chepstow has a good choice of accommodation, which can get booked up in the high season due to its prominent position as the gateway to Wales. In the town itself **camping** is available at *Lower Hardwick House* (☎ 01291-622162, Hardwick Hill) at £5 a tent or £2 per person if there's more than one in the party. You can use the showers in the house and join in the breakfast arrangements.

Otherwise, there is another **campsite** out of town very near the actual start of the path at Sedbury. This is *Upper Sedbury House* (☎ 01291-627173, 🖥 www.smoothhound.co.uk/hotels/uppersed.html, 2D/1T/1F) on Sedbury Lane where tents are £4.50 and they have a pool. B&B is £21.50 and evening meals £11.50. They may also allow you to park your car for the duration of the walk which is a very convenient option.

There are several places at the river end of the town all within a short walk. *The*

First Hurdle (☎ 01291-622189, 9-10 Upper Church St, 1S/2T/2D) is a comfortable and tastefully furnished establishment where en-suite accommodation costs from £25.

Right at the bottom of Bridge St is *Afon Gwy* (☎ 01291-620158, 28 Bridge St, 1T/3D/4F) where B&B will cost you £27.50 per person in an en suite room.

For those who decide to celebrate their completion of the walk with a night of luxury, there are several bigger hotels with prices to match. *Castle View Hotel* (☎ 01291-620349, Bridge St) is ivy clad and would be a good choice but be prepared to pay £50-plus per person not including breakfast.

Where to eat

There's plenty for the hungry to choose from with two Indians, two Chinese and a Pizza house, all centrally located. *Jimmy Dean's* (☎ 01291-630477, St Mary St) is a standard burger joint offering spicy Tex-Mex cuisine including Cagney's Volcano Burger, an explosive experience consisting of an 8oz char-grilled beefburger loaded with jalapeno peppers, salsa and hot Louisiana barbecue sauce which will blow your head off for £10.95.

The best pub in town is *The Boat Inn* (☎ 01292-628192, The Back) down by the river, where they do excellent pub meals. The beer is Theakstons.

Nearly next door is the *Wye Knot* (☎ 01291-622929, The Back), a top-class restaurant catering for a more upwardly-mobile clientele as the prices testify. How about steamed fillets of sea bass filled with a mousseline of langoustines, served on braised fennel and light basil sauce? A snip at £16.95. *Castle View Hotel* (see above) does good food too, specializing in locally-obtained produce of a traditional cuisine either taken as bar meals or in the restaurant. Typical main courses include grilled halibut at £9.95 and herb pancakes filled with a fricassée of courgette and mushrooms at £7.95.

To prepare you for the day's march, the *Baguette Shop* (9 St Mary's Arcade, Mon–Sat 8.30am–5pm) is the place to visit for freshly-baked filled baguettes.

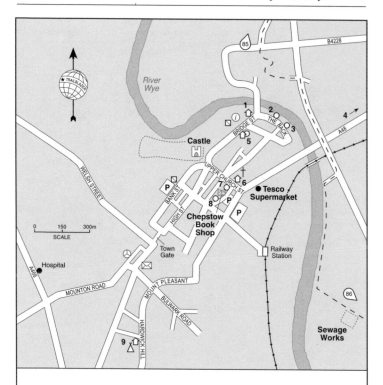

Chepstow   MAP 86a

Where to stay

1 Afon Gwy
4 Upper Sedbury House
  (B&B and Camping)
5 Castle View Hotel

6 The First Hurdle
9 Lower Hardwick House
  (B&B and Camping)

Where to eat

2 The Wye Knot
3 Boat Inn
5 Castle View Hotel
7 Jimmy Dean's
8 The Baguette Shop

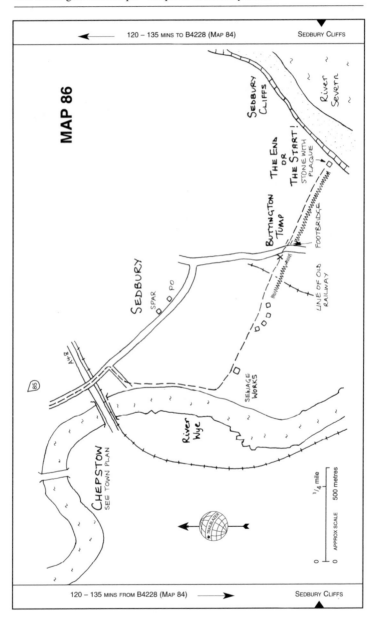

120 – 135 MINS TO B4228 (MAP 84)

SEDBURY CLIFFS

MAP 86

River Severn

SEDBURY CLIFFS

THE END OR THE START!
STONE WITH PLAQUE

BUTTINGTON TUMP

FOOTBRIDGE

LINE OF OLD RAILWAY

SEDBURY

SPAR   PO

A48

85

SEWAGE WORKS

River Wye

CHEPSTOW
SEE TOWN PLAN

TRAILBLAZER

1/4 mile
500 metres
APPROX SCALE
0
0

120 – 135 MINS FROM B4228 (MAP 84)

SEDBURY CLIFFS

❏ **Chepstow Castle**
The Castle (open Apr, May, Oct 9.30am–5pm, Jun–Sept 9.30am–6pm, admission £3) is positioned on the cliffs above the River Wye giving it a commanding presence over the town. It was started the year after the Battle of Hastings, 1067, by the Norman baron William Fitzosbern as a base for subduing South Wales. Its stone-built construction was a vast improvement over the old earth and timber motte and bailey castles, which had been adequate until the introduction of cannon and gunpowder. It was progressively improved and strengthened during the 12th and 13th centuries when it changed hands many times although resisting an assault by Owain Glyndwr. By the time of the English Civil War it was held by the Royalists who surrendered it in 1645 to the Parliamentarians who used it mainly as a prison, but by the end of the 17th century it had begun to fall into disrepair.

CHEPSTOW TO SEDBURY CLIFFS

MAP 86

The final **1¹/₂ miles (2km, 30-45mins)** from the bridge over the A48 to Sedbury Cliffs are possibly the worst you'll have encountered, a rather ignominious end to a superb walk. You go along suburban streets and past a sewage farm; then you slip and slide along the muddy stretch of the Dyke from Buttington Tump to the stone that marks the symbolic end of your 177-mile journey. It seems an anticlimax.

Sedbury Cliffs are overgrown and barbed wire bars a direct way down to the fore-shore; you have to follow a detour to your right if you want to walk out over water-logged grass onto the bank of the river. Whether or not you find it worthwhile covering this last stretch, your sense of satisfaction on achieving your goal will be very real.

**Offa's Dyke Path marker
Sedbury Cliffs**

Unless you've brought a bottle of Offa's Vineyard champagne and a picnic with you, you'll probably want to return to the pubs of Chepstow (only an hour away and all on the pavement) to celebrate your achievement and contemplate the ups and downs, literal and metaphorical, of this magnificent walk.

APPENDIX A: HEALTH & OUTDOOR SAFETY

AVOIDANCE OF HAZARDS

The Offa's Dyke Path is not a hazardous undertaking and should not put the average walker to any greater risk than he or she would encounter on an average day's ramble in the countryside. Always make sure you have sufficient clothes to keep you warm and dry, whatever the conditions, and a spare change of inner clothes. A **compass**, **whistle**, **torch** and **first-aid kit** should also be carried and you should know how to use them.

Take enough **food** to sustain you during the day and always set out with at least one litre of **water**. Drinking from streams is not recommended since they are likely to contain traces of pesticides and other chemicals used on the land. You will find that you will eat more than normal because you are using up more energy. High-energy snacks are worth considering, either proprietary brands or chocolate, nuts and dried fruit.

Stay alert and try to keep track of exactly where you are throughout the day. The easiest way is to use the map to **check your position**. If bad weather comes in, you will then be able to make a sensible decision on what action to take based on your location.

If you enjoy **walking alone** you must appreciate and be prepared for the increased risk. You should tell someone where you are going. One way of doing this is to telephone your booked accommodation and let them know you are walking alone and what time you expect to arrive. Don't forget to contact whoever you have left word with to let them know you have arrived safely.

Safety in wild country

There are parts of the Offa's Dyke Path that fall into the category of wild country, particularly in the Clwydian Hills and the Black Mountains. These parts can feel quite remote and you should always have the means to protect yourself from the worst weather conditions. Besides **extra food** and **map and compass**, you should also carry a **hat** and **gloves** and possibly a **survival bag**. Anyone tackling the route in winter must have sufficient experience to know when not to go out on the hill. Low-level walking in bad weather should not be a problem for the experienced.

WEATHER INFORMATION

Anyone familiar with the British weather will know that it can change quickly. What started out as a warm sunny day can be chilly and wet by lunchtime, so don't be fooled. The daily newspapers, television and radio will always give the forecast for the day ahead and local people will have plenty of advice on the subject.

Telephone and web forecasts

If you are particularly interested you can phone Weathercall (☎ 09068-5004 plus 15 for North Wales; 14 for Powys; 10 for Shropshire and Herefordshire; 09 for Monmouthshire). Calls are charged at the expensive premium rate.

Alternatively internet weather forecasts can be found at 🖳 www.onlineweather.com.

WATER

You need to drink lots of water while walking; 2-4 litres a day depending on the weather. If you're feeling drained, lethargic or just out of sorts it may well be that you haven't drunk enough. Thirst is not a reliable indicator of how much you should drink. The frequency and colour of your urine is better and the maxim, 'a happy mountaineer always pees clear' is worth following.

❑ **Lyme Disease**
Ticks are small blood-sucking insects that live on cattle, sheep and deer and cannot fly. When you are walking with bare arms or legs through long grass or bracken small ticks can brush off and attach themselves to you, painlessly burying their heads under your skin to feed on your blood. After a couple of days of feasting they will have grown to about 10mm and drop off.

There is a very small risk that they can infect you with Lyme Disease, although infected ticks have to be attached to you for 24–36 hours before they are likely to infect you. Check your body after a walk and remove any by pinching the head, not the body, and twisting. Keep the area clean with disinfectant. If you suffer flu-like symptoms, or lasting irritation at the site of the bite for a week or more, see a doctor. Wear boots, socks and trousers when walking through, or sitting on, long grass, heather and bracken.

BLISTERS

You will prevent blisters by wearing worn-in, comfortable boots and looking after your feet. How many people set out on a long walk in new boots and live to regret it!

Look after your feet: air them at lunchtime, keep them clean and change your socks daily. If you feel any 'hot spots' on your feet while you are walking, stop immediately and apply a few strips of zinc oxide tape and leave on until it is pain free or the tape starts to come off.

If you have left it too late and a blister has developed you should surround it with 'moleskin' or any other 'blister kit' to protect it from abrasion. Popping it can lead to infection. If the skin is broken keep the area clean with antiseptic and cover with a non-adhesive dressing material held in place with tape.

DEALING WITH AN ACCIDENT

● Use basic first aid to treat the injury to the best of your ability.
● Work out exactly where you are in case you have to send for the emergency services.
● Try to attract the attention of anybody else who may be in the area. The **emergency signal** is six blasts on a whistle, or six flashes with a torch.
● If possible leave someone with the casualty while others go for help. If there is nobody else, you have a dilemma. If you decide to get help leave all spare clothing and food with the casualty.
● Telephone ☎ 999 and ask for the police or other rescue service.
● Report the exact position of the casualty and his or her condition.

APPENDIX B: GLOSSARY OF WELSH WORDS

aber	river mouth	*heol*	road or street
afon	river	*isaf*	lower
allt	steep hillside	*llan*	enclosure, church
bach	little	*llanerch*	glade
betws	church	*llech*	slab, stone
blaen	head, source	*llwyd*	grey or brown
bran	crow	*maes*	field
bryn	hillside	*mawr*	great
bwlch	pass	*moel*	bare hill
cae	field	*mynach*	monk
caer	fortress	*mynydd*	mountain
carreg	stone, rock	*nant*	brook
castell	castle	*newydd*	new
cefn	ridge	*pandy*	fulling mill
celli	grove, copse	*pen*	head, top
clawdd	dyke, bank, hedge	*pentre*	village
coch	red	*plas*	hall, mansion
coed	wood	*pont*	bridge
cwm	valley	*porth*	gateway
cwrt	court	*pwll*	pool
dinas	hill-fortress, city	*rhos*	moorland
disgwylfa	viewpoint, lookout	*rhyd*	ford
dol, dolau	meadow	*tref*	homestead, hamlet
ffin	boundary	*twyn*	hillock
ffridd	lower part of hill	*ty*	house
ffynnon	spring	*tyddyn*	smallholding
gwaun	moorland, pasture	*uchaf*	higher, upper
hafod	summer dwelling	*ynys*	island
hen	old	*ystrad*	vale, valley
hendre	winter dwelling		

Town plan key

		i	Tourist Information	⊠	Public Toilet
⬆	Where to stay	Λ	Camping Site	⊕	Public Telephone
O	Where to eat	�	Museum	⊕	Bus Station
⊠	Post Office	⊞	Bookshop	●	Other

Trail map key

OFFA'S DYKE PATH

╱ ╱	Offa's Dyke Path (OD)
╱ ╱	Other Footpath
╱ ╱ ╱	Track
╱╱	Tarmac Road
⤙	Slope
⤙⤙	Steep Slope
⊥	Finger Post
GP	Guide Post

🝔	Pile of Stones / Cairn
╱‖‖	Steps
✕	Stile & Fence
∿	Hedge
⚬⚬⚬	Wall
∿∿∿	Offa's Dyke
╱╲	Gate
╱✕╲	Gate & Stile
╱⌀	Kissing Gate

⤙	Footbridge
⤙	Substantial Bridge
⟋	Cattle Grid
▦	Duckboards

NATURAL FEATURES

～～	Water
～	Stream
⟨⟨	River
↓↓	Boggy / Wet Ground

🌲🌳	Trees / Woodland
⌂⌂	Scrubland / Gorse / Bracken / Grazing
◣	Quarry
⋔⋔	Crags
⟋⟍	Scree

MAN-MADE FEATURES

□	Building / Ruin / Barn
✝	Church / Chapel
⊀	Transmitter Mast
✗	Power Lines
P	Car Park
△	Triangulation Pillar (Trig. Point)
⟑	Golf Course

SERVICES

■	B&B / Guesthouse / Youth Hostel
⋏	Camp Site
⌀	Public Toilet
⊕	Public Telephone

INDEX

Page references in bold type refer to maps

❏ Voluntary organizations and campaigns

● **British Trust for Conservation Volunteers** (BTCV) (☎ 01491-821600, 🖳 www.bctv.org) 36 St Mary's St, Wallingford, Oxfordshire, OX10 0EU. Encourages people to value their environment and take practical action to improve it.

● **Campaign for the Protection of Rural Wales** (CPRW) (☎ 01938-552525) Ty Gwyn, 31 High St, Welshpool, Powys, SY21 7YD. Their name says it all.

● **Council for the Protection of Rural England** (CPRE) (☎ 020-7976 6433, 🖳 www .cpre.org.uk) Warwick House, 25 Buckingham Palace Rd, London, SW1W 0PP.

● **Friends of the Earth** (☎ 020-7490 1555, 🖳 www.foe.co.uk) 26/28 Underwood St, London, N1 7JQ. International organization campaigning for a better environment for all, along with: **Friends of the Earth (Wales)** (☎ 029-2022 9577) 33 Castle Arcade Balcony, Cardiff CF10 1BY. Co-ordinating the work of local groups.

● **Greenpeace** (☎ 020-7865 8100, 🖳 www.greenpeace.org) Greenpeace House, Canonbury Villas, London N1 2PN. International organization promoting peaceful activism in defence of the environment world wide.

● **Inland Waterways Association** (☎ 01923-711114, 🖳 www.waterways.org.uk) PO Box 114, Rickmansworth, WD3 1ZY. Looks after the interests of canal users.

● **National Trust** (☎ 020-7222 9252, 🖳 www.nationaltrust.org.uk) 36 Queen Anne's Gate, London, SW1H 9AS. **National Trust Office for Wales,** (☎ 01492-860123) Trinity Square, Llandudno, LL30 2DE.

● **Royal Society for Nature Conservation** (☎ 01636-670000, 🖳 www.rsnc.org).

● **Royal Society for the Protection of Birds** (RSPB) (☎ 01767-680551, 🖳 www.rspb.org.uk) The Lodge, Sandy, Bedfordshire, SG19 2DL. **RSPB South Wales Office**, (☎ 029-2035 3000) Sutherland House, Castlebridge, Cowbridge Road East, Cardiff, CF11 9AB. The largest voluntary conservation body in Europe.

● **The Land is Ours** (TLIO) (☎ 07961-460171, 🖳 www.tlio.org.uk) 16B Cherwell St, Oxford, OX4 1BG. A campaign, not an organization, which aims to highlight the exclusion of ordinary people from the land.

● **Woodland Trust** (☎ 01476-581111, 🖳 www.woodland-trust.org.uk) Autumn Park, Dysart Road, Grantham, Lincolnshire, NG31 6LL. Their aims are to conserve, restore and re-establish trees, particularly broadleaved.

Europe
Trekking in Corsica
Trekking in the Dolomites
Trekking in the Pyrenees
(and the British Walking Series)

South America
Inca Trail, Cusco & Machu Picchu

Australasia
New Zealand – Great Walks

Africa
Kilimanjaro
Trekking in the Moroccan Atlas

Asia
Trekking in the Annapurna Region
Trekking in the Everest Region
Trekking in Ladakh
Trekking in Langtang
Nepal Mountaineering Guide

New Zealand – The Great Walks *Alexander Stewart*
1st edn, 272pp, 60 maps, 40 colour photos
ISBN 1 873756 78 X, £11.99, Can$28.95, US$19.95
New Zealand is a wilderness paradise of incredibly beautiful land-scapes. There is no better way to experience it than on one of the nine designated Great Walks, the country's premier walking tracks which provide outstanding hiking opportunities for people at all levels of fit-ness and proficiency. Also includes detailed guides to Auckland, Wellington, National Park Village, Taumaranui, Nelson, Queenstown, Te Anau and Oban.

Kilimanjaro: a trekking guide to Africa's highest mountain
Henry Stedman, 1st edition, 240pp, 40 maps, 30 photos
ISBN 1 873756 65 8,£9.99, Can$22.95, US$17.95
At 19,340ft the world's tallest freestanding mountain, Kilimanjaro is one of the most popular destinations for hikers visiting Africa. It's possible to walk up to the summit: no technical skills are necessary. This new guide includes town guides to Nairobi and Dar-Es-Salaam, excursions in the region and a detailed colour guide to flora and fauna.

Trekking in the Everest Region *Jamie McGuinness*
4th edn, 304pp, 38 maps, 52 village plans, 30 colour photos
ISBN 1 873756 60 7, £10.99, Can$27.95, US$17.95
Popular guide to the world's most famous trekking region. Includes detailed walking maps, where to stay/eat along the way plus informa-tion on trek preparation and getting to Nepal. Written by a professional trek leader. '*The pick of the guides to the area*' **Adventure Travel**

Trekking in Corsica *David Abram*
1st edition, 320pp, 74 maps, 48 colour photos
ISBN 1 873756 63 1, £11.99, Can$26.95, US$18.95
A mountain range rising straight from the sea, Corsica holds the most arrestingly beautiful and diverse landscapes in the Mediterranean. Among the many trails that penetrate its remotest corners, the GR20, which wriggles across the island's watershed, has gained an interna-tional reputation. This guide also covers the best of the other routes. '*Excellent guide*'. **The Sunday Times**

Trekking in the Pyrenees *Douglas Streatfeild-James*
2nd edition, £11.99, Can$27.95 US$18.95
ISBN 1 873756 50 X, 320pp, 95 maps, 55 colour photos
All the main trails along the France-Spain border including the GR10 (France) coast to coast hike and the GR11 (Spain) from Roncesvalles to Andorra, plus many shorter routes. 90 route maps include walking times and places to stay. Expanded to include greater coverage of routes in Spain. '*Readily accessible, well-written and most readable...*' **John Cleare**

❏ TRAILBLAZER GUIDES

Adventure Cycling Handbook	1st edn late 2004
Adventure Motorcycling Handbook	4th edn out now
Australia by Rail	4th edn out now
Azerbaijan	3rd edn mid 2004
The Blues Highway – New Orleans to Chicago	2nd edn out now
China by Rail	2nd edn mid 2004
Coast to Coast (British Walking Guide)	1st edn Mar 2004
Cornwall Coast Path (British Walking Guide)	1st edn out now
Good Honeymoon Guide	2nd edn out now
Inca Trail, Cusco & Machu Picchu	2nd edn out now
Japan by Rail	1st edn out now
Kilimanjaro – a trekking guide to Africa's highest mountain	1st edn out now
Land's End to John O'Groats	1st edn late 2004
The Med Guide	1st edn mid 2004
Nepal Mountaineering Guide	1st edn mid 2004
New Zealand – Great Walks	1st edn out now
Norway's Arctic Highway	1st edn out now
Offa's Dyke Path (British Walking Guide)	1st edn out now
Pembrokeshire Coast Path (British Walking Guide)	1st edn out now
Pennine Way (British Walking Guide)	1st edn early 2004
Siberian BAM Guide – rail, rivers & road	2nd edn out now
The Silk Roads – a route and planning guide	1st end out now
Sahara Overland – a route and planning guide	1st edn out now
Sahara Abenteuerhandbuch (German edition)	1st edn out now
Ski Canada – where to ski and snowboard	1st edn out now
South Downs Way (British Walking Guide)	1st edn Mar 2004
South-East Asia – The Graphic Guide	1st edn out now
Tibet Overland – mountain biking & jeep touring	1st edn out now
Trans-Canada Rail Guide	3rd edn out now
Trans-Siberian Handbook	6th edn out now
Trekking in the Annapurna Region	4th edn Mar 2004
Trekking in the Everest Region	4th edn out now
Trekking in Corsica	1st edn out now
Trekking in the Dolomites	1st edn out now
Trekking in Ladakh	3rd edn mid 2004
Trekking in Langtang, Gosainkund & Helambu	1st edn out now
Trekking in the Moroccan Atlas	1st edn out now
Trekking in the Pyrenees	2nd edn out now
Tuva and Southern Siberia	1st edn late 2004
Vietnam by Rail	1st edn out now
West Highland Way (British Walking Guide)	1st edn out now

For more information about Trailblazer and our expanding range of guides,
for where to find your nearest stockist, for guidebook updates
or for credit card mail order sales (post-free worldwide) visit our web site:

www.trailblazer-guides.com

ROUTE GUIDES FOR THE ADVENTUROUS TRAVELLER

West Highland Way *Charlie Loram* **Available now**
1st edition, 192pp, 48 maps, 10 town plans, 40 colour photos
ISBN 1 873756 54 2, £9.99, Can$22.95, US$16.95
Scotland's best-known long distance footpath passes through some of the most spectacular scenery in all of Britain. From the outskirts of Glasgow it winds for 95 miles along the wooded banks of Loch Lomond, across the wilderness of Rannoch Moor to a dramatic finish at the foot of Britain's highest peak – Ben Nevis. Includes Glasgow city guide.
'*...the same attention to detail that distinguishes its other guides has been brought to bear here*' **The Sunday Times**

Cornwall Coast Path *Edith Schofield* **Available now**
1st edition, 192pp, 81 maps & town plans, 40 colour photos
ISBN 1 873756 55 0, £9.99, Can$22.95, US$16.95
A 160-mile (258km) National Trail around the western tip of Britain with some of the best coastal walking in Europe. With constantly changing scenery, the footpath takes in secluded coves, tiny fishing villages, rocky headlands, bustling resorts, wooded estuaries and golden surf-washed beaches. It is an area rich in wildlife with seabirds, wild flowers, dolphins and seals.

Pembrokeshire Coast Path *Jim Manthorpe* **Available now**
1st edition, 208pp, 96 maps & town plans, 40 colour photos
ISBN 1 873756 56 9, £9.99, Can$22.95, US$16.95
A magnificent 186-mile (299km) footpath around the stunning coastline of the Pembrokeshire Coast National Park in south-west Wales. Renowned for its unspoilt sandy beaches, secluded coves, tiny fishing villages and off-shore islands rich in bird and marine life, this National Trail provides some of the best coastal walking in Britain.

Coast to Coast *Henry Stedman* **Available Mar 2004**
1st edition, 224pp, 95 maps & town plans, 40 colour photos
ISBN 1 873756 58 5, £9.99, Can$22.95, US$16.95
A classic 191-mile (307km) walk across northern England from the Irish Sea to the North Sea. Crossing three fabulous National Parks – the Lake District, the Yorkshire Dales and the North York Moors – it samples the very best of the English countryside – rugged mountains and lakes, gentle dales and stone-built villages; country lanes and wild moorland; sea cliffs and fishing villages.

South Downs Way *Jim Manthorpe* **Available Mar 2004**
1st edition, 192pp, 50 maps & town plans, 40 colour photos
ISBN 1 873756 71 2, £9.99, Can$22.95, US$16.95
This 100-mile (160km) footpath runs from Eastbourne to Winchester through East Sussex, West Sussex and Hampshire. It follows the chalk downs through several Areas of Outstanding Natural Beauty.

Pennine Way *Ed de la Billière & K Carter* **Available May 2004**
1st edition, 288pp, 130 maps & town plans, 40 colour photos
ISBN 1 873756 57 7, £10.99, Can$22.95, US$16.95
Britain's best-known National Trail winds for 256 miles over wild moorland and through quiet dales following the backbone of Northern England. Crossing three National Parks – the Peak District, the Yorkshire Dales and Northumberland – this superb footpath showcases Britain's finest upland scenery, while touching the literary landscape of the Brontë family and historical legends along Hadrian's Wall.

TRAILBLAZER
BRITISH WALKING GUIDES